A History of
WIRRAL

Coat-of-arms for the Metropolitan Borough of Wirral; designed by Ellis Tomlinson in 1974. The crown has five points: they represent the old local authorities which amalgamated to form the Metropolitan Borough—Bebington, Birkenhead, Heswall, Hoylake and Wallasey.

All the other features were carefully designed to represent aspects of Wirral: the green on the shield's background symbolises its countryside and the waves stand for the Mersey and Dee estuaries; Bog Myrtle— the plant whose Anglo-Saxon name became part of the word 'Wirral'—can be seen sprouting from the helmet; the oyster catcher is a reminder of the birdlife which flourishes along the coast and the horn is the symbol of the authority of the medieval Master Forester.

The people of Wirral look at this coat-of-arms with a mixture of pride, because it is a beautiful representation of the well-loved attractions of their homeland, and sadness, because, officially, it stands only for the northern portion of the peninsula. Southern Wirral is divided between Ellesmere Port and Neston and Chester City Councils.

A History of
WIRRAL

Stephen J. Roberts

To Lynn and John
Love from Your Brother,
the Author, Stephen.

Phillimore

2002

Published by
PHILLIMORE & CO. LTD
Shopwyke Manor Barn, Chichester, West Sussex, England

© Stephen J. Roberts, 2002

ISBN 1 86077 236 6

Printed and bound in Great Britain by
MPG BOOKS LTD
Bodmin, Cornwall

Contents

To the
People of Wirral
and
Wirral Exiles Everywhere

List of Illustrations

Frontispiece: Coat-of-arms of Wirral Metropolitan Borough Council

Illustration Acknowledgements

David Silcock, 1, 3, 8, 12, 14, 15, 19, 26, 28, 30, 31, 36, 37, 39, 40, 46, 47, 48, 56, 69, 73, 79, 102, 105; Jim O'Neil, 51, 52, 53, 65, 66, 67, 68, 74, 103, 104; Ian Boumphrey, 63, 75, 76, 77, 82, 92, 93, 94, 101; Williamson Art Gallery and Museum, Birkenhead, 42, 44, 45, 49, 50, 54, 55, 59, 61 and Cover; *West Kirby and Hilbre A Parochial History*, John Brownbill, 20, 33, 34, 35; Rob Philpott (Copyright the Board of Trustees of the National Museums and Galleries on Merseyside), 21, 22, 23; Merseyside Archaeological Society, 17 (Ray Kenna), 43 (Gill Chitty); Peter Hadwin, 80, 99; *The Romance of Wirral*, A.G. Caton, 2, 13; *Victoria County History of Cheshire*, 27, 29; *Birkenhead Yesterday, Today and Tomorrow*, W.R.S. McIntyre, 95; Walker Art Gallery, Liverpool, 72; *The Illustrated London News*, 78; other pictures are taken from the author's own collection.

Full details of publications can be found in the bibliography.

Acknowledgements

Ambitions can rarely be achieved without the assistance and self-sacrifice of others. This is certainly true in my case. I thank my dear wife Anne, who, by returning to full-time work, allowed me firstly to work part-time and then to spend all my time on the researching and writing of this book. Latterly, she has also greatly assisted in administration. She has, throughout, been understanding and patient. Quite simply, without her, the project would never have been finished. I thank my children—Eleri, Rachel and Samuel for being patient and understanding with their father whilst he was unable to give them the attention they deserve as a result of commitment to this project. I must thank my parents, Fred and Jackie Roberts, for accommodating me during my visits to Wirral and for providing me with resources and contacts. Other family members have also helped me: Peter Hadwin gave me some of his photographs of Birkenhead during the 1960s and was able to describe them in exhaustive and amusing detail; Barbara Mason traced some important sources; Kathryn and Barry Hall and Alison and Bill Ashby gave me several useful books and have always shown an interest, as have Lynn and John Engström, Geoff and Jean Brown and Alan and Val Roberts.

With regard to the arduous process of researching, writing, editing and illustrating the manuscript, nobody has helped me more than fellow Wirral exile and family historian David Silcock. He is not the sort of man who will readily speak about his talents, but I have found him to be a meticulous and creative cartographer and draughtsman, a considerable scholar, a thorough editor and proof-reader and good friend. The quality of his maps and research convinces me that he should aim to write and illustrate a book of his own. I thank him for everything he has done for me.

Professor Stephen Harding is another Wirral exile who has assisted me greatly. I have learned a lot from reading and discussing his *Ingimund's Saga* and he has been a great source of encouragement. I thank him for his enthusiastic and rapid responses to my almost daily e-mails and for sending me copies of some important academic articles and notes.

It seems to me that nobody would be able to write anything meaningful about the north-western corner of the Wirral Peninsula without seeking advice from Jim O'Neil. I thank him for the generous way in which he has discussed the history of Greasby and surrounding villages and kindly lent me some excellent pictures from his collection. We look forward to the day when he is able to turn his years of valuable primary research into a published work.

I thank Ian Boumphrey for, yet again, allowing me to use some of his historical pictures and Colin Simpson for helping me to locate some excellent pictures from the Williamson Art Gallery and Museum, where he is curator. I thank David Roberts of the Merseyside Archaeological Society for answering my enquiry and members of the society whose material I have used, but whom we have not been able to contact.

Merseyside is blessed with a range of distinguished scholars who are not just leaders in their fields but extremely approachable and helpful. The staff at Liverpool Museum have given me a lot of assistance. I could never have written Chapter Two without the help of archaeologists Ron Cowell and Dr Rob Philpott, who have not only discussed the results of their research but given me copies of their articles, commented upon the chapter and lent me photographs. Geologists Alan Bowden, Dr Geoff Tresise and Wendy Simkiss have helped to open my eyes to a discipline about which I previously knew very little, but have since discovered to be both utterly fascinating and extremely useful. I thank them for reviewing Chapter One. I thank Chester Archaeologist Keith Matthews for helping me to understand prehistoric chronologies and the possible story of the Broxton Valley or Deva Spillway and Liverpool University Geographer Dr Andy Plater for sharing some thoughts on Wirral's drainage. Audrey Hall of the Walker Art Gallery has also given assistance.

I have also been greatly assisted by academics who are based nearer to my current home. I thank Professor Ian Whyte for enabling me better to understand the relationship between people and landscape and for quickly and thoroughly reviewing Chapter Three. I thank Dr David Shotter for answering a query about Roman coins and inscriptions and for allowing me to copy part of his work on Roman coins in the North West. Tom Green has been a constant source of encouragement and inspiration and reviewed Chapters Five and Six.

None of the reviewers is responsible for any mistakes which the manuscript might contain.

I thank Wirral librarian and fellow former Carlett Park student Julie Barkway for her interest and support, for answering my enquiries and for supplying me with copies of *Wirral Notes and Queries*. I express similar gratitude to Julie Kennedy and Jill Mason of Carnforth Library who, with cheerfulness and alacrity, have obtained a range of obscure and ancient volumes for me. Angie Maun assisted me by typing up some primary sources and she and her husband Bob generously bought me an expensive and rare copy of one of Wirral's most invaluable works of local history—Brownbill's *West Kirby and Hilbre*. I thank them very much indeed for that.

John Hess has the privilege of residing at Chorlton Hall—the former home of Cheshire's greatest antiquarian, George Ormerod. I thank John for kindly lending me a copy of his excellent book about Ormerod, for giving me copies of his own works of local history, for showing me around his wonderful home and for discussing his eminent predecessor.

Adam Green and Chris Williams deserve gratitude for discussing certain ideas relating to their respective disciplines of Geography and Religious Studies and for giving me copies of relevant and useful books. Ron Tempest lent me his digital camera at a crucial time and he, David Jones and Marcus Mosey have always shown an interest in my work and were very understanding while I was getting the book finished.

I sincerely thank the following family historians for sharing their research with me— Elizabeth de Mercado, Anthony Dumville, Carolyn Macri, Margaret Mulville, Eve Pryde-Roberts, Brian Roberts, Andrew Sutton, Anne Whitehead and Lesley Wright. I ask them not to be discouraged if they cannot find their ancestors mentioned in this work: space would not allow as many genealogical references as I originally thought was going to be possible; but I assure all of them that their work helped me to understand the lives of our

Wirral ancestors. Mike Parker is also a family historian. I thank him for his interest and for lending me a very important article, photograph and notes about Seacombe Pottery.

I have also been greatly assisted by people who have shared their autobiographies—Jack Fairs, Harry Nickson and Leslie Scott Jones. Many others have offered to tell me about their lives. I thank them all very much indeed for their interest and apologise for not taking up their offers. Again, space would not permit me to incorporate any more oral history, but their enthusiasm tells me that there is a need for another book just about the 20th century, so I may yet be asking them for their help after all.

Susan Nicholson provided me with some valuable local information and told me of the availability of the copy of Brownbill. I thank her for her interest and kindness. I thank Julie Fox for sending me a copy of an important family document.

I have not seen Michael Pinnock for some time, but I should like sincerely to thank him for his role in enabling me to write this book. By means of his provocative teaching and lively conversation, he enabled me to acquire the skills and confidence which the project demanded.

For me, the research and writing of this work has been a great personal challenge and I have had frequent cause to remember a proverb from the scriptures: 'Trust in the Lord with all your heart and lean not on your own understanding; in your ways acknowledge him and he will make your ways straight'. I acknowledge Him for fulfilling that promise and echo the prayer of King David, 'Everything comes from you, and we have given you only what comes from your hand'.

Preface

The term 'Wirral' is used to describe the peninsula which is bounded by the Dee and Mersey estuaries, Irish Sea and the Deva Spillway (route of the Shropshire Union Canal between Ellesmere Port and Chester). By 1086 it was an administrative unit called a Hundred, whose boundaries extended as far east as the river Gowy. I make no attempt to discuss the villages which at that time were included in Wirral but were later transferred to Broxton Hundred, apart from in the section which deals with Domesday Book. Unless otherwise stated, the pre-1974 county boundaries and names are employed throughout the text. Similarly, the term 'Merseyside' is used to describe not the short-lived metropolitan county, but the geographical region within the vicinity of the river Mersey, which, for example, includes Ellesmere Port which was never part of the metropolitan county. In order to reduce the necessity for footnotes, only quotations and apparently controversial, specialised or 'new' facts are attributed in that way. The reader can assume that the content of unattributed narratives can be obtained from most of the standard reference works. The names of the classic authors are often mentioned in the narrative, without mention of the exact details of their works. The reader will be able to find all the necessary information in the bibliography.

Introduction

It was early spring 2002. I looked out of the bedroom window of my parents' home, towards Greasby Copse. Grey sheets of hail-laden cloud were scudding in from the south, shutting out the pink light of the setting sun. Desirous of a closer look at the scene, I left the house and walked up the lane. Cars roared past me, but, on the little ridge by the copse, everything was silent. I knew that, some 9,000 years previously, families of stone-age hunter gatherers had lived on that ridge. It was never their permanent home, but one of many seasonal encampments which were scattered in a mystical network throughout the region. I contemplated the world they knew—one in which humans were scarce and plants and animals abundant. I tried to imagine the passage of time and the gradual disappearance of the wild wood. I wondered whether the Romans built a road between *Deva* and Meols and had crossed the same ridge just a little way to the south. Names—Greasby, Arrowe, Irby, Upton, Woodchurch—reminded me of how the Anglo-Saxons and Norse had founded most of the settlements and parcelled up the land. I thought about the the medieval forest and the peasants' efforts to make the land yield more food. Flooded marl-pits in a field behind me were proof that later generations had carried on the tradition. Beyond them lay the park—one of the loveliest in the region, a blessed green haven in a suburban district and the product firstly of the dreams of a businessman and then of the foresight of a local council. Evidences of modernity lay all around—a tower block, the rumble of traffic and the orange glow of street lights reflecting off the base of clouds. I saw that I was the product of that cluttered and noisy world, but also of that silent ridge and of everything which lay between them.

This book's aim is to link us all with the world of that little ridge next to Greasby Copse—to tell the 9,000-year story of people's relationship with each other and with this little portion of the earth's surface known as the Wirral Peninsula. It describes the ways in which successive generations of people have used the district's resources and landscape in order both to survive and to flourish. Attempts are made to describe the lives of the people during every period, to discuss the effects of human life upon the local landscape and to consider modern evidence for past actions and conditions. Wherever possible, local details are explained with reference to regional and national developments, but the main topic is Wirral's uniqueness. Every district in the world is unique, but not many are as easily defined as Wirral. It is after all a 'semi-island', a peninsula—in fact probably one of the world's finest examples of that phenomenon.

Oddly enough, despite the clarity of its geographical definition, it has not so far been the subject of an overall history. George Ormerod described it in his *History of the County Palatine of Cheshire* in 1819; William Williams Mortimer produced *The History of the Hundred of Wirral* in 1847 and Philip Sulley *The Hundred of Wirral* in 1889. All three works follow a similar pattern: they contain an introduction to the area's topography and administrative history and then a gazetteer of its parishes and townships. The emphasis of each chapter is usually on churches, clergymen and the genealogies and arms of local gentry. Little attempt is made to describe the lives of the people or to interpret social and economic developments, although Mortimer does provide us with some excellent information about the growth of Birkenhead. Interestingly, the 20th century saw the publication of several general descriptions of Wirral, typified by H.E. Young's *Perambulation of the Hundred of Wirral* of 1909 and Norman Ellison's *Wirral Peninsula* of 1955, which, even though they did not claim to be histories, used the same gazetteer or 'travelogue' format. There were only two attempts at looking at the peninsula in the round—W. Hewitt's *The Wirral Peninsula* of 1922 and E.H. Rideout's *The Growth of Wirral* of 1927. Hewitt's book was primarily a geographical work, while Rideout's was mainly concerned with demographic and economic history. At the same time, there were several very capable scholars working on specific aspects of the history of Cheshire and on smaller locations within the county. Perusal of the bibliography at the end of this book reveals who they were—R. Stewart-Brown, James Tait, William Ferguson-Irvine, John Brownbill and others. The *Transactions of the Historic Society of Lancashire and Cheshire* was their favoured medium of publication. During the later 20th century, many more excellent works of local history were produced and new fields were explored. P.H.W. Booth, G. Place and the Burton and South Wirral Historical Society must be mentioned in this context. In addition, archaeologists were producing new information about Wirral's more distant past.

I first dreamed of writing a history of Wirral whilst I was a 17-year-old student at Carlett Park College. Many years later, after having studied history at two universities and taught the subject in schools, I felt I was ready to attempt the task. It has been a humbling experience: I have truly discovered the depth and quality of the research which has already been carried out. There have been many unsung heroes and heroines who have lovingly transcribed and edited a range of essential sources. Without their work, it would have taken decades to be able to get to the point of writing a meaningful history. Even amongst the more popular works, there are items of almost equal importance—the *Wirral Journal*, for example, contains numerous succinct and readable accounts of vital topics; the author of the best of them remained consistently anonymous. I offer this work partly in tribute to all such lovers of Wirral who have given the task of sharing their knowledge and reflections about their homeland a higher priority than personal gain or aggrandisement and to all the scholars and researchers who blazed the trail ahead of me.

One

From Creation to the First Settlements

Historians are concerned with the human past, so geological time is not strictly within their domain, but the history of a place is built upon its physical foundations—the lives of humans are influenced by the landscape upon which they dwell, so it is important to know how and why that landscape has ended up looking the way it does. Furthermore, it is interesting to observe how geology and physical geography have so much in common with archaeology and history. They all start by studying the information and trying to see patterns. Then, using the patterns, they make a 'story', which can then be further tested by looking at more information gathered from the field. All the evidence from particular periods is studied in order to construct both descriptions of what happened and explanations for why they happened in the ways in which they did.

Geology as a science emerged during the 18th and 19th centuries. Much of the early work focused on the argument about whether contemporary interpretations of the Bible— notably the one formulated by Archbishop James Ussher of Armagh, in 1650, which said that the Earth was created in 4004 B.C., on Sunday 26 October, at 9 a.m.—could be supported by the evidence. Eventually, geologists were able to put together a 'story'. They analysed the rock layers or strata and studied the fossils which lay within them. By the late 19th century, it had become clear that the days of creation were not literal 24-hour periods, but great eras of millions of years in duration. In addition, glaciation, rather than Noah's flood, had come to be regarded as the main cause of later erosion and deposition. It is the internal structures of Wirral's rocks and the ways in which they have been laid on top of each other and then been affected by ice which enable us to tell the following story.

About 4,600 million years ago the Earth was formed. There was not yet any trace of the Wirral peninsula. The earliest known rocks on Earth are about 3,800 million years old. The oldest rocks now visible in Wirral began to form some 3,555 million years later, that is about 245 million years ago. Their uppermost strata were laid down about 37 million years after that. Wirral's hills—at Wallasey, Bidston, Storeton, Grange, Caldy, Thurstaston and Heswall—are made of these rocks. Look at them carefully—you will see that they are composed of billions of grains of sand which have been compressed and stuck together; they are the product of an ancient environment totally unlike that in which we live today.

Earth's surface is made up of a number of plates which slide around, bumping and grinding against each other. The European Plate had moved to a position near the Equator, so it was drier and hotter than it is today. At certain times, the area might have been as hot and as arid as the Sahara Desert, but at others, for periods of hundreds of years, it would have been more hospitable—wetter and warm rather than hot. It was, perhaps,

1   The distances from Willaston, the notional centre of Wirral.

something like the Nile Delta at the height of Egyptian civilization, where it was quite lush and capable of supporting a variety of animals—Wirral's first residents: the 'Hand Beast', or *Chirotherium* and the 'Snouted Lizard', or *Rhyncosaurus*.

Chirotherium is known mainly by 'trace fossils', or petrified footprints. One matching fossil skeleton was found in Switzerland in 1965. *Chirotherium* was a carnivore which probably ate herbivorous creatures like *Rhyncosaurus*. *Rhyncosaurus* has left skeletons in the Americas, and at Grinshill in Shropshire which have enabled reconstructions of its appearance—to us, the creature would look outlandish, with its long hooked beaks for grubbing up roots, and its powerful jaws and strong teeth for consuming vast amounts of tough plant material. These creatures were large—about a metre high and two metres long; they were heavy enough to make deep impressions in the mud through which they plodded. *Chirotheriums*, who have since been celebrated as the earliest known Wirral residents, plodded along the edge of a shallow lake, which had formed as a result of a sudden downpour.

The cloying ooze through which they squelched was made up of the material which had been eroded from the nearby mountains and washed onto the flood plain. During a subsequent hot, dry spell, loose sand was blown over their tracks, soaking up the dampness, and was then baked by the sun. During the hundreds of millions of years which followed, many more layers were deposited. They were all baked, compressed and stuck together with chemicals such as oxides of iron, which make the sandstone red, and crystals of silica, which make it sparkle. Romano-British people on Wirral certainly knew that the local sandstone was a good building material. By Victorian times, it was being intensively quarried, with the result that hand prints from the old monsters came to light. In fact, they made Storeton quite famous—you will find it mentioned in many a 19th-century geological text. Slabs containing footprints were sent to museums in Liverpool, London, Oxford and Cornwall. Later finds were built into a draper's shop window and into the porch of Bebington church.[1] Many of the early finds were destroyed when Liverpool Museum was burnt out during the May 1941 Blitz in the Second World War. Trace fossils of smaller contemporary animals have been found in Oxton and Hilbre produced further evidence of *Chirotherium* in the 1990s.

Rocks which contain these prints often reveal other evidence from that time—many a Wirral rambler has picked up stones bearing ripple marks caused by floods or cracks resulting from the heat of the sun. It often seems that one moment during a time so

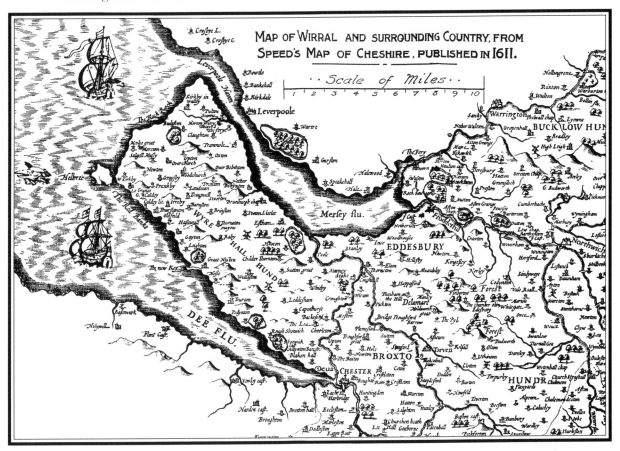

2 Speed's 1611 map of Cheshire. Notice the clear depiction of the lines of hills and the stream running through the Deva Spillway forming Wirral's eastern boundary.

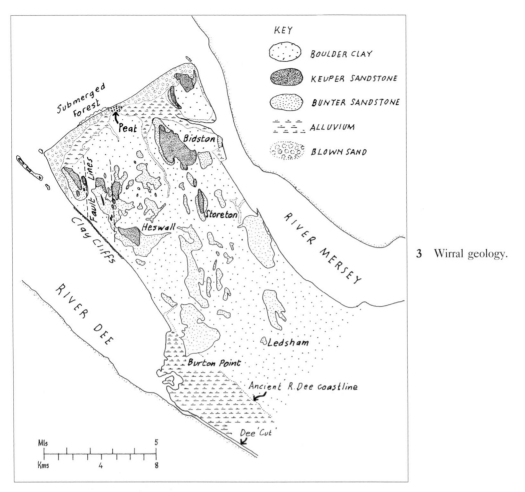

KEY

BOULDER CLAY

KEUPER SANDSTONE

BUNTER SANDSTONE

ALLUVIUM

BLOWN SAND

3 Wirral geology.

immeasurably distant and incredibly dissimilar to our own has been preserved just to remind us that we are neophytes on this beautiful and mysterious globe.

Wirral's older rocks are not visible. They lie beneath the sandstone and were formed some 100 million years earlier, during the Carboniferous period (from the Latin *carbo*, meaning 'coal'), when conditions were warm and humid and the environment fluctuated between being completely submerged in sea water to becoming deltaic swamp. Vegetation of the period is often described as 'coal forest'—it consisted of huge fern-like trees, which were home to a range of creatures, such as giant dragonflies the size of seagulls and millipedes as long as crocodiles. Dead leaves and timber accumulated and rotted on the floor, creating layers of peat, which slowly turned to coal. No carboniferous rocks are visible on the surface of Wirral, but coal measures are found some 150 to 600 feet below the surface at Neston, lying in seams between a foot and six feet thick.

Wirral's rocks have traditionally been labelled 'New Red Sandstone'. It is not a term which seems apposite when we think that they were formed hundreds of millions of years ago, but, of course, they are only 'new' in comparison to many other rocks of the Earth's surface, chiefly the Old Red Sandstone of the previous period—the Devonian, which began about 395 million years ago. In fact, they were laid down during the late Permian and Triassic periods, which lay within the Palaeozoic and Mesozoic 'eras'—an enormous period of time, during which there were animals, who have left fossilised remains of their skeletons (giving the name of the overall geological 'age', covering the last 600 million years from Cambrian to Holocene—the Phanerozoic, from the Greek *phaneros*, meaning 'visible' and *zoion*, meaning 'animal' or 'life-form').

The sandstone actually comprises several distinct strata, which geologists have labelled according to the shape, size and colour of their constituent grains and the presence of pebbles and clay. The uppermost and most recent layers are called Keuper sandstone; the lower and older were traditionally called Bunter sandstone. Both terms are German. The latter comes from *bunt*, meaning 'coloured, bright or mottled'. The more up-to-date title for the Bunter rocks is Sherwood sandstone. Wirral's examples are known as the Thurstaston member of the Helsby Sandstone formation (the other members are Delamere and Frodsham). Keuper Sandstone is usually pale yellow, creamy-white, grey or red. The footprint beds lie within this section of the rock at about 120 feet above its base and mark the strata which are most useful as building material, being tough and gritty, but not pebbly. It has been quarried at Higher Bebington, Storeton, Thingwall, Irby and Heswall.[2] Other layers are either too soft or too pebbly to be used in building. The Bunter sandstone can either be red or yellow (as at Red and Yellow Noses in New Brighton), pebbly (as at Wallasey, Tranmere and Hilbre), soft (as at Burton Point, which is now called Kinnerton sandstone) or hard and coarse grained (as at Caldy and Thurstaston).

It is evident that the sandstone was deposited by water because of the pebbles it contains—they could only have been carried along by powerful, desert flash-floods. Close scrutiny of the grains reveals how they have been sorted out and graded by the action of the flowing water. Some examples, including outcrops on Hilbre, contain fossilised worm tracks. A wonderful example of both the stratification and the tilting or slumping of the

4 Sandstone strata at Thurstaston: the varying colours and depths of the successive layers are evidence of the different environments which existed when each one was deposited. This cross section is visible due to the construction of a cutting for the West Kirby to Chester Road.

5 Evidence of faulting in the sandstone ridge between Thurstaston and Caldy: the valley in the centre of the picture is the result of the downward slippage of a large block of sandstone between two faults which cut through the sandstone ridge. Stapledon Woods are visible at the right of the lower slopes of Caldy Hill on the opposite side of the valley.

Bunter beds can be seen in the cutting for the A540 West Kirby to Chester Road as it passes along the western edge of Thurstaston Common (see illustration 4).

Wirral's sandstone outcrops form two parallel ridges, running north-west to south-east. Grange and Caldy Hills (256 feet above sea level) form the northernmost tip of the western ridge (nearest the Dee), which then includes Thurstaston (300 feet), Heswall (359 feet) and Burton (222 feet). The eastern ridge (nearest the Mersey) comprises Wallasey (188 feet), Bidston (231 feet), Prenton (259 feet) and Higher Bebington (229 feet). These relative highlands are the result of the lifting and sinking of separate blocks of rock, all of which were formed as a result of faults, or deep, linear fractures, in the Earth's crust. The most important faults run north to south, but there are several smaller ones which cut into them at right angles and therefore run west to east, creating the distinctive, separate highs and lows of north Wirral. A good example is the gap which exists between the Grange/Caldy ridge and its continuation at Thurstaston. It is most visible to the traveller heading towards Chester on the A540 from West Kirby, where it descends to the roundabout at Caldy Crossroads where the road levels out for about half a mile. This is a valley formed by geological faults—a huge block of rock has sunk in relation to its neighbours, creating a pass through the ridge, which, in the early 19th century, was actually identified as a possible route for a ship canal running between Birkenhead Docks, the north Wirral coastal plain and Dawpool. Another result of faults is the tilting of the rocks, giving the inclination of the Wirral ridges to dip gently eastwards (looking towards Liverpool) and steeply westwards (looking towards Wales). However, one of the foremost physical geographers of Merseyside—Dr R. Kay Greswell—counselled caution when judging the importance of faults in creating Wirral's landscape:

Whatever degree of relief may have been produced by the Alpine fault movements, their incidence must have been spread over a considerable time, so that [erosion] would operate through the period of their occurrence, and thus prevent the various escarpments, horsts and graben from ever attaining their fullest tectonc magnitude. By the time the area became covered by ice-sheets, it would seem that the solid-rock surface was already one of fairly low relief.[3]

Wirral is, however, a saddle—the product of faults: they determined the pre-glacial drainage of the peninsula—all streams must have flowed north-westwards, or parallel to the current Dee and Mersey estuaries. He also described the formation of the Dee estuary: it is the result of two faults—one on the Welsh side and the other running along Wirral's coast, known as the Wirral Colliery Fault. Both faults had their 'down-throws' on their eastern sides. In other words, a staircase was created. If you had stood on the spot which is now the bank of the Dee at Ness, you would not have seen a drop, but a vertical cliff in front of you. If you had ascended this cliff and looked towards what is now Bagillt, you would see another cliff running along the Flintshire coast—not a propitious beginning for a major river estuary, as the feature was actually the reverse of what was necessary for carrying a flow of water. Erosion, however, completely altered the profile, removing the less resistant layers of sandstone and the older Carboniferous Upper Coal Measures which lay beneath them to create a slight indentation, which was deep enough to form a river bed.

There are no remains from the rest of the Mesozoic 'era' (i.e. from the Jurassic and Cretaceous periods) on the Wirral peninsula, which is doubtless a source of disappointment to many a young dinosaur enthusiast. It is unclear whether the succeeding era—the Cainozoic (from the Greek *kainos*, meaning 'new' or 'recent' and *zoion*, meaning 'life-form')—embraces the Tertiary period (from 66 million years ago) and the Quaternary period (between 1.6

6   The Mersey estuary from New Brighton shore: Wallasey Town Hall is the tall building on the right and Liverpool's Liver Buildings are visible on the left bank of the river. The photograph illustrates the narrowness of the channel between Birkenhead and Liverpool—a condition which has ensured that the tidal flow is always powerful and has prevented the channel from silting.

7 The Dee estuary from Grange Hill, West Kirby: the spire of St Andrew's church and Middle Eye and Hilbre are visible; the expanse of dry sand conveys a sense of the estuary's great width and reminds us of its vulnerability to silting.

million and years ago and the present). The Quaternary is divided into two 'epochs'—the Pleistocene (from the Greek *pleistos*, meaning 'most' and *kainos*) and the Holocene (from the Greek *holos*, meaning 'whole' and *kainos*). The Pleistocene 'epoch' is more commonly known as the Ice Age and lasted until about 10,000 years ago. The Holocene epoch followed it and has not yet finished. During the Quaternary period, the world began to possess environments and life-forms which we would recognise: mammals came into their own and Modern Man or *Homo sapiens* spread throughout the globe. During the Pleistocene, many species of mammal, such as the mammoth and the mastodon, became extinct, while the group of humans whom we call *Neanderthals* had adapted very well to the cold environment and flourished throughout Europe, Central Asia and the Near East. The importance of the epoch for Wirral, however, is less to do with life-forms, but all to do with the gigantic natural forces which now set about sculpting the landscape and bequeathing the stage upon which the history of our ancestors was to be acted out.

During the Pleistocene epoch or Ice Age, the average annual temperature for the entire surface of the Earth was about six degrees lower than it is today. Winter temperatures in Britain were 25 to 30 degrees lower than they are today. It is not clear exactly why this happened: perhaps the heat of the sun had declined, the angle of the Earth's axis in relation to the sun had altered or the solar system was filled with cosmic dust which shielded the Earth from the full power of the sun's rays; but it undoubtedly had a profound effect upon climate, weather and environment: the ice caps were able to creep outwards from the poles; cooler air masses over the north Atlantic meant that there was less evapo-ration, making the seas less salty; icebergs were common; and the lands of northern Europe and North America became vast, chilly plains. The soil never fully thawed (permafrost) and was covered in lichens, grasses, sedges and hardy conifers (tundra) and, therefore, resembled present-day Siberia or Arctic Canada. Of course, the ice was common and widespread. For example, Mount Kilimanjaro in East Africa is only three degrees of latitude away from the Equator—it is estimated that, during the Ice Age, the mountain's ice cap extended 1,200 metres further down its western side than it previously had done, reaching an altitude of 3,400 metres above sea level, instead of the current 5,800 metres.[4] There were four separate major cold periods, which came between warm spells lasting up to 150,000 years. The last great period of glaciation (the Devensian) began about 60,000 years ago and reached its maximum extent 39,000 years later.

The ice which affected Wirral was formed in the Lake District and the Western Highlands of Scotland. It had begun life as snow which had piled up in the hollows on the mountainsides and then been compressed, losing its air content and becoming denser and harder. The subsequent masses of ice resembled gigantic ice cubes which began to slide downwards—these were the glaciers. Where they met neighbouring glaciers, they coalesced to form even bigger ones and continued to slide southwards into the hollow which we now call the Irish Sea, which, at that time, was dry. The ice attained a depth of 450 metres and was carrying debris which it had gouged out of its native hills; it now proceeded to scrape up and carry countless thousands of tons of material from what was to become the seabed. As we have seen, the bedrock was sandstone, so the ice was now carrying a red, sticky mud as well as many loose rocks and pebbles. When it reached the Wirral area, it was deflected

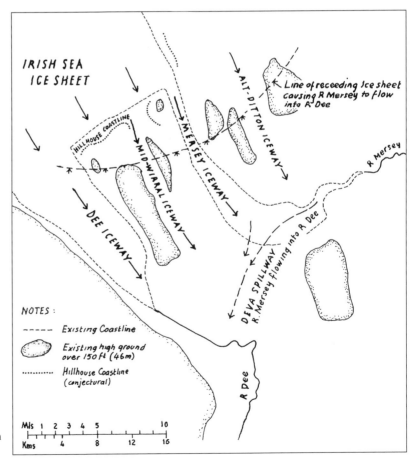

8   The effects of glaciation on the Wirral Peninsula.

9 The view across the northern end of Wirral from Grange Hill, West Kirby towards Wallasey: the shallow valley in the centre is the northern end of the mid-Wirral iceway, lying between the Deeside and Merseyside sandstone ridges.

by the harder rocks of the Clwydian Hills and effectively funnelled into a tighter and more powerful south-easterly flow. It found its way over the Wirral sandstone, using its layer of accumulated debris to abrade and scoop up the softer rocks in its path. Only the harder rocks remained proud. The ice's course can be traced on the local landscape, chiefly in the form of four great parallel ice ways, or valleys, which it carved between the outcrops of harder rock. They are the Dee and Mersey estuaries, the Mid Wirral Valley (now occupied by the M53 Motorway) and the Alt-Ditton Gap in southern Lancashire.

The Dee estuary is wide and shallow, demonstrating the disposition of the harder rocks—they lie at the northern edge of Wales and at Red Rocks near Hilbre Point. Hilbre Island itself withstood the glacial onslaught because its rocks are harder. The Mersey has a very distinctive shape—its narrow mouth is a result of the ice being funnelled between two outcrops of hard sandstone, one of which underlies Liverpool and the other Wallasey and Birkenhead. The channel at this point is partly filled with boulder clay; excavations for the Kingsway road tunnel revealed that the solid rock at this point lies at 90 feet below sea level. The inner part of the Mersey estuary, lying between Speke, Runcorn and Eastham, is much wider and shallower and must have been the resting place of a large body of ice. A bore hole in the Mersey at Ellesmere Port showed that solid rock lies at 146 feet below sea level.[5] On the land, any remnants of previous glaciations were completely erased, along with any possible evidence of human settlement in the area. In addition, the courses of Wirral's rivers were redefined. At last, the peninsula was taking shape, but the work was still not complete.

The above description is of the erosive or destructive power of the glaciers. Of equal, if not greater, importance for Wirral was their constructive ability: remember all that mud, which was made up from the grains of pulverised sandstone from the bed of the future Irish Sea and from the surrounding rocks; it was now suspended at the base of the glaciers—

as the ice retreated, between 14,000 and 12,000 years ago, it began to leave this glutinous mass behind and effectively to act like a plasterer, coating an ancient, rugged stonewall with a layer of cement, filling in the hollows and disguising the bumps. This wonderfully cosmetic material used to be called till, but is now known as boulder clay. It makes up about 65 per cent of the surface area of Wirral and its thickness ranges between one and 150 feet;[6] it is, therefore, the chief determinant of the peninsula's appearance, vegetation and agriculture. Many Wirralians will identify with the experience of Norman Ellison as he scrutinised the boulder clay cliffs at Thurstaston: 'With our penknives we dug out several small stones ... and found a thrill in exposing to daylight again something that had been buried for a million [*sic*] years.'[7]

He reminds us of the reason why the word 'boulder' is used to describe the clay: it contains tons of eroded material—everything from sand and gravel to large rocks, many of which are not native to the district and are, therefore, termed 'erratics'. There are rocks from all the homelands of the glaciers—greenstones and other basaltics, granites, grits, andesites, tuffs, quartzites, limestones, shales and mudstones, revealing provenances in Ailsa Craig, Buttermere, Criffel, Galloway, Shap and many more localities in the Lake District and Scotland. Poetically, the prehistoric transport of these beautiful rock specimens to Wirral seems to presage many of the human immigrations which were to occur in historic times and were similarly to enrich the peninsula. During the 1920s, Hewitt recorded bore holes which were designed to measure the depths of the glacial deposits on dry land: the one at Ellesmere Port revealed clay and gravel to a depth of 90 feet and the one at Hooton showed glacial deposits to a depth of 169 feet; solid rock was discovered at 62 feet below sea level, revealing just how important glacial deposition has been in creating the substance and profile of the Wirral peninsula.[8] Wirral's surface is generally smooth. This indicates that the clay was deposited gradually by ice which was moving slowly as it melted.

Clay is heavy, sticky, acidic and wet. It enables the growth of good pasture and woodland, but can be difficult to work. Fortunately for Wirral's farmers, nature seems to have provided a remedy in the midst of the boulder clay itself—marl—a versatile substance, which, when added to the soil, can improve both its chemical composition, by making it less acidic, and its physical character, by making it lighter, more workable and better drained. Marl is simply certain parts of the boulder clay which contain a higher proportion of lime (calcium carbonate), often in the form of shells—material which was scooped up by the glaciers on their way southwards from Scotland and the Lakes and deposited here during the thaw. The social history of marling will be discussed in later chapters; suffice it to say here that the substance was found in pockets throughout the peninsula and was extensively dug, leaving flooded pits, which we now know as ponds.

The ice affected the sea level, which, in turn, affected the appearance of Wirral's coast. The weight of the glaciers depressed the Earth's crust, but the sea level was low because much of the water was stored within the ice. It is estimated that global sea level was 120 metres lower than it is now. As the ice melted, the crust began to rise (the process is called isostatic rebound or equilibrium), but so did the level of the sea, possibly at a faster rate than did the land. Dr Gresswell identified a feature which he believed to be the result of wave erosion, which occurred around 5000 B.C., while the sea level was much higher than it is now, during the so called Flandrian Maximum. He called it The Hillhouse coast, and demonstrated its existence between the Lleyn peninsula and south Lancashire,

10 Marlpit at Arrowe, July 2002: a heron looks for fish on the edge of a pond which was the result of man's exploitation of a natural resource which the glaciers bequeathed to the landscape. Marl is a natural fertiliser made mainly of shells and found in pockets in the boulder clay.

where the eponymous village of Hillhouse lies. It takes the form of a step in the landscape. Its landward side is a fossil cliff, rising to a height of 50 feet above sea level, which the sea cut into the boulder clay. Its seaward side is effectively the former beach at about 17 feet above sea level, which runs down to the modern actual beach.

The identification of the Hillhouse cliff at the northern end of Wirral is not easy, but Gresswell claimed that it could be seen running from the northern edge of Grange Hill, through Moreton, inland a little at the Fender Valley, along the edge of Bidston Hill and then to Wallasey. The former beach is the coastal plain, now containing Hoylake, Meols, Moreton and Leasowe. In order to gain an impression of this feature, stand in any of these settlements with your back to the sea and look in a south-easterly direction—you will notice the way that the flat area continues inland for about a mile and then the ground begins to rise at the point where the ancient cliff existed. The motorist travelling towards Upton along the A551 from Moreton Cross will notice how the road climbs gently for about half a mile until it reaches the junction of the M53 Motorway, which is effectively at the top of the former cliff. This is a good place to turn around and look towards the sea and try to imagine how the area might have looked when the sea level was higher: there would have been water right up to the primary school on Upton Road, engulfing the centre of Moreton. The urbanisation of the district does not aid the pinpointing of physical features, but the real problem is that the cliff is unspectacular: it has been eroded or degraded—

its angle is less acute than it used to be, but it can be traced on the 1:50000 Ordnance Survey map, along the 10-metre contour line.

Dr Gresswell did most of his fieldwork in Lancashire and admitted: 'There is considerable uncertainty regarding the distance to which the Hillhouse tidal estuary penetrated the Fender Valley, and whether or not Wallasey was an island with the sea occupying The Floats.'[9]

Perhaps Gresswell was getting carried away with his theory: his mind's eye might have been over stimulated by the eagerness to see a continuity, running southwards, in a line which he had found north of the Mersey and which he knew existed in Scotland. We will find a similar phenomenon amongst those keen to trace routes of Roman roads through Wirral. Certainly, his theory is widely disputed: recent work has questioned Gresswell's chronology—calculations of former sea levels show that, at the time when the Hillhouse coast was supposedly being formed, sea levels were about three metres lower than would have been required to erode land at this height. In addition, analysis of the sand found on the former beach area of the Hillhouse coast in Lancashire has revealed the existence of the same sort of sand over 20 kilometres inland—much further than the sea is believed to have penetrated. This questions both the notion that it was deposited by the sea in the first place and also the possible date of deposition—it is postulated that it must have been laid down about 11,000 years ago, but no firm conclusions have been reached and more research is needed.[10] Here we see a good example of the evolution of knowledge about the past—observations were made and stories or hypotheses put forward, which were subsequently re-checked with the help of new data and consequently altered. It is a process which occurs in all the disciplines being employed in this book—geology, geography, archaeology and history.

The precise chronology and details of Wirral's coastal changes are disputed, but nobody doubts that they actually occurred. Change, both natural and caused by humans, is a phenomenon which the reader must constantly bear in mind whilst considering the history of the district, especially with regard to the coast. Much exciting work has been done on the environmental history of north Wirral, mainly stimulated by the numerous archaeological discoveries from Meols and the former visibility of the remains of great forests on the foreshore. There have been important scientific advances in archaeological techniques over the last 40 years, including Radio Carbon 14 dating, pollen analysis and other methods of studying ancient environmental evidence. They have enabled detailed pictures of the evolution of the local coasts to be drawn. A central fact which all the studies prove is that the coastline has fluctuated: the tree trunks on the beach, for example, are evidence of dry land having lain much further out to sea than it does at present—the opposite condition to that which is implied by the Hillhouse coast. As the evidence deals chiefly with the human prehistoric period, further discussion of this topic will be found in the next chapter.[11]

During the early 20th century, William Ashton studied the coasts of the Irish Sea and developed a theory, which is relevant to the history of Wirral, concerning the course of the River Mersey. He observed that 19th-century local historians, such as Mortimer and Ormerod, as well as local tradition, had assumed that the Mersey had not emptied into the Irish Sea in the Liverpool Bay as it does today, but had flowed across the southern neck of the Wirral Peninsula, through a depression called the Broxton Valley, now occupied by the Shropshire Union Canal, and joined the Dee just north-west of Chester. As evidence,

11 Boulder clay at its most spectacular—Thurstaston shore: this promontory is some thirty feet high and was formed by melting and receding glaciers which plastered their great loads of mud, sand and boulders over the bedrock. The cave at the centre is the result of a pocket of sand which has been exposed by sea erosion and has trickled onto the shore; 'erractics' or rocks which were transported to Wirral from Scotland and the Lake District are visible on the shore.

he cited the existence of sands, gravels and shells in this valley and the fact that it has no significant gradient, making it an ideal host for the canal. He asserted that the inner part of the Mersey estuary (bounded by Speke, Runcorn and Eastham) was a freshwater lake into which the streams of north Wirral once drained via Wallasey Pool. He even quoted historical evidence to show that the Mersey estuary is a relatively new feature: the second-century Roman geographer Ptolemy did not mark it on his map and the *Antonine Itinerary* did not mention it. He went on to say:

> It is probable that when the Romans in the year 79 A.D. marched from Anglesey along the coast to the north of England they would cross the Dee at the ford which Flint Castle was built to defend, and would cross on foot from the Wirral to Seaforth, where a Roman coin of Vespasian's reign has been found: they would march north through Harkirke (Little Crosby), Formby, Birkdale Common, and Far Banks, at all of which places Roman coins of the era also have been found.[12]

Is this another example of wishful thinking resulting from enthusiasm for a theory? Does a supposed line of extremely infrequent Roman coins constitute proof of a land crossing where the Mersey estuary now exists? It might have been just such thinking which undermined enthusiasm for the hypothesis in later years, but Ashton did cite other evidence which supported the claim that the sea level had once been lower but had since risen and broken through whatever obstacle was lying at the mouth of the Mersey and flooded previously dry land: the supposed Roman bridge at 15 feet below high tide which was discovered at Wallasey Pool in 1845; a possible ford across the Mersey which was found 15 feet below sea level at Eastham; and the inclination of roads on the coastal plain to head towards the sea, indicating the former existence of a land mass between Wirral and Lancashire. He suggested that the floods occurred between the fourth and eighth centuries A.D. and quoted Camden who had written that, in A.D. 563, 'There occurred in Cheshire an inundation of the sea by which 5000 persons and an innumerable quantity of cattle perished'. Ashton, therefore, presumed that the modern course of the lower Mersey estuary was formed in historic times and that the Broxton Valley would have silted up and dried out after that event.

Ashton's theory is not now accepted. As a result of more advanced scientific analysis of coastal strata near Meols, Ray Kenna was able to say this in 1978:

> There is no evidence for the Mersey flowing into the Dee through the Broxton Valley in historic times or during the last 10,000 years; neither is there evidence for the main channel of the Mersey having entered the sea to the north west via Wallasey Pool. During the Roman period, a navigable entrance may not have been in evidence due to the existence of sand bars, spits and banks formed from glacial and periglacial sediment already in Liverpool Bay ... During the Roman period and earlier times the Mersey may have been more deltaic in appearance, backed by uninviting saltmarsh.[13]

This is not completely to dismiss Ashton's work because it is accepted that the Broxton Valley was a kind of river course, but its official title is now the Deva Spillway or Backford Gap: it seems that the mouth of the Mersey *was* blocked either in the way in which Kenna described above or by a large remnant of ice. The melt waters from the inland ice sheets gathered in what is now the inner Mersey estuary and then overflowed at the lowest point they could find—the Broxton Valley—and ran to the Dee. The barrier eventually either melted or was eroded away and the waters were released, leaving the Broxton Valley high and dry. This happened during prehistoric times. Again, the reader is being reminded that, on Wirral, environmental changes have been dramatic and must have presented differing challenges and opportunities to human settlers.

Wirral had a belt of spectacular sand-dunes along its Irish Sea coast. Due to urban development, they are now visible only in pockets. They were the same as the sand-dunes of North Wales and south Lancashire and were probably formed at the same time and in the same way: some 5,000 years ago, once sea levels had stabilised, prevailing winds blew dry sand onshore from the offshore sandbanks as they lay exposed at low tide. The sand-dune belt reached a width of half a mile and the dunes achieved heights of between 50 and 60 feet. They probably took 2,500 years to form. Residents at the tip of Wirral are familiar with the accumulation of sand next to kerbs, walls and other urban features during windy weather and are, therefore, being reminded of nature's continuing desire to replace its lost sand-dune belt.

Wirral's streams are noted neither for their width nor their power, but they have generated particular vegetation, shaped settlement and land use and affected the psyches of Wirral people, colouring their ideas of place and home. As has been said, due to faulting,

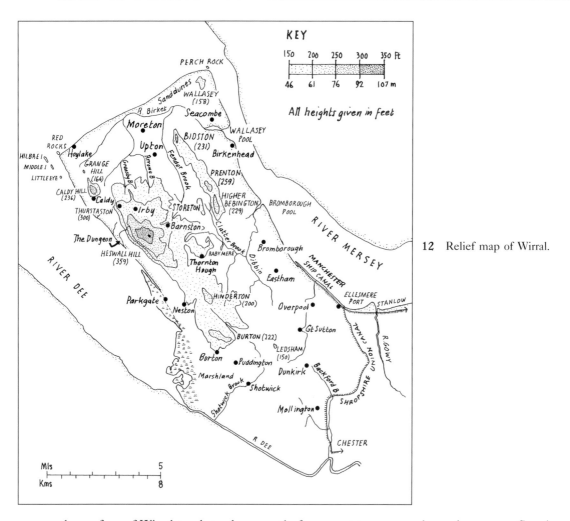

12   Relief map of Wirral.

the surface of Wirral tends to slope gently from west to east, so the main streams flow into the Mersey estuary. There are three drainage basins. The largest centres on the River Birket in the north; it drains an area of about 30 square miles and flows into the Wallasey Pool. The river was named 'Birket' after Birkenhead by the Ordnance Survey in the 19th century. Its course has been altered by man, but the strange way in which it runs parallel to the north coast, rather than emptying into the Irish Sea, is thought to be natural and a result of the sand-dune barrier. It emerges at the foot of Grange Hill and is augmented by Caldy, Arrowe and Greasby Brooks and the River Fender, which emerges at the northern end of the Mid Wirral Iceway, next to the A553 Bidston by-pass. Eric Rideout wrote this enchanting description of the course of Greasby Brook in 1922:

> The brook, though at present hardly larger than a ditch, arises on the extreme southern edge of Irby Heath and crossing the heathland its course is better marked for the distinctive vegetation on either bank. On the left is a grove of overhanging birch trees and on the edge of the moor a grass slope; on the right are the fields hardly won from nature sloping down

from the pine-clad summit of Irby Mill Hill. The confluence of Greasby and Arrowe Brooks near the footpath from Greasby village to that of Saughall Massie is an extremely characteristic and pretty sight, the volume of water being sufficient to illustrate on a small scale the formation of bars and shoals where sand and clay with small pebbles brought along by flood waters have been deposited with the slowing of currents.[14]

The reader will be able to compare the description with this modern scene and to ask why, 80 years later, certain parts of the course of the brook are so different. The author, even though he grew up in the area over forty years after Rideout's account, can recognise the features he describes, particularly the area near Saughall Massie, where many a long summer afternoon was spent knee-deep in water, pushing a net through the weed in pursuit of sticklebacks, sometimes shrieking with delighted horror after landing a water scorpion or staring in whispering awe at a kingfisher on a fence post. The Irby Heath section resonates with the memories of older and more contemplative years spent walking home from Thurstaston on winter afternoons as the sinking sun's beams were fractured by the sighing birch trees. It all serves to remind us of the importance of the landscape in helping to mould our sense of who we are and particularly of the ability which streams and rivers have of creating places upon that landscape for us to love and remember. It is unsurprising that the ancient Celts said that rivers were gods.

The second largest drainage basin covers 25 square miles and empties into Bromborough Pool. This also includes exciting and picturesque localities, especially Dibbinsdale, home of the River Dibbin or Dibbinsdale Brook. It is an area of woodland which was never cleared by man due to its lying in a deep valley which the stream has carved both through the boulder clay and sandstone and is, thankfully, today a nature reserve. The river originates as two unnamed branches—one near Street Hey in Willaston and the other betweeen Hooton and Childer Thornton. It passes along the eastern edge of Bromborough Golf Course, creating another picturesque haven for nature called Plymyard Dale. The Clatter Brook emerges to the west of Storeton Hill, passes through the Clatterbridge Hospital complex and creates a similarly wooded valley as it runs south-east to join the Dibbin between Raby Dell and Dibbins Green in Bromborough. The Dibbin is fed by a nameless stream which rises just south of Thornton Hough and another which emerges near Willaston and flows just west of Hargrave Hall Farm and down to Raby Mere, which is where it has been dammed to create a millpond.

Backford Brook drains some 12 square miles; it emerges at Dunkirk near the A5117 and flows south, through Backford and Mollington, under the Shropshire Union Canal and into the River Dee at Chester.

Another nameless stream emerges just south of Capenhurst and flows through Great Sutton, then along a valley between Overpool and Little Sutton and down to the Manchester Ship Canal, where it forms the heart of Rivacre Country Park.

There are only really three streams which flow into the Dee estuary—Shotwick Brook, which emerges in Ness Wood on Mill Lane just west of the A540 Chester High Road and then flows south-east, parallel to the main road until it reaches Woodbank, where it diverts to the south-west and flows through Shotwick down to the Dee. Between Heswall and Thurstaston a stream rises at the top of the Deeside ridge and flows down to the estuary, cutting a beautiful gorge through the sandstone and creating a waterfall and another enclave of woodland known as the Dungeon. There is a further brook to the north of Thurstaston which emerges in fields, cuts through the boulder clay, where it provides shelter for a dense growth of gorse and blackthorn, and then trickles onto the shore.

It is clear that, without the streams, there would be far less surviving natural vegetation on the surface of Wirral, as the land would probably have been totally cleared between Prehistoric and Medieval times in order to provide more space for both the plough and pasture; it would then have been swallowed up by the urban development of the last 150 years. The reader is advised to peruse local maps and to notice the many other ways in which humble streams have helped shape the landscape: by determining field, township and parish boundaries, by dictating local land use, by acting as ornaments at the heart of country estates or by carrying away industrial effluent and sewage. Also observe how man has diverted, sunk and canalised the water courses for his own purposes.

The Wirral peninsula took hundreds of millions of years to become an inhabitable part of the Earth's surface. The above description should have revealed how this came about and given an idea of what obstacles and resources lay in wait for the people who were going to make it their home. The ensuing chapters will attempt to discover who these people were, how they got on and what they did to the landscape upon which they lived.

Two

From the First Settlers to the Romans

Part One: Trifling Relics of Primeval Races?

Prehistory is so called because nobody wrote anything. The traditional definition says that the historian is primarily interested in documents, so the study of illiterate past societies is the domain of the archaeologist who studies objects. Emphasis of the dichotomy of the two disciplines is unhelpful: of course, their respective exponents use different skills, but they do want to achieve the same end—the reconstruction and explanation of the human past. The local and regional historian must be prepared to compare the evidence produced by both disciplines and explore the continuity of human settlement from prehistory to history within the chosen area. Indeed, even when exploring historic times, archaeology assists the historian in this aim.

Learned people had always revered the literate civilisations of Greece and Rome: they had been taught Greek and Latin at school and encouraged to admire and copy the great men of those societies, such as Socrates, Aristotle, Alexander the Great and Julius Caesar. The period when these heroes flourished is known as Classical Times or the Ancient World and everything which preceded it was thought to be virtually unknowable.

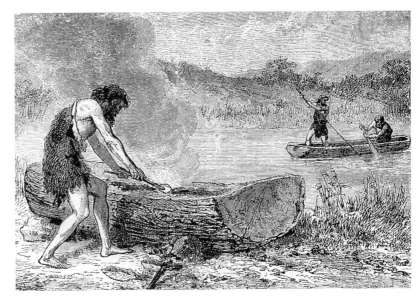

13 Artist's impression (*c.*1947) of prehistoric Wirral boat scene somewhere on the Wallasey Pool. The shaggy beards and ragged clothes were typical features in earlier ideas about the appearances of prehistoric people; they are not based on evidence—nobody knows how our early ancestors would have looked, but perhaps they were not as wild as this.

Prehistory was a heathen and savage time, 'wrapped in a thick fog' and about which 'we can do no more than guess'.[1] Progress occurred in the 19th century when Christian J. Thomsen (1788-1865), curator of the Danish National Museum, categorised the archaeological exhibits according to the materials from which they were made in the now familiar order of stone, bronze and iron, believing, on the basis of his own extensive fieldwork, that this was a chronological succession. The system was adopted throughout Europe and was refined by numerous subsequent scholars. We still use it today. Tentative dates were placed on the various ages as a result of cross-referencing between the prehistoric and classical worlds: bronze and iron objects, which must have been traded from the non-literate prehistoric people from northern and central Europe, were discovered at sites in the Mediterranean belonging to the literate Greeks and Romans whose history is datable from written sources.

Thus the prehistoric ages of man are categorised as follows: the Stone Age was the earliest period and is subdivided into the Old Stone Age or Palaeolithic, Middle Stone Age or Mesolithic and New Stone Age or Neolithic; the Bronze Age came next; and was succeeded by the Iron Age. The reader's attention is drawn to Table 1 on page 22 which gives the dates and characteristics of these ages as well as a summary of their representation on the Wirral Peninsula.

Prehistory in England was notionally brought to an end by the Roman conquest of A.D. 43, when a large part of the British Isles was supposedly incorporated into a literate civilisation. In the case of Wirral, this event did little to change the nature of the sources available to us, as, apart from the words found upon the various coins from the period, there is not a single piece of written evidence directly relevant to the district. This fact, together with the paucity of archaeological evidence, dictates, sadly, that the 400-year story of Roman Wirral must be told in the same chapter as the prehistory.

The evidence from prehistoric Wirral has been collected in a variety of ways. Nineteenth-century urbanisation led to the random discovery of valuable items. The very first volume of the *Transactions of the Historic Society of Lancashire and Cheshire* (1849) contains a transcription of a lecture given by the famous Wirral antiquarian and philanthropist Mr Joseph Mayer about several clay funerary vases. He told the story as follows:

> These vases ... were found in 1840 ... about two hundred and fifty yards from the column erected on the top of the hill above, as a sea mark, by the Dock Corporation of Liverpool. There were several Vases found, but only three of them perfect, the others being broken in digging.

There is imprecision in the description of 'several' vases and a limited attempt to analyse the context of the finds. Typically, the vases were inadequately recorded and preserved and have since disappeared. Interestingly, during the rest of his lecture, Mr Mayer tried energetically to relate the finds to the Romans, even though they must have been made up to 1,800 years before the Romans ever came to Britain. He concluded by saying: 'I hope during the summer to be enabled to lay before you something more on the subject, as I think, by a careful examination of that part of country, to find other remains with works of the Romans'. He obviously found it difficult to think about anything ancient unless he could relate it to a classical civilisation and, in this respect, he was a man of his times.

Many items have been found accidentally by observant ramblers or landowners. The *Journal of the Chester Archaeological Society* for 1952 (Volume 39) contains the following entry:

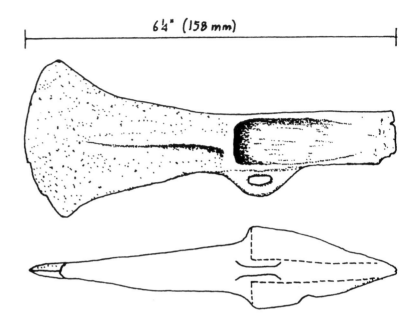

6¼" (158 mm)

14 A single-looped palstave found at Great Sutton was a type of axe made in the Bronze Age and evidence of prehistoric settlement in Wirral.

PALSTAVE FROM GREAT SUTTON. [A Bronze-Age axe] A single-looped palstave was found a few years ago under a bush by a hedge in Church Lane, Great Sutton. It may have been brought to that position recently in road-building material, though this seems unlikely. It is 6¼ inches long and weighs 15¼ oz. The blade has a shallow midrib on each side below the ridge. The palstave is unusual in having the loop above the stop ridge.

This comes from the same journal for 1957 (Volume 44):

STONE AXE FROM OXTON, BIRKENHEAD. [A typical New Stone-Age artifact] Another polished stone axe was dug up in 1951 in the grounds of Westridge, Oxton, Birkenhead (National Grid Reference 303872) and has been placed on loan at the Grosvenor Museum ...

And this from 1962 (Volume 49):

FLINT ARROW-HEAD FROM THURSTASTON. A barbed and tanged flint arrow-head of Bronze-Age date was found in 1946 in a mole-hill west of the main ridge of Thurstaston Hill (precise find-spot not known) ...

Norman Ellison described a similar experience during a visit to the site of Shotwick Castle in his popular work *The Wirral Peninsula* in 1958: 'The Earthworks seemed isolated and forgotten; lonely, silent and brooding. Moles had been busy all over the mound throwing up 'tumps' of new earth. I turned over several with my foot; a mole had once excavated a flint arrow-head for me.'

15 A barbed and tanged flint-arrow head found at Thurstaston. It was made in the Bronze Age and probably lost by a hunter who missed his target.

Table 1

Dates and Characteristics of Wirral from the Old Stone Age to Roman Times

Name of Age	Dates (B.C.)	Characteristics	Examples on Wirral
Old Stone Age/ Palaeolithic	*c.*500,000	Hunter Gatherers; small nomadic groups	None
Middle Stone Age/ Mesolithic	11,000	Hunter Gatherers; small nomadic groups living in temporary encampments; use of microliths	Evidence of flint manufacture at Red Noses, Hilbre Point and Greasby Copse; settlements at Irby and Greasby Copse; cereal pollen at Bidston Moss
New Stone Age/ Neolithic	4,000	Farming and hunting; woodland clearances; polished stone axes	Evidence of flint manufacture at Red Noses and Hilbre Point; pottery at Meols; polished axes from Bidston, Birkenhead, Burton, Little Meols, Moreton, Neston, Wallasey, Woodchurch
Bronze Age	2,500	Farming and hunting; continued woodland clearances; first metal objects made, but flints still used— barbed and tanged arrow-heads; cremations and burials; ritual landscapes; monuments in southern England	Arrow-heads at Burton, Eastham, Little Meols, Shotwick and Thurstaston; perforated tools at Wallasey; bronze axes and other blades at Bidston, Little Meols, Little Sutton, Storeton, Wallasey, North Wirral shore; cremations and burials in West Kirby area
Iron Age	*c.*800	Celtic Languages; pressure on land; hillforts; investment in weapons manufacture	Fortified camp at Burton, Mediterranean coins at Meols = evidence of overseas trade; villages at Meols and Irby; pottery at Irby and Barker Lane, Greasby
Roman	A.D. 43-*c.*400	Large part of Britain incorporated into the Roman Empire; increased urbanisation; roads, military bases and villas; relative villas; relative peace and order established; British people gain opportunities for 'career advancement'; people from diverse geographical origins settle in Britain; introduction of Christianity	Garrison established at Chester; Wirral forms part of *Prata legionis*? Sandstone from Storeton used in Chester; coins used lost and hoarded; rural settlements in North Wirral; Meols continued to flourish as a port; possible Roman Roads between Chester and Birkenhead and Meols; wooden Bridge in Birkenhead?

It is not hard to imagine how the arrow-heads got there: perhaps 5,000 years ago, hunters were roaming the countryside in search of game and either aimed and missed, losing their arrows in the undergrowth or hitting animals which were not killed, but crept away and died in secret where their bodies and the arrow shafts rotted away, leaving only the imperishable stone heads. The axes are a little more problematic: they could have been lost accidentally, deliberately buried or thrown into a pool or other sacred site as an offering to a local god or goddess.

During recent years, many more isolated finds have been made by metal detectorists. When they have been handed over or shown to archaeologists, they have significantly added to our knowledge of the distant past. But for finds to be truly meaningful, their contexts need to be analysed as well. But isolated finds are better than no finds at all—at least they simply reveal that people were present at the time when it is deemed that the objects were made in that particular way with those particular materials.

By far the most satisfactory way for artifacts to be discovered is by competent archaeologists, who take great pains to analyse all the material in an objective and meticulous fashion. Happily there is a growing number of examples of such work relevant to prehistoric Wirral, two of which will be described later in the chapter.

This is a good point at which to introduce the fascinating case of Meols. It is certainly the most important archaeological site in Wirral, perhaps even in England, but one of the least understood. According to Philip Sulley, at least 7,000 antiquities had been picked up from the Meols shore in the 50 years up to 1889.[2] They dated from prehistory to the later Middle Ages and attracted the attention of several antiquarians, the chief of whom was the Rev. A. Hume of Liverpool, whose interest was sparked by seeing several items on the mantelpiece of the vicar of Hoylake, whom he was visiting. The items had been found by a local fisherman and Hume soon discovered that there were many more where they had come from. His subsequent study of the artifacts resulted in his beautiful and monumental work, *Ancient Meols or Some Account of the Antiquities Found near Dove Point on the Sea-Coast of Cheshire* (1863). Fascination with this section of coast was further stimulated by the presence of a submerged forest, visible only at low tide, on the beach between Meols and Leasowe. Other local antiquarians then became involved, such as Edward Cox, Charles Potter and Henry Eckroyd Smith, all of whom made numerous contributions to *The Transactions of the Historic Society of Lancashire and Cheshire*. In Volume 46 for the year 1894, Cox recorded these intriguing and haunting observations about a surface which had been exposed by wind and sea erosion on the foreshore:

> About a foot below the Medieval floor-level, and about eighteen inches below the line of spring tides, a circular hut was exposed, which I only saw after it was broken up by the tide; but in April, 1892, I was fortunate enough to find the foundation of another circular hut, one half of which was visible beyond the scarp of the sand hill. The stones were partly rough, but had a few pick-marks and holes cut in them, in which to set the stakes for the conical roof ... All these residences have their upright stakes preserved, but in soft condition, to a uniform height of about 15 to 18 inches; above this height all trace is gone.

The huts were probably Iron-Age or Romano-British and seem similar to what has been revealed at the Irby excavation which will be described later in the chapter.

How our current archaeologists, with all their scientific techniques, would love to discover such remains today. The Meols area no longer yields such an archaeological bonanza, because the ancient settlement lay offshore from the present town and has been eroded away by the sea. The context of most of the finds was simply destroyed, leaving us guessing about the place's true nature. Suffice it to say here that, due to the remarkable representation of most historical periods up to about A.D. 1500 in the Meols finds, there will be many references to the district during the rest of this work and that the site has stimulated a good deal of subsequent archaeological work, giving this account of the early periods an inevitable bias towards the north coast of the peninsula.

16   The submerged forest at Meols.

Part Two: Prehistoric Wirral

Wirral's prehistoric evidence tells us that people lived here continuously between the Middle Stone Age and the end of the Roman Empire—a period of about 7,500 years. Most of the evidence was found on the coast, on rocky outcrops or on the thinner soils, probably because these areas were less densely wooded and were closer to the wetlands which provided a variety of food and materials.

Some discussion of the ancient woodland will improve our understanding of the environment in which the earliest settlers lived. About 15,000 years ago, where the ice was retreating, short, tough plants began to establish themselves, forming a tundra-like landscape of the type which today can be seen in Siberia and Northern Canada. There were many mosses, lichens, herbs and shrubs. As the climate warmed up, trees like birch and juniper began to take root and large mammals such as reindeer, elk, wild horse and giant deer lived amongst them. About 2,500 years later, temperatures declined again and the tundra returned for about 500 years. When temperatures began to rise, the larger plants returned: pine, birch and then hazel trees formed a canopy which starved the shorter species of sunlight and killed them off. Deciduous trees became more dominant after about 5,500 B.C. The great wild wood of prehistoric times was taking shape. It covered the Wirral peninsula, apart from marshes, sand dunes, lakes and beaches. Alder grew in profusion along the banks of rivers and in the wetlands (notice their continuing preponderance beside streams such as Arrowe Brook today); other common species included beech, hornbeam and pine. Smaller species included buckthorn, ivy, honeysuckle, guelder rose, wild cherry and bog myrtle (the plant which, in Saxon times, gave its name to the peninsula itself). The 'submerged forests' of the Meols and Leasowe seashores are remnants of this natural wonderland. Radio carbon 14 tests on various samples have shown that they were growing between 4500 and 1900 B.C. At that time it was warm and wet enough to enable the woodland to flourish; it became uniformly dense throughout Cheshire and southern Lancashire. Wirral, however, presented more opportunities to prospective settlers—it had a coastline of which the northern part was fluid and exciting, possessing a variety of features such as dunes, tidal inlets, freshwater lakes, streams and marshes, all of which have left evidence for their existence in the layers of deposits which lie under the surface in the coastal area. Each type of feature attracted its own range of wildlife which people could capture and eat.[3]

There is no evidence of Old Stone-Age settlement on Wirral. It might be awaiting discovery, irrevocably lost or never have existed. The nearest places containing such evidence are caves in North Wales, Derbyshire and on the north shore of Morecambe Bay. The first known settlers in Wirral were Middle Stone-Age hunter gatherers. Their habitation sites are identifiable by the distinctive stone work which they left behind. The most important materials of the 21st century are plastic and metal. Our Stone-Age ancestors are so called because their most important material was flint (and other stones with similar properties). With it they were able to make extremely sharp tools and weapons.

The process of manufacturing flint blades is called knapping. The knapper starts with a large raw flint which he or she strikes with another stone or heavy piece of antler whilst holding it steady on a solid base or anvil. The resulting fragments are called blanks and are then chipped down to the required shape and usually mounted on wooden shafts or handles in order to be employed as knives, spears or arrow-heads. The process inevitably causes a lot of waste material which can sometimes be seen lying about on the modern soil surface, thus indicating the probable former existence of prehistoric people in the vicinity. Other clues can include remains of the parent flint itself (known as the core), stores of blanks awaiting further work and examples of the finished tools. Middle Stone-Age material has been found at Red Noses in New Brighton, Meols, Red Rocks near Hoylake, Little Eye, Thurstaston, Irby, Greasby and Newton Carr, so people from that period were certainly living, for some of the time at least, in north Wirral.

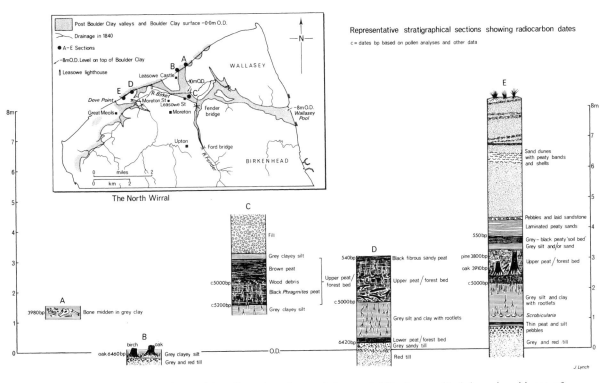

17 Stratigraphical sections, with radio carbon dates, of the north Wirral coast. Each layer is evidence of one phase in the development of the coastal environment.

In recent years two sites have been thoroughly investigated by field archaeologists from Liverpool Museum—a suburban area near Irby Mill Hill and Greasby Copse. The Irby site was inhabited between the Middle Stone Age and Romano-British times; Greasby Copse is a Middle Stone-Age encampment or settlement site. They have both been studied by highly skilled archaeologists and, as a result, tell us a lot about early Wirral.[4]

In 1987, following its discovery during the Second World War in a suburban garden in Irby, a Roman bowl was handed in to Liverpool Museum. Many more pottery fragments were discovered in neighbouring gardens, so excavations were carried out during the late 1980s and 1990s. By 1996, 40 small portions of the gardens, amounting to 2,500 square metres, had been dug and much archaeological evidence recovered. The leading archaeologist, Dr Robert Philpott, identified nine 'building phases'. Prehistoric material was found in phases one and two, indicating 'intermittent and repeated occupation over many thousands of years'. Over half of the prehistoric evidence is deemed 'insufficiently diagnostic', but 30 per cent of it is fragments of tools and waste from the Middle Stone Age. The implication here is that early habitation created the foundations for a settlement which flourished right up to the present day.

Also in the late 1980s, in the neighbouring township of Greasby, field walking by Liverpool Museum staff led to the discovery of one of the most important Middle Stone-Age sites in Britain. It lies in the vicinity of Greasby Copse (a dominant landmark of the area and site of a good deal of archaeological investigation and speculation relative to many past periods), on farmland at an elevation of 50 metres above sea-level. The excavations were carried out during the winters between 1987 and 1990 under the leadership of Ron Cowell. About 14,000 flints were discovered in two adjacent rectangular concentrations, each measuring roughly six by seven metres. Stake holes and a hearth were identified. One area was lined with pebbles and contained chemicals associated with plant material; another showed signs of having been a store for animal products—its eastern side seemed to have contained bone material and its southern side meat or offal. There was plenty of evidence to show that flint knapping was executed on site. Here was a dwelling place for hunter gatherers who, some 9,000 years ago, did not pay just one fleeting visit to the place, but used it regularly.

Much of the material is chert from the area between Prestatyn and Holywell. This indicates that the people travelled freely across the Dee estuary, perhaps in dugout canoes. They must have had a very broad view of the landscape—'home' included a network of camps throughout the region which would be occupied at different times of the year and for different purposes. It has been estimated that, around 7,000 B.C., given the productive land area available in Britain, population densities would have amounted to no more than 0.01-0.02 people per square kilometre, giving a total British population of between 2,750 and 5,500.[5] The people's impact upon the environment must, therefore, have been minimal. They were probably the last people in England to live on a completely natural, virgin landscape. Meditation upon what that would have been like momentarily takes one's breath away: great whispering woodlands, replete with birds and animals; crystal streams where salmon would leap; shining meres guarded by phalanxes of waving reeds; still and silent marshes; sand-dunes and then ... the sea—home to such a range and such a multitude of creatures as can no longer be seen off any European coast— shellfish, crabs, shrimps and prawns, eels, flat and round fish of every size, dolphins, porpoises and whales. Man's survival did not necessitate destruction of this world—he used what he needed; he co-operated with nature.

During their seasonal treks, the families must have followed the routes which their ancestors had blazed through the wild wood. Footprints, individual trees, streams and lakes must have helped them find their way; local smells and subtle textures and hues of soils and rocks as well as the sun, the moon and the stars would have directed them to that little campsite, where a season's undergrowth was starting to cover the old familiar spots—the fireplace, work area, kitchen and dormitory. A few hours' work would restore the old place to homeliness; water would be fetched in skins from the stream at the foot of the slope, the fire lit and the folks sit down around it. As the night drew in, deer skin cloaks would be drawn over hunched shoulders and the sound of crackling wood would mingle with the murmur of voices. Sparks leapt upwards seeming to merge with the stars, as the children listened to their parents and grandparents discussing the plans for tomorrow's hunt. Sometimes the talk would be of less utilitarian topics such as the deeds of ancestors or the spirits of the forest; it all helped to nurture the confidence, trust and unity of the group.

18 Archaeologists from Liverpool Museum at work on Hilbre Island, 23 July 2002. The wall forms the eastern boundary of the Custodian's Garden and is to be moved away from the cliff to protect any evidence of past human ativity. The archaeologists are digging the trench for its foundations and recording all resulting

The Liverpool Daily Post for 15 January 1990 contains an interview with Ron Cowell, the archaeologist at the Greasby site, wherein he said this: 'You feel something really special here. I don't know whether it is because we have uncovered so much stuff, or whether it is something undefinable about the atmosphere.'

It is pleasing to hear a man whose occupation demands rigorous, scientific methods and strict personal objectivity feeling free to talk about a natural human feeling when encountering what might be called the 'numinous of place'—the ability of certain parts of the Earth's surface to arouse a feeling of awe, possibly engendered by the knowledge that people lived there so inordinately long ago or by the beguiling of the senses by subtle combinations of colour, light and shade, shape, sound and smell. It is an experience which can enrich the life of the individual and is not to be despised. We cannot know for sure, but it is possible that those early hunters felt the same way when they looked down the slope from their little camp across the tops of the countless trees to the distant sea. Perhaps they articulated the sensation in the form of a religion which revered either the spirits who dwelled in the woods and waters or the one Great Spirit who brooded in the shades of his creation. Later on, in correspondence with the author, Ron Cowell expanded upon the theme: 'I would think that the repeated visits to the hillside over countless generations would have invested the place with special meanings, beyond the practical shelter, fire and food. You only have to look at the Aboriginal attitude to the landscape to give you a feeling for it.'

Those who walk along the footpath which runs parallel to the edge of Arrowe Park from Arrowe Brook Lane towards Thingwall are encouraged to look to their right across the field and over Arrowe Brook Lane towards Greasby Copse. The hunters lived on that humble ridge in the middle distance. It lies upon land belonging to Greenhouse Farm. The ridge also draws the eye when one is travelling down Arrowe Brook Road towards Greasby with the factories on the right and Arrowe Park on the left. It becomes visible as an attractive rural vista over the top of the trees of the park.

The land provided the people with everything they needed. Meat would have come from deer, wild pig and ox. Smaller animals such as otters, beavers and pine martins, as well as birds, were also available. Fresh and saltwater fish enriched the diet. Berries and nuts could be gathered from neighbouring trees and, doubtless, a range of plants was exploited for medicinal content and natural dyes. Animal carcasses provided more than just meat: there was sinew for bowstrings, bone for needles, antler for pickaxes and hammers, teeth for jewellery and skin for clothes and shelters. Stomachs and bladders might have been used as sacks or containers. Studies of living groups of people with similar technologies have shown that the hunter-gatherer lifestyle is the least laborious—the hunt itself is the most demanding activity, but is not carried out every day: once the kill has been brought in, there is a period of processing, cooking and storing, followed by extended sessions of relative idleness. In view of this, the eventual adoption of an agricultural economy, which generally requires a lot more sustained and arduous work, is a little more difficult to explain. Pollen analysis has revealed the presence of thick undergrowth during the later Middle Stone Age, which might have been making the hunting more difficult and coastal change might have removed some of the old hunting grounds, making agriculture appear a bit more secure. Certainly the transition occurred over a very long time and, of course, for some of the time, people would, simultaneously, have been carrying out both cultivation and hunter-gathering.

North Wirral has produced some unique and revealing evidence which is helping us further to explore the transition from a hunter-gatherer economy to an agricultural one: Ron Cowell's studies of Bidston Moss have shown that people were disturbing the woodland as early as about 6400 B.C.[6] Analysis of the pollen content of sections from the underlying strata shows a decline in tree pollens and an increase in those from grass and weeds. It would seem that the landscape was being divided into separate zones which were exploited in different ways: it is possible that trees were originally removed in order to provide grazing for the wild ox and deer who would thus be enticed in and killed; but, from about 4900 B.C., the people appear to have gone a step further and started to plant cereals in the clearings in order to supplement their diets. This is a remarkable discovery, as the traditional account says that agriculture did not begin for another 500 years, during the New Stone Age. People were clearly combining some degree of deliberate cultivation with hunting and gathering.

Although his vocabulary is a little dated, the spirit of Mr Varley's assessment of the contribution of Old Stone-Age people to the development of the area is apposite: 'I incline

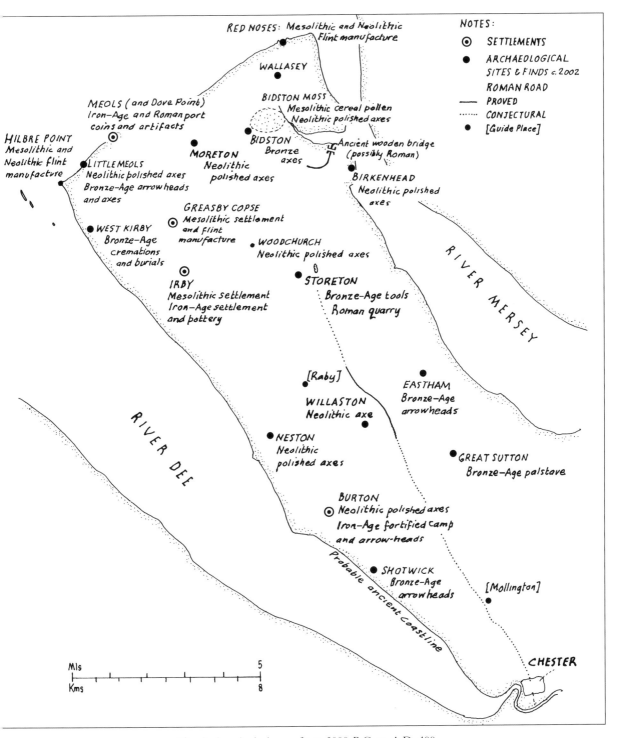

RED NOSES: Mesolithic and Neolithic
Flint manufacture

WALLASEY

BIDSTON MOSS
Mesolithic cereal pollen
Neolithic polished axes

MEOLS (and Dove Point)
Iron-Age and Roman port
coins and artifacts

BIDSTON
Bronze
axes

Ancient wooden bridge
(possibly Roman)

HILBRE POINT
Mesolithic and
Neolithic flint
manufacture

MORETON
Neolithic
polished axes

BIRKENHEAD
Neolithic polished
axes

LITTLE MEOLS
Neolithic polished axes
Bronze-Age arrowheads
and axes

GREASBY COPSE
Mesolithic settlement
and flint
manufacture

WEST KIRBY
Bronze-Age
cremations
and burials

WOODCHURCH
Neolithic polished axes

IRBY
Mesolithic settlement
Iron-Age settlement
and pottery

STORETON
Bronze-Age tools
Roman quarry

RIVER MERSEY

[Raby]

EASTHAM
Bronze-Age
arrowheads

WILLASTON
Neolithic axe

NESTON
Neolithic
polished axes

GREAT SUTTON
Bronze-Age palstave

RIVER DEE

BURTON
Neolithic polished axes
Iron-Age fortified camp
and arrow-heads

[Mollington]

Probable ancient coastline

SHOTWICK
Bronze-Age
arrowheads

CHESTER

NOTES:

⊙ SETTLEMENTS

● ARCHAEOLOGICAL
SITES & FINDS c. 2002

ROMAN ROAD
—— PROVED
········ CONJECTURAL
● [Guide Place]

Mls 5
Kms 8

19   Archaeological map from 2000 B.C. to A.D. 400.

more and more to the belief that Mesolithic man was the foundation stock both racially and culturally throughout those areas he occupied'.[7]

True agriculture became widespread during the New Stone Age. The technology of the period shows an increasing interest in chopping down trees and creating space for animal husbandry and cereal growing. The polished axe is a characteristic artifact of the time. Many examples, from throughout Britain, are so beautifully smooth that they were probably possessions which could be both traded and offered up to the gods. As well as the above-mentioned example from Oxton, stone axes have been found at Birkenhead, Wallasey, Bidston, Moreton, Little Meols, Woodchurch, Neston and Burton.[8] The obvious conclusion, once again, is that, at that time, people were both living throughout Wirral and changing its appearance.

The most significant site from the period is Red Noses in New Brighton which was explored by Mr C. Roeder during the late 1890s.[9] Erosion had revealed a floor upon which Roeder counted between 600 and 700 flints—'still unworked raw flint material, spoiled and chipped cores, splinters, flakes, knives, scrapers, spear- and arrow-heads, and burnt flakes ...' Stones which had not been obtained from the local boulder clay had been imported from Antrim in Ireland; they are evidence of trade and travel over a wide area around the shores of the Irish Sea. Notice also that the tools are designed for hunting not farming, so there had not been a complete adoption of agriculture.

Pottery from the New Stone Age in the north-west of England is rare, but a fragment was discovered near Meols during the 19th century. It is held by the Grosvenor Museum, Chester and, of all the objects there from Meols, it is perhaps the most attractive, not because it is fine, but because it contains a personal link with the nameless ancestor who made it—his or her fingerprint. The clay from which the pot was made is obviously local and very stony, making the fragment difficult to distinguish from the surrounding earth and indicating that its discoverer must have had a very sharp eye. It bears a characteristic design of the period, known as whipped cord, which was perhaps originally intended to make the vessel look like a basket. The pot must have been for the storage or cooking of food or drink. It implies the existence of a more permanent population.

North Wirral would have continued to provide the resources which attracted the Middle Stone-Age people, but farming was being further developed. Pollen analysis at Bidston, although not especially anywhere else on Merseyside, shows that trees were declining in number, while weeds from the species which today are so familiar to gardeners—ribwort, plantain, dock, mugwort, knapweed, goosefoot, thistle and chickweed—were multiplying. In north Wirral, the elm declined between about 4034 and 3790 B.C. and the man-made clearings in Bidston expanded a little. The great wild wood was gradually disappearing and human settlements taking shape. Dr N.J. Higham makes the following provoking observation: 'The clearing of land and ongoing decisions concerning land use began the long process from which the territories, land units and estates of the early historic period eventually emerged'.[10]

He reinforces the point, made earlier in the chapter, about the necessity of exploring the links between the prehistoric and the historic and the need to contemplate the very ancient origins of Wirral settlements. Places such as Meols bear names from the Early Middle Ages, but even the most cursory viewing of the archaeology shows that their physical roots go back much further than that.

The Bronze Age is so called because people had worked out how to manufacture a special metal; it was an alloy of copper and tin which was useful for making sharp tools and weapons as well as jewellery and other valuable personal items. During the New Stone Age, people were already making a huge impact upon the landscape by intensifying their agriculture and building burial mounds and stone circles. Bronze-Age people continued the tradition. Stonehenge is the most famous monument from the time. People were expressing their affinity with and communal ownership of parts of the earth's surface by building focal points, and designating sacred or ritual areas by setting out avenues, enclosures and ancestral tombs. In the north west, there are nowhere near as many great monuments—the most spectacular examples are the Calderstones in Liverpool and the Bridestones, a chambered tomb, near Congleton. There is a tiny bit of evidence for the possible existence of some kind of mound or earthwork in Storeton: Edward Cox, in his 1897 article entitled *The Antiquities of Storeton*, drew attention to a local field name—Umlinson's Meadow, which had appeared in various records as *Homilston, Homelston* and *Umberstone*. It comes from the Old English words *hamol* and *stan* and means 'mutilated stone or rock' and might refer to 'some lost megalithic archaeological feature'.[11] The only other possible examples of such features are the famous Bonks in Birkenhead Park—they are certainly very old landmarks because they were used to define part of the boundary between Claughton and Birkenhead. Such clues are tenuous, but there is plenty of other evidence to show that the area was inhabited.

Meols and New Brighton have produced evidence of continued occupation during the Bronze Age. Indeed, the excavation of the mainly Romano-British farmstead in Irby have revealed evidence of Bronze-Age houses a little before 1000 B.C., which might only have been inhabited for a short time. Isolated objects have been picked up from all over the peninsula. At least half of them are actually made of stone; it is their design and not their material which tells us when they were made. Barbed and tanged arrow-heads of the type mentioned earlier in the chapter are typical of the period. They have also been found at Little Meols, West Kirby, the Isles, Burton and Eastham. Their existence shows that people still hunted and that, just because bronze had been invented, it did not mean that everything was made out of it. Holed or perforated stone axes are another product of the age and examples of these have been found in Bidston, Tranmere, Wallasey and Meols. They were probably employed either as agricultural hoes or woodworking adzes. Again, they might have had a role as high status possessions or in trade. Given the labour and skill which they required, actual bronze objects must have been extremely valuable. In addition to the Little Sutton palstave, another was found at Bidston; a 'rapier' was picked up in Storeton and a 'dirk' on the north Wirral shore; other axes were found at Little Meols and Wallasey.[12]

These tools speak of continuing woodland clearance and the people's desire to control their natural environment. Pollen samples from north Wirral reveal that, on the coast, the wild wood had virtually disappeared by 2000 B.C. Sea inundation had destroyed a lot of trees, but human activity had also contributed to their decline. Inland areas were probably not as badly affected, but the density of woodland was certainly declining.

The funerary vases, found at West Kirby and described earlier in the chapter, date from the Bronze Age. They had been placed in a significant spot—a cleft in the sandstone hill overlooking the Dee estuary and Irish Sea. Those familiar to the the area will testify to its special atmosphere: breezes vary with the tides, carrying the clouds which alter the

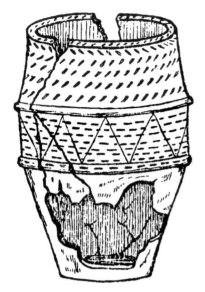

20 A Bronze-Age funerary urn from West Kirby, was recorded by Joseph Mayer in 1840 and was the subject of his lecture to the Historic Society of Lancashire and Cheshire of that year.

light, changing the hue of sea and sand; the Clwydian Hills can appear green or black; and sunsets during any season are usually delectable. West Kirby Cemetery and Grange Hill War Memorial are not far away—the ancient practice of expressing the ties between people and their home ground clearly, therefore, continues today with the lodging of the remains and commemoration of the lives of loved ones on this attractive piece of upland.

Other Bronze-Age burials have been found in the area— a damaged funerary urn was exposed by sea erosion next to the shore in 1965 and a bucket-shaped urn was discovered on Middle Eye. A crouched burial was discovered under a cairn on Little Eye and 'a partly cremated inhumation, dug into the forest peat at Great Meols'.[13] Those whose cremated remains were buried in this fashion were probably the leaders or richer members of the local community. It seems that the majority of people were not given such honours; perhaps their ashes were simply scattered over open ground. In 1967, however, a pit containing deer antlers and boar and ox bones was discovered at Leasowe. It was dated to about 2000 B.C. Why certain animal remains were accorded greater apparent ceremony than were the remains of most humans is unknown. The pit might, of course, simply have been a midden or dump, but no other examples of such practice have been found. The bones could, therefore, be evidence of an offering to the gods or spirits of the land.

Evidence from the Iron Age is scarce. The dig at Irby has increased the amount of available data, but there are still very few local clues to work from. It is believed that, in Britain as a whole, it was a time of great change. The iron technologies themselves might have been imported by immigrants from the continent—the Celts—or simply have been the result of the evolution of ideas brought about by trade and communication with people in other parts of Europe. Celtic languages were spoken in what we now know as England, Wales and Southern Scotland right up to the 6th and 7th centuries A.D., when the Anglo-Saxons began to found the English kingdoms. Its modern descendants are Welsh, Breton and Cornish.

The majority of the names which the Celts gave to their settlements and local features have been lost, but, as is the case elsewhere in the country, some of their river names remain and tell us a little about their beliefs and feelings. The river goddess *Deva* gave her name to the Dee where she is believed to have dwelled. The Romans appear to have adopted the local custom of worshipping this river spirit, but absorbed it into the cult of their own goddess, Minerva, who had a shrine at Handbridge near Chester. The name of the river to the east of Wirral, Gowy, is also a Celtic word.

There was tension in Iron-Age Britain: the climate had deteriorated, upland soils became less fertile due to over exploitation and population growth. There was competition for land and the tendency which had begun in the Bronze Age for groups to invest resources and effort in the manufacture of weapons and the construction of hillforts for self-defence was intensified. As yet, no Iron-Age weapons or high status goods have been found in Wirral. It was probably not rich enough to be able to produce them, but the remains of a small, fortified site can be seen at Burton Point. Its existence led the very name of the parish in which it sits: Burton means 'the farm or enclosure at a fortification' (deriving from the Anglo-Saxon words *burh* and *tun*). It takes the form of an enclosure on a south facing sandstone promontory overlooking the Dee Estuary. There is a 60 metre long, arc-shaped defensive bank on one side which rises to about 3.5 metres above the level of its ditch and 2.5 metres above the internal ground surface. There does not appear ever to have been any major archaeological exploration of the site. Perhaps it was a temporary refuge for local people when neighbouring groups invaded. The smallness of the fort implies that it was only designed to accommodate the immediate locals, certainly not the population of the whole of southern Wirral.[14]

Again, north Wirral has produced the most significant evidence: Meols was a busy little port and the farmstead at Irby was still inhabited. The relevant items from Meols are remarkably exotic and reveal that it had contacts with the classical Mediterranean world: there are three coins (*drachmae*) from Carthage, which is in present-day Tunisia, dating from 220-210 B.C., two base silver coins from the Channel Islands and two swan neck pins. There might not have been boats actually plying between the Mediterranean and Meols, but there were certainly trade links. The Irby site contains evidence of houses and also 590 fragments of Iron-Age pottery—certainly the largest collection of pottery from Prehistoric Wirral. All the pieces are typical examples of Cheshire Very Coarse Pottery (V.C.P.), but the site's archaeologist, Dr Robert Philpott, states that they really need further analysis. A steatite spindle whorl reveals contacts with North Wales. It would seem that north Wirral was a distinct area of settlement: perhaps there were a few tiny settlements such as Irby on the sandstone ridges with a linked local economy and with access to the outside world via their own port at Meols.

Part Three: Roman Wirral: A.D. 43 to 400

According to the traditional story, the Roman invasion, which was ordered by the Emperor Claudius and carried out by his general Aulus Plautius in A.D. 43 with an army of 45,000 men, civilised Britain and brought it out of prehistory into history: the Romans conquered, unified, policed, modernised and defended a once barbarous collection of peoples. The true picture is more complex. Before the Romans arrived, the peoples of lowland southern and eastern Britain were already trading and allying with the Romans, as well as copying some of their ways especially in the use of coins and towns. In northern Britain the peoples were more isolated and traditional—they did not live in towns nor did they use coins. So, at the heyday of the Roman occupation, the trend had persisted, with the result that southern Britain was more visibly Roman, possessing towns, villas, civilian institutions and a strong economy, whereas northern Britain was essentially a zone of military occupation, where the main focuses of economic activity were garrisons and fortresses and where Roman influences on the average hearth and home were virtually non-existent.

Roman literature gave the British their first mention in written histories—the main accounts of the invasion come from the works of Cassius Dio (*c.*A.D.150-235) and Gaius Cornelius Tacitus (*c.* A.D. 55-120). Sadly, neither author had anything to say about either the North West of England or the Wirral Peninsula. However, three of Tacitus' works— *The Life of Agricola*, *The Histories* and *The Annals*—together with a certain amount of archaeology, enable some description of the probable events of the period. The evidence shows that 'conquest' is not an accurate word to describe the Roman occupation of Wirral— apparently, there were no battles or uprisings of any sort. The district was simply absorbed into the Empire and people appear to have got on with their lives much as they had done before. An awareness of what was happening in the wider region would, however, enable a better understanding of the times.

Tacitus was keen to record the great deeds of his father-in-law, Gnaeus Julius Agricola (A.D. 40-93), who was Governor of Britain between A.D. 77 and 83. Agricola certainly won a great victory over the Britons at the Battle of Mons Graupius in Scotland and, therefore, conquered the far north, but Tacitus' claim that he had, earlier, been solely responsible for the conquest of northern England is probably an exaggeration. It would seem that it had actually been achieved by earlier leaders. General Ostorius Scapula fought the *Deceangli* of North Wales in A.D. 48. Given the strategic value of the River Dee, it is possible that a turf and wood fortress was erected on the site which was to become *Deva* (i.e. Chester) at that time. In A.D. 71, Quintus Petellius Cerialis Caesius Rufus became Governor of Britain. He took on the largest tribe of the north—the *Brigantes*, whose territories lay north of the Mersey and stretched between the Irish Sea and North Sea coasts—by launching two land attacks: a western column led by Agricola (before he became Governor) and an eastern which he himself led. As the advance moved northwards, the armies were probably reinforced and supplied by naval expeditions sailing out of established bases, down the Dee and Mersey estuaries and up those of the Ribble, Lune and Kent. The Romans, noticing the usefulness of the River Dee in gaining access to the whole north-western region, would, therefore, have begun to build *Deva* as a permanent military base in the A.D. 70s. Agricola must have used it in his later northern campaigns.[15]

The people of Wirral were probably no more than bystanders: some would have seen the *Classis Britannia* or Roman Navy working its imperious way along the Dee or Mersey; others might just have heard rumours of these conquerors from afar and nervously kept their distance; more adventurous souls might actually have sought contact with Roman soldiers with a view to making some money or seeking opportunities to leave the drudgery and boredom of home. The presence of so many soldiers certainly encouraged people to settle around the outskirts of the legionary fortress, effectively creating suburbs. By the time the fortress was fully established, there were collections of cottages and booths, called *canabae*, to the west, south and east of the walls, which were occupied by merchants, shop-keepers, ale-sellers, craftsmen and retired soldiers and their families. It is reasonable to suppose that some of these settlers had come from Wirral. Anybody who was fed up with the remoteness and unyielding routines of life in Wirral and had a bit of entrepreneurial acumen would have been attracted by the unprecedented business opportunities offered by the Roman soldier: after all, he could buy 800 boot nails, 32 eggs, 7½ lbs. of bacon or 144 pints of beer with a *denarius*, or single day's pay.[16]

The garrison constantly needed supplies. It has been suggested that, in common with other garrisons in Europe, *Deva* was surrounded by officially designated *prata legionis* ('meadows of the legions'), which would have included at least part of the Wirral peninsula. It was an area designed to provide the Roman Army with some of its necessities—not grain or produce, but horses and mules for transport (a legion needed 640 mules) and oxen for transport, meat and sacrifices. The local peasantry were required either to give or to sell these items to the military authorities. Doubtless many more of Wirral's resources were also sent to the garrison, but the only one about which we can be sure is building stone: fragments of a Roman circular mausoleum and a frieze from a temple as well as a substantial part of a military tombstone had been built into Chester's medieval city wall and discovered in the 19th century. They were made out of keuper sandstone from Storeton Quarries.

The tombstone is especially interesting (see appendix 1 for full details) as it introduces us to the soldiers themselves—in other words, to the type of people who were living and dying, not only within the confines of the legionary fortress, but perhaps also in the surrounding countryside, including Wirral. The soldier's name has been broken off, but we can read that he was 61 years old and that he had served in four separate legions, finishing up in the Twentieth *Valeria Victrix* which had come to Chester from Inchtuthil in Scotland in A.D. 87. He was probably one of the first soldiers from that legion to arrive at the garrison. Soldiers served for 20 years, so, prior to his death, he could have been retired for up to 23 years, but had obviously stayed in the area. It was common practice to do so. It is, therefore, possible that similar veterans settled in Wirral. They probably married local girls and acquired small farms which met their basic economic needs. It is likely that the favoured locations for such farms were close to roads and that most of the Roman coins which have been discovered on Wirral once belonged to such settlers.

Appendix I is a list of all the Roman coins found in Wirral. There are representatives from the full duration of the Roman occupation, indicating that Wirral was continuously inhabited. The frequency of coin finds is typical for the North West of England, so, using this basic indicator, we are also able to say that the density of population was average. Five coin hoards have been discovered. One was discovered in Birkenhead in 1900; there are no existing details of the collection. The others were found in Eastham, Hooton, Neston and Willaston and all date from the fourth century. In the days before banks, the hoarding of coins was a simple way of protecting one's savings. The money would be wrapped in cloths or placed in a leather bag and then put into a bottle or jar and buried. Jesus described just such a practice in his parable of the talents, implying that it was quite a common thing to do in the ancient world. The owner would expect to retrieve his or her money later on. In the five Wirral cases, the owners obviously never did. They must either have died or moved away and failed to tell anybody where their little caches could be found. The fact that they all date from the fourth century could reveal that it was a time of uncertainty or upheaval, when the slightly better off people became worried about their assets and took such measures to protect them.

Meols has produced the largest single collection of coins in Wirral: 91 have been recorded and at least six were picked up on the foreshore during the 1980s. Others have been found at Moreton and Leasowe. It is, therefore, the fifteenth largest collection of Roman coins from a settlement site in the North West (i.e. from the counties of Cumberland, Westmorland, Lancashire and Cheshire); Carlisle has so far produced the largest collection— 2,073; and Chester the second largest—2,035.[17] Clearly Meols, or whatever it was called at that time, was an important little town. Its trade had continued to flourish and it housed the largest population in Wirral. Many other items from the Roman period have been discovered. Brooches are particularly common and are well described and depicted in *Ancient Meols*. They were used for fastening cloaks and other loose-fitting garments at the chest or shoulder. It was obviously important to wear an attractive and fashionable brooch and the wearers would have been reasonably well-off to be able to buy them, showing us that the settlement was, by the standards of the region, quite prosperous. Other domestic items include two pairs of iron shears (either for cutting hair or wool), an ornamental pin and a fragment of dark red decorated glass. Two categories of finds are conspicuous by their absence—pottery and military material.

Most Roman sites in Britain produce immense amounts of pottery. Only a few bits have been found at Meols. This is a mystery. It is possible either that environmental conditions did not allow its preservation or that the original collectors did not recognise it when they saw it or were uninterested in it. Alternatively, perhaps very little pottery was kept in the settlement because the locals preferred to use other methods of storage. The only military item is a belt buckle. There is no evidence of equipment or buildings This was not, therefore, an outpost of the Chester garrison, but a local, village or town which was carrying on much as it had been doing before the Roman invasion. The trade contacts which Meols had been enjoying during the Iron Age must simply have been strengthened by its incorporation into an empire which controlled all the shores of the Mediterranean and protected all its trade routes with Europe, Africa and Asia. The military authorities were probably quite content not to interfere in the affairs of this little port, although they might have placed a small watch or signalling station on the coast for the benefit of their navy and almost certainly taxed the inhabitants as much as was practicable.

On the basis of Mr Cox's observations of the remains of some apparent Romano-British houses on the foreshore in 1894, which were quoted earlier in the chapter, we can begin to imagine the appearance of this little town: to our eyes, it would appear ramshackle and dirty; there would have been huddles of little, circular cottages made from wooden uprights sunk into the ground with wattle and daub walls and thatched roofs. Each cottage, regardless of season, would have been permanently veiled in its little pall of smoke; smaller replicas of the same buildings acted as storehouses, workshops and animal pens. At least the dirt was natural—creeping up from the surface of the pathways and lanes, it clung to the walls of the cottages and the clothes of the people, making them all look as though they were emerging from the earth itself. Dotted about the complex were great steaming piles—the families' waste tips awaiting distribution on the fields. The smells would have been rich—wood smoke, damp earth, human and animal excrement, cooking, fish, the sea—and the sounds diverse: the chatter of children and the grumble of adults, the slapping of bread-making and the chipping and tapping of craftsmen. Nearer the shore, boats would have lain beached, awaiting repairs or tides; their owners would have stood nearby, negotiating deals on the latest cargoes of lead ingots, olive oil, jewellery, wine or fish. It seems likely that there was no harbour or dock area, but perhaps simply a beach up which boats could be dragged or a pool similar to the Hoyle Lake which accommodated the fishing fleet during the 19th century.

There is one inland site from the Roman period which confirms the above picture—Irby. Again, nobody knows what it was called at the time, but it had been inhabited in various ways since the Middle Stone Age and was certainly inhabited now. During the early 1990s, Dr Robert Philpott discovered evidence of there having been a collection of cottages built in the style which is imagined above in Meols. There were post holes which revealed the former existence of circular houses with diameters of between 11 and 12 metres. One contained evidence of three buildings having stood consecutively on the same spot, so they obviously had a natural life-span and were then rebuilt. The roofs had decayed without trace and must, therefore, have been made from straw, grass, turf or heather. The cottages stood close together and were encircled by a modest ditch which was not really a defensive feature, but more of a boundary marker. During the second century, the houses were replaced with structures of a slightly different design—polygonal instead of circular, with wattle and daub panels between each upright. Perhaps a hundred years later, these cottages were abandoned, but not demolished and the settlement was expanded. The earlier ditch was filled in and new rectangular, instead of polygonal, houses were built. Sites from elsewhere in the region have contained evidence of a similar change during the mid-Roman period. It might have been the result of the spread of Roman towns and building fashions.

Irby is very different from Meols in one obvious way: it has so far produced 2,400 pieces of pottery. They came from the local Roman settlements of Wilderspool and Holt as well as from Warwickshire, Oxfordshire, Northamptonshire, Dorset, Lincolnshire and Yorkshire and from the continent. All the pots could have been brought to the area via Meols. Only seven Roman coins were recovered from the site, but numerous other items have come to light, including 2,700 fragments of metal-work; pieces of tools such as a saw, chisels and awls, a padlock, nails and shoe-nails; farming implements, such as a rotary quern for grinding grain; and equipment for spinning and weaving wool. Apart from some small items of personal ornament and a piece of window glass, there is not much evidence of great material wealth. It might have been expressed in other ways, such as land holding, and the local people might have favoured traditional methods of storing food and drink in perishable containers like skins, which do not show up in the archaeology, but the site is typical of the north west of England—it does not appear greatly to have prospered as a result of the Roman occupation. It is possible that the Romans might actually have reduced its wealth by taxation, but it is more likely that the farmstead was in a rural backwater and that it was largely self-sufficient: the people grew their own crops, made their own cloth and metal ware and fashioned quern stones from local rock. Any trade which took place did not require Roman coinage because it was done locally by means of traditional family and tribal ties.

21 View of Romano-British farm excavation at Irby.

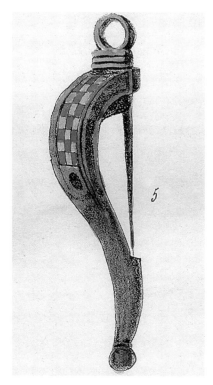

22 'Wirral-Type' brooch from the second century A.D. and recorded by Hume in 1863.

The site at Irby was preserved by chance—it lay in a hollow which protected it from the plough; but many more such sites might have been destroyed by either agriculture or urban development. Other places might be awaiting discovery. It would, therefore, be sensible to suppose that Irby is representative of the type of settlement in which people lived, at least at the northern end of Wirral, between the first and fifth centuries A.D. Any or all of the older settlements of north Wirral might be standing directly upon the remains of villages or farms which existed in Romano-British times. It is possible that disturbance of buildings in settlements like Greasby, West Kirby, Frankby or Upton could expose new evidence about life in both prehistoric and Roman Wirral.

Dr Philpott has shed further light on Roman Wirral with his highly stimulating analysis of a design of Roman brooch which he has labelled 'Wirral Type'. Hume depicted an example in *Ancient Meols* in 1863. Since his day, several more brooches of this type have been found. Of the 31 Roman brooches found in Wirral, Philpott states that 15, or 48 per cent of them (found at Barnston, Frankby, Heswall, Irby, Ness and Thurstaston), are of this distinctive 'trumpet brooch' design. He proposes that they were made by one craftsman during the second century A.D., who probably moved from farm to farm making his characteristic little item of jewellery to order. Other examples of the design have been found in the English North and Midlands, North Wales and Scotland, with a particular concentration around Hadrian's Wall. This could be further evidence of the importance of Meols for exporting local goods, but might also imply that the craftsman himself eventually moved up north in order to exploit the greater business opportunities offered by the garrisons along the Roman Wall.[18]

Roads are probably the most popular relics of the Roman occupation of Britain. During the last 150 years, people have looked at Chester and at Meols some 20 miles away and thought, 'there must have been a road between them'. They have then gone to the landscape and almost forced it to yield proof of their theory. Let us be circumspect about the supposed necessity of a road between the two settlements and then be a little more objective when viewing the evidence. Yes, both places flourished during Roman times, but one was a garrison and the other a small port serving the farmsteads of north Wirral. Need there have been a formal relationship between them? The Romans would certainly have been interested in the place, if only in order to tax the inhabitants and place a watch and signalling station nearby, but access could more easily be achieved by sea—a road was not necessary.

In fact, the best evidence for a Roman road in Wirral derives from Mr K.E. Jermy's work during the early 1960s.[19] He analysed field names, road, track and boundary alignments and carried out some small excavations. He concluded that there is only one definite section of Roman Road—Street Hey Lane in Willaston. It is certainly convincingly straight in the recognisable Roman style and the use of the word 'street' might indicate that a road has been in use there for a very long time. According to the 1843 tithe map of Willaston, there were eight adjoining and neighbouring fields names which contained the element 'Street'. Jermy's small trenches revealed cobbles in a disposition which had already been seen on the known Roman road between Chester and Manchester, confirming that Street Hey Lane certainly follows the course of the Roman road. The northerly continuation of the road is indicated, not by a modern road, but by features such as banks, ditches, parish boundaries, disturbed ground and parch marks. Its apparent direction at this point does not indicate that it went to Meols. There might have been a junction for Meols, but no evidence for this has yet been found. Indeed, it seems that the road headed for Birkenhead and Wallasey.

There is additional evidence for a road to north-eastern Wirral: during the 19th century, small sections of possible Roman road had been spotted in Storeton and Poulton Lancelyn and the name Blake Street (deriving from the Dark-Age and medieval practice of calling a Roman road a *Black Street*, because of the cobbles which lay on the surface) was used in a document of 1305 to describe Street Hey Lane. The name 'High Street' was used in a 1396 document to describe a lane which led 'from the centre of the country of Wirral' to a ferry across Wallasey pool in Claughton. In 1845 engineers constructing the Birkenhead Dock to Chester Railway found the remains of a wooden bridge in Birkenhead, buried in river silt and submerged in water some 15 feet below the level of high tides. To its discoverers, its dimensions and construction certainly seemed Roman; it might have been a continuation of the road from Chester and implies that the Romans had some economic interest in the area of Wallasey Pool, perhaps oyster fisheries.

Enthusiasts for a road to Meols have not been idle. Mr Peter France carried out various surveys between the 1960s and '80s, the findings of which he summarised in the *Wirral Journal* in 1986. He traced the road from Dove Point in Meols, along Dove Point Road and past Meols Station, where:

> ... Roman cremation urns and coins said to have been found when the bridge over the railway was constructed. The whereabouts of these finds and their authenticity is not known, but as the Romans made burials alongside roads, the finds may well have been genuine. The alignment next takes us to Heron Road, where the author was fortunate to be able to examine trenches dug for pipe laying early in 1985. A partial section here revealed that the present road surface is laid directly on a foundation of broken sandstone rubble. Beneath this was a substantial earlier road which was at this point directly beneath the modern road, but separated from it by about a foot of brown sandy humus.

He said that the humus was decayed brushwood which the Romans had laid as a foundation in the boggy earth for the clay and cobbles which constituted the road surface. He noticed wheel ruts and sandstone kerbing which had been laid to prevent the road from spreading. He averred that the road surface must have stood higher than the surrounding land. The line was then traced through Pump Lane, Mill Lane and Barker Lane in Greasby. A Roman coin from the first century had apparently been found at the top of Barker Lane in 1976, but has since been lost. In 1985, Mr France carried out some small keyhole excavations in the field to the east of the course of an old lane which runs up the hill beside Greasby Copse. Further evidence of cobbles was discovered. The old lane had already yielded a variety of finds, such as Romano-British pottery, flints and a medieval pilgrim's token, all indicating the former importance of the route. Mr France then identified

23 Spindle whorl from the Romano-British farm at Irby.

the road's continuation along Limbo Lane to Thingwall, Barnston Dale, Thornton Hough and finally Street Hey in Willaston, where he suggested that it joined the main road between Birkenhead and Chester which was described earlier.

Mr France obviously passionately believed in the validity of his evidence and makes us want to agree with him, but there is no concrete dating evidence, merely a coin and a cremation urn, both of which were never properly recorded and have since disappeared. We are also required to trust Mr France's identification of the various construction features as definitely Roman. One's inclination is to believe in the existence of this route, but more evidence will have to be produced before the theory is completely accepted.

Between the mid-first and early fifth centuries then, Wirral, along with the rest of England and Wales, was a part of the Roman Empire. The life of the people must have been affected by the proximity of the garrison at Chester which almost certainly either appropriated or traded natural and agricultural resources from the peninsula and taxed the people. Retired soldiers probably settled in small farms throughout the district and were responsible for most of the coins which have since been found. There could have been two main roads—one to Birkenhead and another to Meols. There were small settlements at the northern end of the peninsula which were inter-related and served by the port at Meols, but had few formal ties with the Roman authorities and carried out traditional rural economies in much the same way as had been done in the Iron Age. Further divisions and patterns were inscribed on the landscape: remember how the line of the road in Willaston had been adopted as a field, township and parish boundary; the Irby excavation revealed how an Anglo-Saxon or medieval parish boundary followed the course of a Romano-British earthwork. These are small examples of a phenomenon which must have occurred in many other parts of the peninsula.

By this time, the ancient wild wood had probably all but disappeared, as the land was exploited for agriculture. It brings to mind Sir Christopher Wren's epitaph in St Paul's Cathedral—*si monumentum requiris, circumspice*—'if you seek a monument, look around you'. It could just as well act as the epitaph for the anonymous people of Wirral from the immense period of time which we have just discussed: they left no visible buildings; their legacy is the essential form of the landscape itself and the foundational outlines of many of the settlements and land divisions which were to become so vital for life later on.

Three

Celtic, Saxon and Viking Wirral, A.D. 400-1066

Part One: Dark Ages or Middle Ages?

Nobody is quite sure how to label the period between the departure of the Romans and the arrival of the Normans. The old title, The Dark Ages, will not do due to the

enormous amount of historical, archaeological and linguistic research which has shed light on the period. The alternative term, Early Middle Ages, even though it aptly describes the way in which the era falls in the early part of the time which fits neatly between ancient and modern times, does not roll off the tongue and gets confused with the period just after the Norman Conquest. Perhaps we should simply be content not to give it a title and to study the people of the time in their own right. When we do so, certain themes become apparent: it was a time when people invaded and settled in Britain; the outlines of the modern countries of the British Isles and of some of the counties of England were delineated; most English places acquired the original versions of their modern names; English displaced British or Welsh as the main language in the centre of the island of Britain; and the foundations for many of the political and religious institutions, with which we in 21st century Britain are familiar, were laid. The period produced more literary and archaeological evidence than the one covered by the previous chapter, making it possible for us to survey a shorter timespan.[1]

24 Looking north along Street Hey Lane, Willaston. Many people have longed to find a Roman road running between Chester and north Wirral. This lane has been excavated and surrounding features surveyed. It is the only section of road in Wirral whose Roman origins seem likely.

Wirral was a microcosm—it experienced every major development which occurred in England as a whole: the departure of the Roman Army; a period, termed Sub-Roman, when the native British people carried on with their lives as best they could without the help of the Romans; a time of Anglo-Saxon or early English settlement when most of Wirral's villages acquired their shapes and names and when the great county in which it was wholly to lie until 1974 began to take shape; a subsequent period of Scandinavian colonisation when some settlements were taken over and renamed, new ones were founded and marginal land was brought into cultivation; and the final conquest by a group of French aristocrats of Scandinavian ancestry from Normandy, who began to build the great institutions which dominated people's lives during the following 500 years. The peninsula also acquired the name by which we know it today and, for the first time, was mentioned in written sources. The rest of this chapter will tell Wirral's story by looking at each episode in turn.

Part Two: Sub-Roman or Celtic Wirral

The Roman Empire, despite its many great qualities, was not eternal. By the end of the fourth century, it was crumbling. The Roman soldiers of Britain were ordered back to Rome to fight off the barbarians. The people were left to defend themselves as best they could. In certain areas the British authorities employed mercenaries from Northern Germany to help them fight the raiding Scots and Picts, not realising that these Germanic warriors themselves would become permanent settlers and, therefore, rivals for British living space. Life in Wirral, however, seems to have been able to continue in much the same way as it had done during the Roman occupation. By the early fifth century, the Chester garrison had certainly gone and the settlement was left in a dilapidated state. The people who had prospered from its existence must have felt bereft and desirous of other sources of income. The small amount of available evidence, however, implies that the apparent detachment of the people of north Wirral from Roman influences was perpetuated after the Romans had left: they continued to trade overseas and to maintain their religion regardless of the great upheavals which were afflicting southern and eastern Britain.

25 Possible northern end of a Roman road—Barker Lane, Greasby. The hedge running down the hill follows the route of an old lane; excavations in the summer of 1985 in the field this side of the hedge revealed some sandstone blocks which might have been part of a road, but there was no evidence to prove that it was Roman. The road's assumed destination, Meols, is visible in the distance.

Meols, or whatever it was called at that time, was a prosperous little port. It had been during the Iron Age and continued to be so during the Roman occupation. The Roman departure did not significantly disrupt its economy. Amongst the many thousands of items from all periods found on the Meols shore, there are two late Roman buckle plates and some sixth century brooches. During the 1980s, metal detectorists in the neighbouring township of Moreton found three sixth-century Byzantine coins—a bronze *decanummium* from Carthage (from the reign of Justinian I (527-65), a bronze *follis* from Constantinople from the reign of Justin I (518-27) and a bronze *follis* from the reign of Maurice Tiberius (582-602).[2] These items show, not only that the site was still inhabited during the 200 years after the Romans left, but that its long-standing business links with Europe and the Mediterranean were still flourishing. In 1955 a pilgrim's flask from the Shrine of St Menas near Alexandria was discovered in the sand

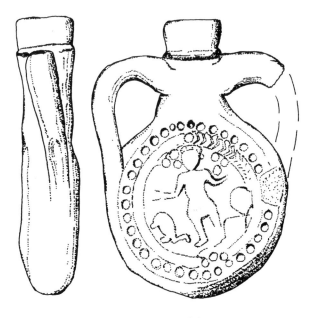

26 St Menas pilgrim's flask, one of the many exotic items recovered from Meols shore and evidence of its continuing importance after the departure of the Romans.

300 yards offshore from Dove Point. St Menas was martyred for his Christian faith in A.D. 296 and, from the fourth century until its destruction in the seventh century, his burial place was a popular destination for pilgrims. The flask was designed to carry holy water.[3] Again, this is evidence of settlement, trade and travel, but also hints at the importance of the Christian religion on the Wirral Peninsula in post-Roman and pre-Anglo-Saxon times.

Christianity had taken root in Britain during the last century of Roman rule. During the fifth and sixth centuries, in what we now know as North Wales and Cheshire, the British Church was strong. There was a large monastery at Bangor Iscoed (Bangor on Dee). In 603 the national importance of the monastery was revealed when its abbot, Dinooth (or Donatus), attended an important meeting with St Augustine of Rome who had come to convert the English. A Welsh chronicle, called the *Annales Cambriae*, for the year 601 records that, during the previous year, a gathering of British bishops included representatives from *Urbs Legionis* ('City of the Legions'—Chester), implying that the town was an important ecclesiastical centre.[4] The landscape of north and central Wirral contains further evidence for the presence of Christianity—the churchyards at Bromborough, Overchurch, Wallasey, West Kirby and Woodchurch were all originally circular.[5] This is a sign that they were probably founded by Celts and not Anglo-Saxons, Scandinavians or Normans. In addition, Wallasey parish church is dedicated to St Hilary of Poitiers, who was, in the words of J.D. Bu'Lock: '... a correspondent of the fourth century British Bishops. A church where his memory was respected and possibly where some putative relics were enshrined, could quite possibly have originated in the fourth or fifth century ...'[6]

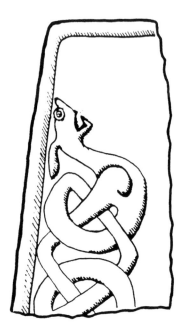

27 Overchurch runic stone—
evidence of Anglo-Saxon
settlement in Wirral.

Place-names themselves indicate the continuing presence of British settlements during the time when the Anglo-Saxons were moving into Wirral. Wallasey means 'Welshmen's or Britons' Island' (from the Anglo-Saxon *wala* and *eg*); Liscard means 'Hall at the rock' (from the Primitive Welsh *lis* and *garreg*);[7] Pensby means 'Farm at a hill called Penn' (from Primitive Welsh *penn*—'top or end' and Old Norse *byr*; the word *penn* probably referred to Heswall Hill and was treated as a proper noun by the English). There are two British field names which were recorded during the Middle Ages and have since been lost: *Knuckyn* in Irby (1307-23) and *Kneckyn* in Caldy (1454). They might both derive from the Old Welsh word *cyncyn*—'little hill'. Landican means 'Tegan's Church' (from Old Welsh *lann* and the personal name *Tegan*). Landican church is the one we now know as Holy Cross parish church in Woodchurch. Woodchurch is not mentioned in Domesday Book, but Landican is and is described as having a priest. It is, therefore, logical to suppose that the old parish of Landican included what we now know as the township of Woodchurch and that the original church dedication to St Tegan was subsequently changed and the arrangement reversed, so that Landican came to be a township lying in the parish of Woodchurch. The fact that the Woodchurch churchyard was curvilinear is further evidence that it is the site of the original church of St Tegan.[8]

The above evidence leads us to the conclusion that, during the 200 years after the departure of the Romans, Wirral was inhabited predominantly by Britons. They spoke a Celtic language which was the ancestor of modern Welsh, lived in distinct settlements, practised the Christian religion in at least five church buildings on the peninsula and were involved in overseas trade through the port at Meols. The ensuing discussion of the English settlements will show that the Britons were not wiped out, but that they acquired a more lowly social and economic position in the area and were either gradually absorbed into the eventual majority invading population or simply acquired its language and culture and ultimately became part of it.

Part Three: The English Settlements

In order to illustrate the heritage of the modern English language and the roots of the founders of England, the reader is encouraged to carry out a simple experiment. Write down an ordinary, everyday sentence; take an etymological dictionary and look up the origin of each word. As a result of his own experiments, the author is confident that some three quarters of the words in the chosen sentence will prove to be derived from Anglo-Saxon or Old English. This fact makes English a Teutonic or Germanic language. More complex and abstract sentences might contain words which derive from Latin, Greek and French, but most English simple naming words (common nouns) are similar in sound, if not in spelling, to their German equivalents.

The English language and the homeland in which it evolved is the result of invasion and settlement by people from Germany, Denmark and the Netherlands. They started to arrive during the last days of the Roman Empire. They had been recruited by the British authorities to help defend the island against invaders from Ireland and Scotland, but eventually rebelled against their employers and began to settle here themselves. It was the beginning of a vast and sustained migration of people from northern Europe to Britain. They were the Angles, Saxons, Jutes and Frisians, but are usually simply called the Anglo-Saxons or English. Nobody is sure what made them want to leave their homelands. Perhaps, as a result of westward migration of people from central and eastern Europe, there was increasing competition for living space on lands which were largely waterlogged and where the climate could be difficult. Britain might have offered opportunities which were not available to them on their native plains—it was green, warm and undefended. The south and east of Britain were the first areas to be settled; the north-west remained largely untouched until the seventh century. By the eighth century, in the centre of Britain, the English had become the dominant linguistic and cultural group. The area was divided into seven English kingdoms—Kent, Sussex, Essex, Wessex, Northumbria, East Anglia and Mercia. The English remained pagan until after the missions of St Augustine of Rome in 597 and St Aidan of Iona and Lindisfarne in 635. The native Celts were able to maintain their language and culture only in the western and northern peripheries. Under the rule of King Egbert of Wessex, England became a united and recognisable entity between 802 and 839.

During the 1960s, John McNeal Dodgson expounded his theory about the way in which place-names can help us to perceive the progression of the English settlement of Cheshire. It deserves respect, not least because nobody has yet managed to produce an equally detailed and well-argued hypothesis which neatly correlates linguistic and historical evidence and because it is an intriguing and stimulating way of helping us to understand the events of that mainly unrecorded time.[9] He brought his enormous scholarship and knowledge of southern English place-name history to bear on the question of the Anglo-Saxon settlement of Cheshire. His first observation concerned the lack of any names containing the elements -ingas and -ingaham, which mean 'the folk of—', 'the folk named after—' and 'the village of the folk named after—'. Such names are known to occur where there were 'English communities in a newly taken country'. In other words, they are associated with the first wave of English settlement in Britain. The Wirral place names which apparently belong to this category do not actually contain these elements. They are made from the slight variants,—ingas and inga, which do, however, have the same meaning. The examples are: Bebington—'Farm of a person called Bebba' (from the Anglo-Saxon personal name and *ing* and *tun*); Mollington—'Farm associated with a man named Moll' (from the Anglo-Saxon personal name and *ing* and *tun*); and Puddington—'Farm associated with a man called Put(t)a' (from the Anglo-Saxon personal name and *ing* and *tun*). They are the result of a 'secondary stage' of English settlement. In this case, it must have been after the end of the seventh century when Wirral was absorbed into the kingdom of Mercia.

Another type of name which is associated with the early settlements contains the element *ham*, meaning 'village' or 'homestead' joined to a personal name or 'simple modifier'. Dodgson put Eastham in this category, which means 'Homestead in the East [of Wirral]' or 'East Village'. He never mentioned Ledsham, but it must surely be a classic example of the same type, because it simply means 'Leofede's Homestead or Village' (from the Anglo-Saxon personal name and *ham*). It is probable, therefore, that the two villages were founded or colonised and renamed by early, independent English settlers sometime in the late sixth or early seventh centuries. They were moving into an area inhabited by Britons in advance of the expansion of the kingdom of Mercia which was eventually to incorporate the Wirral peninsula. The first English settlers were pagan. The British were Christian.

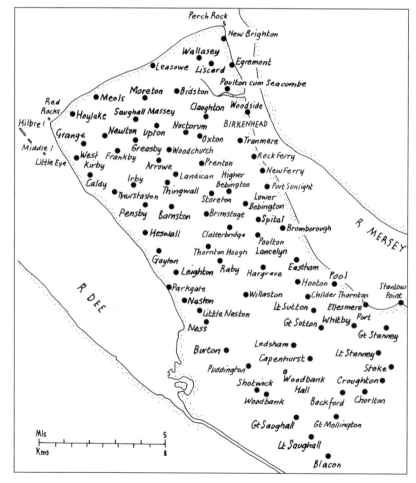

28   Wirral place-names.

Apart from documentary references to *le Dedemonnes Greve* (i.e. 'The Dead Man's Grove or Wood') in 1323 in Storeton, and to a field called *Harrowe* (i.e. 'Heathen Shrine' from Anglo-Saxon *hearg*) in about 1293 in Heswall, there are no known pagan English burial mounds in Wirral. This fact does not contradict the argument for early settlement because the newcomers were a minority and would have conformed to the funerary practice of the majority which in this case was, of course, the burial of the dead in Christian churchyards.

Meols has produced a little evidence from the possible English settlements of the early seventh century in the form of a quoit brooch and several Anglo-Saxon coins known as *sceattas* and *stycas*. A blue glass bead with yellow and green ornament, of a type associated with seventh-century cemeteries, was found on Hilbre. Of course, these items might not be evidence of settlement but of trade. The district could easily have continued to be mainly British.[10]

The traditional story states that it was the Battle of Chester of about 616 which

29 Neston: sculptured stone believed to be fragments of grave crosses from the Viking period.

opened Cheshire up to further English colonisation and to its eventual inclusion in the kingdom of Mercia. The Northumbrian monk and historian, Bede, in his great *Historia Ecclesiastica* (popularly known as the 'Ecclesiastical History of the English People') gives us the following account of the battle:

> ... The powerful king Aethelfrith [of Northumbria] ... Raised a great army at the City of the Legions—which the English call Legacestir, but which the Britons more correctly name Carlegion [i.e. Chester]—and made a great slaughter of the faithless Britons. Before battle was joined, he noticed that their priests were assembled apart in a safer place to pray for their soldiers, and he enquired who they were and what they had come there to do. Most of the priests came from the monastery of Bangor ... Most of the monks, who had kept a three day fast, had gathered to pray at the battle, guarded by a certain Brocmail, who was there to protect them from the swords of the barbarians while they were intent on prayer. As soon as King Aethelfrith was informed of their purpose, he said, 'If they are crying to their God against us, they are fighting against us even if they do not bear arms.' He therefore directed his first attack against them, and then destroyed the rest of the accursed army, not without heavy loss to his own forces. It is said that of the monks who had come to pray about twelve hundred perished in this battle, and only fifty escaped by flight. Brocmail and his men took to their heels at the first assault, leaving those whom they should have protected unarmed and exposed to the enemy. Thus, long after his death, was fulfilled Bishop Augustine's prophecy that the faithless Britons, who had rejected the offer of eternal salvation, would incur the punishment of temporal destruction.[11]

[47]

The battle was clearly a severe blow to British prestige and to their ability to control west Cheshire. It did not, however, enable the kingdom of Northumbria to conquer the area. Aethelfrith's army had been depleted. He was exposed to further attacks by alliances between his English enemies and the British and withdrew to his homelands in the north. He was killed in 617 by the East Anglians. Aethelfrith's rival, Edwin of Deira, was then made King of Northumbria. From that date until the end of the seventh century, the kingdom of Mercia maintained an alliance with the British in order to oppose the kingdom of Northumbria. Overall, the Mercians kept control of Cheshire. The British were perhaps allowed to keep an enclave west of the river Gowy (which at that time bore the name Tarvin—from Welsh *terfyn*—'boundary'). It would obviously have included Wirral. We must further conclude, therefore, that any early English settlement in Wirral must have been subject to the approval of British leaders.

During the early part of the eighth century, the kingdom of Mercia became more dominant and less worried about Northumbria. It no longer had need of an alliance with the British. A huge physical statement of the English claim to former British lands west of the river Dee was constructed, probably by king Aethelbald of Mercia between 716 and 757. It is known as Wat's Dyke and is not a defensive wall, but a boundary marker, running northwards from Oswestry to Basingwerk. It is possible that, during the reign of Offa (757-796), an even more impressive earthwork was built further west and beginning much further south in Chepstow. It is known as Offa's Dyke and strikes northwards from the Dee along the ridges of the Clwydian Hills, terminating near Prestatyn. Both structures speak of power, ownership and division. They show that both banks of the Dee estuary were now in English hands and that the British were regarded as foreigners, enemies and inferiors.

Mercia means 'Land of the Boundary Folk' (from the tribal name *Mierce*). In other words, its name was acquired as a result of its position next to Wales. Mersey means 'Boundary River' (from Anglo-Saxon *maeres* and *ea*). It was Mercia's boundary with Northumbria. Wirral, therefore, lay in the north-western corner of Mercia. Now that the English were clearly in charge, either more intense immigration into Wirral could take place or the English-speaking people already resident on the peninsula could assert their higher status and acquire more authority. In order to have been able to survive in this changing world, the British inhabitants would have had to adopt the language and customs of the their political masters. Thus we can see that, for Wirral along with the rest of Cheshire to become English, it would not have been necessary for the Anglo-Saxons to massacre their Celtic neighbours, but merely to have dominated them politically and psychologically and eventually culturally and genetically to have absorbed them.

The linguistic evidence helps us further to understand the story. As every Wirralian who has ever travelled into Wales along the A550 Queensferry Road knows, the Welsh word for Wales is *Cymru* (pronounced 'kuhmri'). It means 'Land of the Fellow Countrymen'. The Welsh word for the people of Wales is *Cymry*, meaning 'Compatriots' or 'Countrymen'. The word 'Welsh' comes from the Old English *walh*, meaning 'foreigners', 'outsiders', 'strangers' or 'serfs' (i.e. inferior or lowly people). Thus, according to this anglocentric view of Britain, the Welsh are, in the words of the great Welsh historian Gwyn A. Williams, 'Aliens in their Own Country'.[12] The name Wallasey, therefore, is evidence of contemporary English disdain for a surviving remnant of the former Celtic population of Wirral. The remnant had survived because it was separated from the rest of the peninsula by the Wallasey Pool to the south and marshy ground to the west. If the English had regarded the inhabitants of that semi-island as equals, they would probably have used the people's name for themselves, as was the case at Combermere (from Anglo-Saxon *Cumbre*—adopted from the Welsh *Cymry*—and *mere*—'lake') and Comberbach (from Anglo-Saxon *Cumbre* and *bece*—'stream in a valley') on the Cheshire Plain. Notice that the other British place names, which were explained earlier in the chapter—Landican and Pensby—are also at the northern end of Wirral. We are, therefore, able to imagine that this was the last area to be anglicised; and that, for a considerable time, a rough line between modern Heswall and Wallasey Pool would have marked the transition zone between Anglo-Saxon and British Wirral.

It is difficult to exaggerate the importance of the Anglo-Saxon or English settlement of Wirral. It was a revolution. The British had not been annihilated, but their language survived only in pockets, eventually to fall into complete disuse and to be remembered only in the form of a few place names. The majority of places and features of the peninsula acquired English names.

Some settlements might have existed already and been renamed; others would have been started from scratch. It is possible that the townships of Wirral are hiding the evidence of their early history beneath the foundations of their existing buildings. The reader is encouraged to visualise the older buildings which lie in the centre of villages such as Greasby, Saughall Massie, Bidston, Eastham, Burton, Puddington and Shotwick. The fact that there are so many old buildings must mean that the settlements were successful—they had the resources and conditions which made life possible. Most of the old farms, barns and cottages date from the 17th and 18th centuries, but they could well be standing on the sites of much older structures. The actual habitation sites might even have come into being during prehistoric times. Most of these old buildings are, thankfully, protected by law but, should their foundations ever be disturbed as a result of repair or alteration work, the archaeologists must swoop in and retrieve any clues which might be exposed.

The Anglo-Saxons have given us most of our words for units and types of land. Obvious examples are land (*land*), meadow (*maed*), ditch (*dic*) and croft (*croft*). Less obvious words include furlong (*furlang*—'furrow long', referring to the standard length of a ploughed strip of ground which was a product of the length of a plough team), nook (*noc*—'corner'), pingo or pingel (*pightel*—'small enclosed field'), pike (*pic*—'sharp pointed instrument', referring to a long narrow field), hay (*gehaeg*—'fence' or 'enclosure') and flash (*flasshe*—'pool' or 'marshy place').

Below are some examples of field-names with Anglo-Saxon elements and taken at random from Dodgson's *Place-Names of Cheshire Volume 4*. It illustrates the importance of Old English in Wirral.

Township	Examples of field names with Anglo-Saxon Elements
Backford	Glugg Meadow, Long Meadow, Mill Croft, Pingo, Three Nook Croft, Pool Hay, Prior's Hay.
Childer Thornton	Acorn Hay, Price's Cow Hay, Golden Nook, Land Hay, Meadow, Hay.
Heswall	Bank Hay, Land Hay, Pingle, Rye Croft, Meadow, Fellings (from *furlang*).
Neston	Marled Hay, The Pikes, Three Nooks, Ditch Way.
Willaston	Adfalant ('top furlong'), Flashes Meadow, Marled Hay, Fox Hay, Three Nooks.

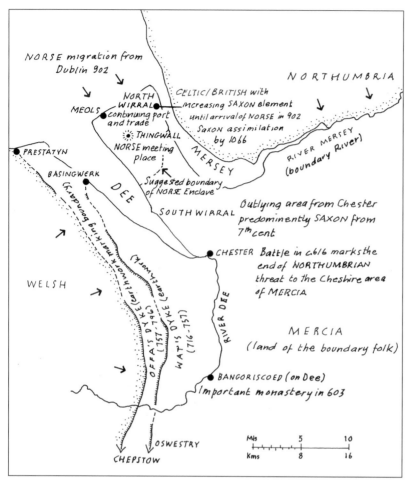

NORSE migration from
Dublin 902

NORTHUMBRIA

NORTH
WIRRAL
MEOLS ● continuing port
and trade

CELTIC/BRITISH with
increasing SAXON element
until arrival of NORSE in 902
Saxon assimilation
by 1066

☼ THINGWALL
NORSE meeting
place

MERSEY

RIVER MERSEY
(boundary River)

PRESTATYN ●

BASINGWERK ●

DEE

Suggested boundary
of NORSE Enclave

SOUTH WIRRAL

Outlying area from Chester
predominently SAXON from
7th cent

30 Saxon-Norse settlements.

WELSH

(Kathpound network boundary)

OFFA'S DYKE
(757-796) (early)

WAT'S DYKE
(716-757) (early Mercworth)

RIVER DEE

CHESTER ● Battle in c.616 marks the
end of NORTHUMBRIAN
threat to the Cheshire area
of MERCIA

MERCIA
(land of the boundary folk)

BANGORISCOED (on Dee) ●
Important monastery in 603

Mls   5   10

Kms   8   16

OSWESTRY

CHEPSTOW

As a result of the urbanisation of Wirral during the last 150 years, many of these elements have been preserved in modern road names. Thus, at the beginning of the 21st century, there are numerous avenues, closes, drives and lanes joined to the words croft, meadow and hay.

The Anglo-Saxons also left their imprint upon the land itself. They must have worked with some of the units which had begun to take shape well before they arrived, but would also have created new ones. Eastham was probably a new one. As has been shown, its name indicates that it was probably the first English settlement in Wirral. In 1086, Domesday Book described it as being the largest manor (in other words an area of land belonging to a lord) in Wirral. It covered most of the eastern side of the peninsula—all the shores of the Mersey as far north as Wallasey Pool. Before 1066, it had belonged to the English Earl Edwin, but had probably originally been a royal estate. It was the most important place in Wirral and effectively the basis of the Anglo-Saxon administrative unit called the Hundred of Wirral. There was no church in Eastham in 1086. Bromborough had a priest and its church contains some small fragments of pre-Norman stonework. It is, therefore, believed that Eastham lay within the parish of Bromborough. Eastham gained its own chapel in the

12th century and became a separate parish later on. Bromborough churchyard was originally curvilinear, indicating that it was in existence before the English arrived. They had, therefore, combined a pre-existing ecclesiastical centre with their own economic land division. It speaks of two important developing features of the history and landscape of Wirral—feudalism and administrative boundaries.

Feudalism was the chief characteristic of the Middle Ages. It has always been thought to have begun properly in 1066 when the Normans arrived. It is clear, however, that feudalism had taken root in pre-Conquest or Anglo-Saxon times. The essence of the system was the overlordship of powerful individuals over areas of land, which were called manors, and over the people who lived there. Originally, the lord lived in the centre of his manor; he owned a house, associated farm buildings and a piece of ground (called a demesne) where his own produce was grown. In return for services and various kinds of payment, the lord let people live upon and cultivate portions of his manor. Eastham is a classic example of the way in which the system emerged. It was probably settled by a powerful leader who would have been either royal or at least noble. The centre of the manor could have been the stronghold which gave Bromborough its name. It means 'Bruna's fortified place' (from the Anglo-Saxon personal name and *burh*). Perhaps Bruna was the founder of the settlement. The stronghold was closely related to the church. The alliance between the church and the overlord is another typical feature of the feudal system.

This large manor and parish left its mark upon the face of the peninsula. Illustration 46 (p.95, parishes) shows Brimstage as a detached portion of Bromborough parish. It is an odd arrangement and results from the way in which Bromborough parish once covered most of the eastern and central part of the peninsula. The former predominance of Eastham manor/Bromborough parish has been gradually eroded by the creation of other units, resulting from increases in population and developments in local economic and political history during the early Middle Ages. The rest of the peninsula must have been shared among the parishes of Wallasey, West Kirby, Landican/Woodchurch (which, with its ten townships dominated the centre of north Wirral) and Neston. The first three of these sites had curvilinear churchyards and all of them have produced pre-Norman stonework, indicating their importance. There was also the small and enigmatic parish of Overchurch—the only place to have produced any pre-Viking stonework and which, by the Middle Ages, included only the township of Upton. Burton parish is an example of the way in which the dominance of Bromborough/Eastham was gradually broken down. Burton had a priest in 1086 and had belonged to the Bishop of Lichfield for some time. Perhaps he had created it in order to gain a stake in Wirral at the expense of the Bromborough/Eastham parish/manor, depriving it of its former access to the shore of the Dee.

By the 11th century, most of England south of the river Tees had been divided into shires (from the Anglo-Saxon *scir*—'office' or 'authority'). Chester was the administrative centre of one of them—the future county of Cheshire. Wirral was a hundred, an administrative unit within the shire. It was called a hundred because it contained 100 hides. A hide was an Anglo-Saxon unit of land area. In contemporary Latin documents, hides are described as *terra unius familiae*, 'one family's land'. So the term does not describe a precise acreage but a concept. It could have different dimensions in different regions according to the relative abilities of the soil to sustain families. The Hundred Court of Wirral met at 'Eada's Mound' or Hadlow in the village of Willaston (from the Anglo-Saxon

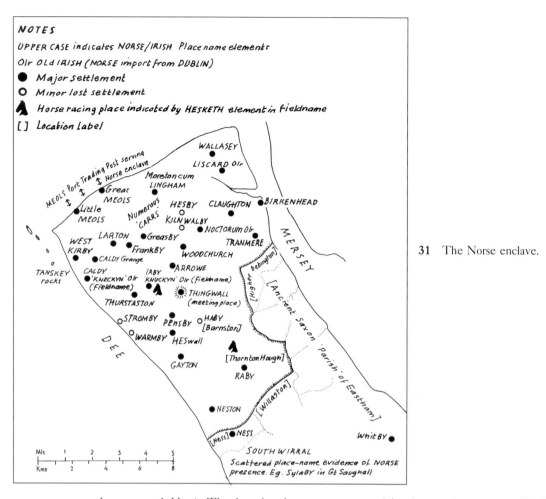

NOTES

UPPER CASE indicates NORSE/IRISH Place name elements

OIr OLD IRISH (NORSE import from DUBLIN)

● Major settlement

○ Minor lost settlement

▲ Horse racing place indicated by HESKETH element in fieldname

[ ] Location label

31 The Norse enclave.

personal name and *hlaw*). The location is commemorated in the modern names Hadlow Road and Hadlow Wood. If it operated in the manner which is implied by the records from other parts of England, the people would have gathered in the open air and problems relating to local taxation, land use and law and order would have been discussed and resolved. Officers with specialist legal knowledge and representatives of the aristocratic authority would have been present. The Germanic peoples of Europe had a tradition of dealing with their communal problems in this way. As will be described later in the chapter, the Vikings practised a similar form of local administration. It was one of the foundations for both modern British local government and national parliamentary democracy.

Although it was the most important one, Hadlow was probably not the only meeting place in Wirral. Dodgson mentions that a house name *Motelawe* was recorded in 1471 in Moreton. He suggested that it stood on the piece of slightly higher ground which underlies the main part of the settlement. The name probably came from the Anglo-Saxon words *mot*—'meeting' or *motere*—'speaker' and *hlaw*—'hill'. There was also a field called Mutler in Brimstage and another called Mutlow in Thornton Hough, which probably had the same derivation.[13]

Imagination will bring those times to life. The peninsula was green and quiet. Its precious soil was parcelled by lines of trees, hedges, streams, hillocks and small remnants of the wild wood. People had shaped the landscape but it was still natural: man-made structures did not deface it. The houses were wooden and small; the largest buildings were the few churches and the lords' mansions. There was a network of well-known tracks leading from one tiny cluster of cottages to another and between the various plots of ground. This was the only land which the people knew. They could not read and probably did not travel far. Their knowledge was narrow but they were not ignorant—they knew the soil and the foliage which sprouted from it, not as an occasional aesthetic stimulant but as a daily source of food, medicine and colour. They knew what land belonged to whom and, in their constant quest to ensure survival and perhaps to gain a little enrichment, they would both fight to preserve the perimeters of their crofts and to extend them to the waste or woods beyond. When neighbours allowed weeds to encroach, fences to collapse or animals to stray, or dared surreptitiously to extend their furrows onto another's patch, then the grievance would be taken to the Hundred Court. On the allotted date, the folk—expectant, anxious, angry, curious—would gather at the mound in the centre of their homeland. It was a time to see old friends and enjoy a bit of spectacle as well as to do business. Picture the gathering: to us, a ragged huddle; to the folks of the time, the largest accumulation of people any of them would ever see—brown-faced, grimy-handed farmers, all in their dull, earthy, woollen clothes—the forefathers of English Wirral.

By 1086, the district was known as *Wilaveston* Hundred after the name of the township where the court met, but, in the *Anglo-Saxon Chronicle* for 894 and 895, it had also been called *Wirhealum* and *Wirheale*—'The nooks where the bog-myrtle grows' (from *wir*—'bog-myrtle' and *halh*— 'nook, corner or secluded place').

The only piece of writing from Anglo-Saxon days comes from Overchurch. It is an inscription in runes (from the Germanic word *run*—'mystery') on a sandstone monument. It has been transliterated as: 'Folca(ae) araerdon becun biddath fore Aethelmund(e)'. Giving the translation: 'The people raised a memorial. Pray for Aethelmund(e)'. It was a kind of 'bidding-stone'—a memorial to a respected leader, requesting prayers from passers-by. An Aethelmund appears as a witness on several Mercian charters and is described in the *Anglo-Saxon Chronicle* as having been killed in a raid on Wessex in 800. Perhaps this is the man who came from Overchurch or held lands in the area. He was respected as a warrior and leader and the people wanted to remember him.[14]

There is very little archaeology from the time. Meols has produced a reasonable collection of artifacts, including bronze and silver pins, buckles, strap-ends and five pre-Viking coins—two silver *sceattas* from about 725 and three Northumbrian copper *stycas* from about 850. The old place was carrying on its business just as it had done during the previous thousand years. The site of a possible early modern chapel has been excavated in Moreton and produced evidence of habitation during Anglo-Saxon times in the form of drainage ditches, signs of a hearth or oven and remains of a timber building. A coin from A.D. 955-59 and some beans, peas and cereal grains were recovered.[15]

The Anglo-Saxons were undoubtedly the founders of England—they gave it its language and drew the outlines of its political geography. We have seen how and when they came to Wirral and how they related to the existing British or Celtic population. They both adopted some of the existing settlements and institutions and created new ones. They worked within some of the old boundaries and created others from scratch. They gave Wirral, as well as most of its townships and the river which forms its eastern perimeter, their names. Their leaders were in charge of the neighbourhood in 1066. But there was another group of immigrants who were to arrive in Wirral long before the Normans and who were to make their distinctive contribution to the language, landscape and culture of the district—the Vikings.

Part Four: Viking Wirral

According to the *Anglo-Saxon Chronicle*, the first time the Vikings came to England was in 793 when they raided the monastery at Lindisfarne in Northumbria. They had a reputation as savage, pagan invaders bent on looting, raping and destruction. This was actually only part of their story: their real legacy in Europe is far more positive and is the consequence of their being sailors, colonisers, craftsmen, farmers, businessmen, town-builders, artists and writers. Raiding and fighting were features of their early search for wealth and living space, probably incited by population growth and the pressure on the southern frontiers of Scandinavia which was being exerted by the people of central Europe. The movement of people from Scandinavia to the British Isles is a later stage in that remarkable restlessness of the peoples of Europe during the post-Roman and early medieval periods. Scandinavians settled mainly in eastern Ireland, north-west Scotland and the north of England. In the north-west of England the most striking evidence for their presence is of a linguistic nature—place-names and dialect, but they bequeathed us very little archaeological or literary material. There is much debate about just how much the Vikings actually did influence the history of the region. After all, we do now all speak English and not Norwegian; our institutions are English with a Scandinavian flavour and not the other way around; and our capital city is London and not Oslo or Reykjavik.

The Vikings' fearsome reputation, artistic energy and colourful mythology, combined with the mysteriousness of their history, has traditionally made them attractive both to the scholar and to the dreamer. Wirral has been home to a fascinating example of this interplay between self-delusory myth-making and serious scholarship. All Wirralians know and love Thurstaston Common. It is a beautiful tract of uncultivated land which the public is free to roam. At its heart there lies a large block of sandstone, standing separate from the surrounding terrain. Nobody could deny that it is an enchanting location where it is possible to forget that one is standing on a tiny remnant of nature in a built-up district. The best time to visit is dusk in early winter: as the chill air sinks into the hollows and the sky changes from riotous red to steely grey, nothing may be heard but the rustle of bare branches and the occasional shout of a fox. In the gloom, the rain-sculptured rock-forms become petrified people and animals. Here is a cathedral of the wild, a chapel of reveries and a womb for wonderings. It is called Thor's Stone. During the 19th century, it spurned some glorious nonsense. Sir James Picton, Liverpool antiquarian and businessman, said that it had once been a Viking religious site and that it was '... a record of Danish heathendom ... [a] gigantic rock altar ... How far its original shape has been modified it is impossible to say, but human labour has been largely expended upon it.' Philip Sulley, a later Wirral historian, continued the theme: 'The great stone of Thor was reddened with the blood of priests and captives'; and Hilda Gamlin concluded: 'The stone was probably raised by the Danes to commemorate the great battle of Brunenburh.'[16] (The Battle of Brunanburh is discussed in detail in Appendix II.) Their fantasies were encouraged by misinterpreting the name Thurstaston to mean 'Village of Thor's Stone', instead of the

32 Thor's Stone in July 2002, a beautiful sandstone feature on Thurstaston Common. Was it a Viking sacrificial altar or the result of modern quarrying?

correct, but prosaic, 'Thorsteinn's Farm'. Even if Thorsteinn himself was a first generation Norse settler, he would have been a Norwegian from Ireland, not a Dane. He is unlikely to have been interested in human sacrifice as he would have been a Christian. Even if he did have a secret passion for immolating his neighbours—clerical or lay—he would doubtless have been too busy cultivating his land to be able to indulge his anti-social hobby. Indeed, the supposed Rock of Thor itself has a much more mundane origin—it is probably a portion of poorer quality sandstone which 19th-century builders, who must have been free to cut sandstone from the common land, have left behind.

We are fortunate now to be able to review the history of Viking Wirral in the light of some excellent and innovatory work which has been carried out by a group of Viking scholars led by exiled Wirralian Stephen Harding. It consists of a unique combination of scholarly historical analysis, a sympathetic attention to local Viking mythologies and scientific research related to Professor Harding's professional specialism in biological science. The ensuing discussion is based mainly on Harding's book, *Ingimund's Saga* and the one to which he contributed, *Wirral and its Viking Heritage.*[17]

The story begins with the expulsion of the Norwegian or Norse people from Dublin in A.D. 902. It is told in an Irish Annal and partially supported by another one from Wales. This makes it the only Norse settlement in England which is described in writing. Wirral is not mentioned by name, but the Irish Annal states that the leader of the group of Scandinavians was called Hingamund or Ingimund. First of all, he attempted to settle in Anglesey, but was ejected, so he applied to Aethelflaed, 'Queen of the Saxons' (in Mercia) and was allowed to settle on some land 'near Chester, and he stayed there for a long time'. Wirral's proximity to Chester combined with its numerous Scandinavian place-names tells us that this was the district in which Ingimund and his people settled. The Irish Annal goes on to say that Ingimund later decided to capture Chester itself, but was beaten back by the Saxons. The *Anglo-Saxon Chronicle* supports this by saying that Aethelflaeda reinforced the city walls in 907.

Actual Norse colonisation of Wirral might have taken longer than is implied by the records. Margaret Gelling proposes that the manors near to Chester were taken over by the first wave of Norse overlords, who preserved the settlements' English names. The way was then opened for more colonists to come to the peninsula via the port at Meols. The later arrivals settled on the less desirable or marginal areas of north Wirral. They brought waste and boggy land into cultivation and revitalised Meols itself, giving it the name by which we now know it. It is certainly difficult to imagine an entire population arriving with Ingimund at the same time, especially when we try to visualise him sailing first to Anglesey, then to Chester and then spreading onto the Wirral Peninsula with a huge following of men, women and children constantly in tow. It is easier to picture him arriving with one or two ships manned by his closest supporters and some community leaders and then sending back to Ireland for the rest of the people once the way had been opened for them.

Of all the evidence for the importance of the Norse colonisation of Wirral, the most apparently persuasive is of the linguistic variety. There are 600 possible examples of Norse names in Wirral—townships, small and lost settlements, field and road names. In *Ingimund's Saga*, Professor Harding says '... nowhere else in the U.K. is there such a density in such a small area'. In addition to Meols, there are the following names which are either wholly Norse or contain Norse elements or other evidence of Norse influence: Birkenhead, Caldy, Claughton, Frankby, Gayton, Greasby, Hargrave, Irby, Larton, Mollington Torold, Moreton-cum-Lingham, Pensby, Raby, Storeton, Thingwall, Thurstaston, Tranmere, West Kirby, Whitby and Woodchurch. In addition, there are five names of Irish origin. Three are still in use—Arrowe, Noctorum and Liscard and two have been lost—*Knuckyn* in Irby and *Kneckyn* (possibly Caldy Hill) in the parish of West Kirby. They reflect the fact that, even though the immigrants were Norwegians, their most recent home had been in Ireland and that some of them were Irish-speakers. The fact that Irby means 'Irishmen's Farm' endorses this conclusion. Some of the Norse settlements have not survived into modern times. Their former existence is revealed only by documentary evidence and field-names. They were Haby (in Barnston), Heskeby/Eskeby (in Bidston), Kiln Walby (in Overchurch/Upton), Stromby (in Thurstaston), Syllaby (in Great Saughall) and Warmby (in Heswall).

In addition to the settlement names, there are numerous names of fields and other smaller locations which contain classic Norse elements: there are 96 rakes (from *rak*, 'lane'), 50 carrs (from *kjar*, 'marsh'), 37 intakes (from *inntak*, 'enclosure'), 24 holms (from *holmr*, 'island in marshy or flooded ground'), and 11 slacks (from *slakki*, 'hollows' or 'shallow valleys'). Harding has also pinpointed some special sites. Both Irby and Thornton Hough contain fields with the name Hesketh. It means 'Horse Track' (from *hestur*, 'horse' and *skeith*, 'track'). Wallasey had a rocky outcrop called The Clynsse (from *klint*, 'projecting rock') and Bromborough had areas called Wood Clints and The Clints with the same derivation. The full list of names would seem to be proof that Wirral was both colonised and radically changed by the Norse settlers from Ireland.

Linguistic evidence on its own, however, contains some inherent ambiguities. Place-names imply that the Norse language was once predominant, but there are few if any signs of its legacy in current speech. Modern Wirralians speak with an accent which is shared, with subtle variations, by the people of Liverpool, south-west Lancashire, Chester and the North Wales coast between Sealand and Abergele. The classic form of the accent grew up in Liverpool and is called Scouse. Ironically, even though the word scouse itself was introduced to Liverpool by 19th-century Scandinavian sailors (from *lapskaus*, a stew made from leftover meat), the dialect owes nothing to Old Norse: it is the result of the mixing of the speech of the city's two largest 19th-century immigrant communities, the Welsh and the Irish, with the native Lancashire accent and perhaps a little Scots. It is a metropolitan accent which has gradually superseded other local accents within Liverpool's hinterland. London's accent, Cockney, has followed a similar course in south-east England. It is not clear exactly how Wirralians spoke before the expansion of Liverpool, but the few available clues lead this author to the tentative conclusion that the local accent contained elements which were similar to the speech of the West Midlands. If this was so, it would indicate that it was based on the Mercian dialect of Anglo-Saxon and not Norse.

Clearly Norse words had entered the English language but their former and current use does not necessarily imply that the Scandinavians were ever the dominant linguistic, cultural or political group. Despite the fact that Britain has not been colonised by Indians, there are many words in modern English which derive from Indian languages (eg. punch, khaki, shampoo, pundit, bungalow, canoe and pukka). The truth is that they are loan-words: they were adopted in order to describe things which formerly were unheard-of or whose previous titles were inadequate. The parallel is not completely accurate but it illustrates the nature of the phenomenon. It is possible, therefore, that not every Wirral location with a Norse name was given it by an actual Viking. The names could have been awarded centuries after the Norse settlement, by people who spoke English and were of largely Anglo-Saxon ancestry. Their forebears had simply adopted the Norse words to describe features, like marshes and other marginal lands, which were coming into greater use as a consequence of improvements in agriculture.

West Kirby is a possible classic Norse settlement: it has a namesake in Iceland, *Vestri Kirkjubaer*; its church is dedicated to St Bridget of Ireland and it is home to a small collection of Viking stonework. Table 2 on page 58 has a list of field-names from the township and, therefore, shows the relative importance of Norse words in the district. Only three out of the 30 names (10 per cent)—Flat, Rugs and Slack—have Norse origins. The rest are Old, Middle or Modern English words. One field is called Sandhills: an English term has been used in preference to the Norse word, *melr*, which was used in creating the name of the adjoining township, Little Meols. This shows us how Norse had fallen into disuse. Their names might contain Norse elements but they are classic examples of loan-words and are clearly not evidence of Viking settlement.

In order to lend more substance to the argument, Table 3 on page 60 summarises the West Kirby analysis together with that of ten more townships—two more with Norse names from north Wirral, three with Anglo-Saxon names from north Wirral, one with a Norse name at the southern end, three from the southern end with an Anglo-Saxon name and one from outside Wirral altogether. For the sake of argument, the table accepts two types of words whose status is ambiguous, but are assumed to be evidence of Norse influence: elements like Dale (of which there are four in Thingwall, one in Oxton and two in Whitby) and Gate (there is one in Whitby) which could have come either from Anglo-Saxon or Norse originals; and words with Norse roots but which are obviously now current in Modern English—Crook(ed) and Cross. In addition, repetitions of single words which are describing divisions of the same geographical feature (eg. The Holm, Holm Bridge, Lower Holm, Top Holm and Five Acre Holm in Prenton) have been recorded as separate examples. Four personal names are taken as Norse field-name elements—Arni in Oxton, Ufaldi in Saughall Massie, Ingrith in Shotwick and Reynold in Whitby. The last two are problematic: Ingrith could be either Danish or Norwegian and Reynold is broadly Germanic

Table 2: Field Names from West Kirby (from Dodgson, *Place-Names of Cheshire, Vol. 4*, pp.295-300)

Abbreviations for Lang. (Language): O.E. = Old English; M.E. = Middle or Modern English; O.N. = Old Norse. The annotation in the Explanation is only where known and necessary).

Field Names	Date	Lang.	Elements	Explanation
Back Field	1844	M.E.		
Bawk	1844	O.E.	*balc*	Unploughed ridge of land between the strips in the open field
Brow	1844	M.E.		
Butchers Bank	1844	M.E.		
Common Allotment Kirby Common	1844 1831	M.E.		The Common Field for everybody's use
Le Conyngre Le Conygre	1547 1553	French M.E.	*cony*	The Rabbit field
Cowhay -Hey	1639	O.E.	*(ge)heag*	
Croft Mellon	1844	O.E.	*croft*	
Flat	1844	O.N.	*flatr*	Level piece of ground or enclosed section of the former open field
Gobbins Butts	1844	O.E.	*butte*	Ellen Gobbin was a beneficiary of the will of Robert Wigan of Hilbre in 1550
Grass Hey-Hay	1639	O.E.	*(ge)heag*	
Hoo Headlands	1844	O.E.	*hoh, heaford-land*	Spur of land, low projecting piece of land in bend of a river or on level ground; headland—the top of something
Kiln Hay	1844	O.E.	*(ge)heag*	
Little Hey-Hay The Parson's, Little Hey	1844 1639	O.E.	*(ge)heag*	
Longtonn Field The Field Under the Ton	1844 1325	O.E.	*lang, tun*	The long field connected to the town(ship)
Lower-, Middle, Higher-, Brown-, & Linacre's Loohon	1844	O.E.	*land*	Linacre was a common surname in West Kirby parish. Loon referred to a former strip from the open fields
Marl Hay/Marled Hey	1639	O.E.	*(ge)heag*	
Mellons	1844			
Croft Mellon Crockmellin	1844 1639	O.E.	*croft*	
Mill Ditch	1844	O.E.	*dic*	
Mutch Hay	1844	O.E.	*(ge)heag*	The Mutch family had lived in West Kirby since the 18th cent.
Nottrills	1844			
The Rugs	1844	O.N.	*hryggr*	The Ridge
Little Salver The Sarvor	1844 1639		*server*	
Sandhills	1844	M.E.		The English word has been chosen in preference to the Norse word *melr*
Slack	1844	O.N.	*slakki*	Shallow valley
The Stones, Lower Stones	1844	O.E.	*stan*	
Swithen's Green	1844			
Town Field Little Town Field	1844 1639	O.E.	*tun*	The open field of the town(ship)

Table 3: Field-Name Analysis from 11 Townships (from Dodgson, *Place-Names of Cheshire, Vol. 4*).

Township	Description	No. of Field-Names	No. with Norse Elements	%
Thingwall	Norse township name; in north Wirral; believed to be site of *thing* or Norse meeting place	25	7	28.0
Great and Little Meols	Norse township name (*melr*); in North Wirral; Viking archaeology on shore; believed to be the port for the Norse enclave in Wirral	56	6	10.7
West Kirby	Norse township name; Irish church dedication; Viking stonework; in north Wirral	30	3	10.0
Oxton	Anglo-Saxon township name; in north Wirral	48	13	27.1
Prenton	Anglo-Saxon township name; in north Wirral	28	7	25.0
Saughall Massie	Anglo-Saxon township name; in north Wirral	57	5	8.8
Whitby	Norse township name; in southern Wirral	77	9	11.7
Chorlton	Anglo-Saxon township name; in southern Wirral	33	3	9.1
Shotwick	Anglo-Saxon township name; in southern Wirral	36	2	5.6
Lea	Anglo-Saxon township name; in southern Wirral	47	2	4.3
Malpas	French township name; not in Wirral (A 'control' example)	126	2	1.6

and could have come to England with the Normans. The other words—Carr, Holme, Intake, Rake and Slack—are, as we have seen, Norse topographical words which were adopted by English speakers. We are gaining the impression that it is dangerous to use local names alone as evidence of a large Scandinavian presence in Wirral. Indeed, if we pursue our questions about the validity of the list of Norse words to their logical conclusion, we will even begin to doubt that any Scandinavian people ever set foot on the peninsula at all: the entire collection of 600 'Norse' names could simply be the result of loaning.

Table 3 reveals that Norse field-names are in the minority in every township. In north Wirral, there is little correlation between whether the settlement has a Norse name and its proportion of Norse field names. For example, 'Anglo-Saxon' Oxton has the second highest proportion of Norse names; 'Norse' West Kirby has the next to lowest. We must conclude that the language from which the name of the township is derived need not be an indication of the ethnicity of the people who lived there. Furthermore, the use of Norse words within a township must owe more to the nature of the local landscape than to the number of Norse people dwelling within it. Thus, the boggy lands of the north Wirral coastal plain and the valleys of the rivers Fender and Birket have attracted relatively intensive use of the words *holmr* and *kjar*; while the widespread practices, during the Middle Ages and early modern period, of bringing waste ground into cultivation and enclosing the former open fields, have ensured that the elements *inntak* and *flatr* can be found virtually everywhere. Indeed, both of the Norse names in Malpas on the Cheshire Plain (Intake and Dun's Flatt), a long way from any Viking settlement, contain these elements. At this point in the discussion, we might feel inclined to decide that Scandinavian settlers did not, after all, make a large impact on Wirral. But let us not be so hasty—to do so would turn the Wirral Vikings into 'ghosts in the machine' or spirits who die from a thousand definitions. It must be remembered that the Viking scholars have also used archaeological and literary evidence to support their argument for the former significance of the Scandinavians in Wirral. In looking at the origins of local place-names we have drawn attention to the complex way in which our language has evolved. It has borrowed words from a range of roots. Our field-names are fascinating and attractive because they are the result of over a thousand years of human relationships with the landscape. Unfortunately, however, they have not, so far, furnished us with conclusive proof that the Scandinavian settlers were numerous.

Table 3 does, however, illustrate some subtle trends: south Wirral settlements with Anglo-Saxon names have smaller proportions of Norse field-names. This might be due to the failure of the local topography to attract the classic elements *kjar* and *holmr* which are associated with marshy ground, but it also correlates with an argument, which has been propounded by most of the Wirral Viking scholars in the last 50 years, that most of Wirral's Scandinavian immigrants settled at the northern end of the peninsula and formed an enclave which was quite distinct from Anglo-Saxon southern Wirral. They have identified a boundary between the two parts of the peninsula. Its chief indicators are the name Raby (from Old Norse *ra byr*, 'Border village') and the natural features, such as Dibbinsdale and Prospect and Storeton Hills, along which it is likely to have run. To the south of the border, in Bromborough, there were two fascinating names—*Gremoteland* (recorded in 1330) which means 'Place of meeting under a truce' and *Lathegestfeld* (recorded in 1412) which means 'Unwelcome guest field'. They speak of activities which would have occurred around a frontier between Norse and Anglo-Saxon people in Wirral.

Domesday Book (see Appendix III for all Wirral Domesday entries) refers indirectly to the existence of the Wirral Norse enclave. It lists the properties of the Norman barons who had come to England with William the Conqueror. Robert of Rhuddlan's Wirral properties, apart from Great and Little Mollington, lay north of the Raby boundary. They were in a compact parcel, whereas, in the rest of Wirral, lords' properties were dispersed. In the words of John Dodgson: 'It looks as though the Norse enclave in Wirral was so politically distinctive that it justified a special feudal administration'. He goes on to say that a document of 1182 refers to 'Caldy Hundred' (*Caldeihundredun*), implying that even by that time it was still a separate administrative unit, based within the larger Hundred of Wirral. The fact that it had the Anglo-Saxon title of Hundred instead of the Norse Wapentake is, however, significant: the former area of Norse home rule had become an English unit of local government.[18]

The Norse enclave would effectively have been a 'mini-state' with its own public meeting place at Thingwall (from *thing-vollr*, 'Field where an assembly met' or 'Meeting-place') and a port at Meols. Noticeable in the collection of artifacts from the Meols shore is a comparative lack of ninth-century coins. The port must have been suffering from a trade recession just before the Vikings arrived. Offa's Dyke had claimed the Welsh shore of the Dee estuary as English territory. Little harbours between Flint and Point of Ayr might have stolen some of Meols' trade. Alternatively, Chester itself might simply have been acting as Mercia's north-western trade outlet, making Meols superfluous. There are numerous coins from the 10th and 11th centuries from places such as Canterbury, Chester, Shrewsbury, Winchester and York. The implied change suggests that the Vikings revitalised Meols and were able to exploit its position as a 'marginal' and 'neutral' site on the coast of the Irish sea in order to trade with a wide area. As stated above, Chester was refortified by the Queen of Mercia in 907. It was emphatically an Anglo-Saxon city and port. Meols, however, lay in the Wirral Norse enclave and operated outside Chester's orbit. Perhaps it stole a lot of Chester's trade. As well as the coins, there are numerous other items from the Viking era, including an impressive collection of distinctly Irish-Norse bronze ring-headed pins. Here was a small but prosperous settlement whose wealth must have come from its trade and not its agriculture.[19] Again, however, there is no concrete evidence that the town was inhabited either completely or substantially by Scandinavians. It was certainly named by them, but its Viking objects could just be the result of its role as a centre of trade in the Irish Sea Province. Its residents could have been British, Anglo-Saxon or a mixture of the two groups with little or no Viking presence at all.

Ironically for a people who are popularly imagined as evil, pagan marauders, the most visible legacy of the Wirral Vikings is a collection of stone crosses. No complete, standing cross has ever been found, but various pieces of heads and shafts have been discovered at Hilbre, West Kirby, Wallasey, Bromborough and Neston. Some of the fragments have clearly been broken and reshaped in order to become building blocks in later structures. Scrutiny of the Hilbre cross reveals more about their original appearance: it has a small hole in its centre which was designed to house a coloured bead. Its intricately carved patterns would have been painted red, blue and yellow. W.G. Collingwood asserted that the West Kirby examples would have been made around 1030. He said that, by that time, the Scandinavian population would have been both stable and prosperous enough to invest money in such luxurious statements about their faith and further suggested that the individuals who had them erected 'wished to be in the fashion' and that demand for the crosses was possibly 'created by the supply'. The craftsman probably lived in Chester and executed his carvings in a workshop connected to the Collegiate Church of St John. Collingwood went on to observe that one of the pieces had been 'bungled' and said that this was evidence of the mason having come to West Kirby in order to make the cross on site. He might have been anxious to finish early and rushed the job or gone home and left one of his less experienced assistants to complete it.[20]

All of Wirral's Viking crosses could be viewed as examples of conspicuous consumption—statements by a Scandinavian social elite that they had sufficient wealth and importance to justify the erection of striking works of art. Investment in crosses might have accompanied even greater expenditure on church or domestic buildings. Peace and prosperity had arrived. Additionally, the Vikings could have been telling their Anglo-Saxon neighbours that they were here to stay and that this was their land. They particularly used Christian symbols in order to emphasise that they were civilised and, therefore, just as worthy as the Anglo-Saxons not only to settle here but politically to rule and economically to dominate the people who lived within their north Wirral mini-state.

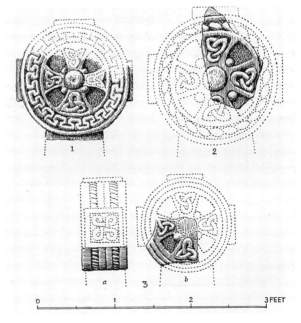

33 Pre-Norman cross-heads from West Kirby.

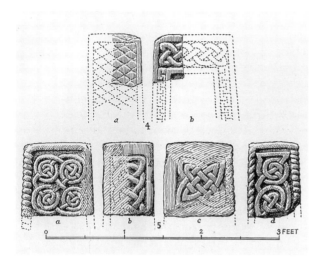

34 Pre-Norman sculptured stones from West Kirby.

Later on in the 10th century, vertical crosses seem to have gone out of fashion and were replaced by 'hogbacks'. These are odd-looking recumbent tombstones which have central ridges with apparent drops of water running down their vertical sides. The drops originally represented roofing tiles and the complete carvings were meant to depict houses. Collingwood says this about the West Kirby example: 'Some important person had died and a memorial was put in the hands of an artificer who was hardly a professional monumental mason, but had seen hogbacks in Cumbria and he did his best.'[21]

By the 12th century, hogbacks had fallen out of fashion and been replaced by flat slabs which had crosses carved upon them.

About all Wirral's Viking stonework, J.D. Bu'lock said this: '... these stones, whether today they are preserved in museums, or exposed to the weather, cared for, or piled in some neglected corner of a church, were the memorials and testimonies of men, and these were our ancestors.'[22]

Science is beginning to enable us to discover to what extent the Vikings were really the ancestors of modern Wirralians. It is fortunate that Professor Stephen Harding is three things—a Wirralian, a local historian and a scientist. As a result of his first two attributes, the important subject of Viking Wirral, which had lain dormant for half a century, has been revived and it is hoped that analysis, debate and popular interest will continue to flourish. But due to his latter qualification as a bioscientist we are beginning to gauge the strength of the genetic inheritance from the Vikings. Professor Harding was able to link his research

35 'Hogback' tombstone from West Kirby.

with wider surveys which were being carried out by scientists from the University of London and which were later described in the B.B.C. Television series *Blood of the Vikings*. During 2001, volunteers in Wirral and south-west Lancashire were asked to give samples of their D.N.A. They were all men whose paternal grandfathers had come from the local area. Samples were taken from the cells in their cheek linings by mouth swabs and analysed by means of 'PCR-technology' in Professor David Goldstein's laboratory at the University of London. The researchers were looking for two types of Y-chromosome—the so-called '+2.47' and '+3.65'. These are carried by 38 per cent and 20 per cent respectively of men in modern Norway. They are comparatively rare in men from Denmark and North Germany and virtually absent amongst Welshmen, so they are good indicators of Scandinavian ancestry. The Y-chromosome is passed from father to son and is, therefore, a link with an ancestor of some 40 generations ago, but an individual's D.N.A. analysis will not necessarily reveal a Viking ancestor. The research is only meaningful when performed on populations. Thus, some 300 samples were assessed and the results have been published. In Harding's words:

> ... show a strong correlation of the genetic and place name maps. The north Wirral data appears statistically similar to the other 'Scandinavian place name rich' areas of South Wirral and SW & West Lancashire, but completely different from North Wales and, significantly, Mid Cheshire. Geographically, with their closeness to Wales, SW Lancs and particularly Wirral might be expected to be far more Celtic than they actually are—indeed, to be like Mid-Cheshire. Strong Viking settlements may appear to adequately explain the difference. So although the genetic results by themselves are not conclusive proof of Vikings, their combination with the place name (philological) evidence is compelling. The only other genetic demonstrations of Viking influence in UK ... have been in the Scottish Isles, Isle of Man and the North Lakes, areas which have a strong Celtic rather than Germanic background, which makes Vikings easier to detect. No Vikings have for example been detected in York! This is not because there aren't any, it is just the technique as its stands can't pick them out.[23]

Non-scientists were perhaps a little disappointed with the results of this survey—not because they failed to reveal Viking ancestry, but because a more definite story cannot yet be told. Historians will not be surprised at the outcome; the truth about the past is never easy to discover. Thankfully, the movements, motivations and inter-relationships of people are far too complex and rich to yield simplistic definitions and assertions. We remain both humble and sceptical, being constantly aware of the ambiguities of all our evidence and alive to the weaknesses in every argument. Of one thing there can be no doubt—more work is needed. We look forward to the next stage in the genetic survey which will attempt to take samples from people whose ancestors lived in the chosen areas prior to 1600 or whose surnames will have been identified as being strongly local. The results will undoubtedly open up more avenues of inquiry and increase our understanding of local population and family history.

By the middle of the 11th century, Wirral had been settled by two important groups of Germanic people. The Anglo-Saxons gave the peninsula its name and created most of the settlements. The Viking contribution to the history of the district was significant but is yet to be fully understood. We have seen that linguistic evidence alone cannot prove that there were large numbers of Scandinavian settlers but, when it is combined with the literary and archaeological evidence, we must conclude that, at the very least, their impact on Wirral was second in importance to that of the Anglo-Saxons. There is a good case for believing in the existence of a Norse mini-state in north Wirral and the archaeological evidence shows that some people must have been prosperous and wanted to make it clear that they were here to stay, but ultimately it is an inescapable fact that Wirral became English. Examples of 'Norseness' appear in Wirral sources possibly as late as the 16th century, but, in all important respects, the peninsula owed more to its Anglo-Saxon heritage than to that bequeathed by the Vikings. John Dodgson's explanation of the failure of the Celts to hold on to Cheshire in the face of the Anglo-Saxon invasion because of their weak political institutions seems apposite. The reverse situation pertained when the Vikings arrived: Anglo-Saxon Mercia stood its ground, forcing the Vikings to stay largely within an agreed pocket in northern Wirral. Within this pocket, they were able to dominate the population. They need not have even been numerically superior, but just have become the political elite. As a result, perhaps for a period of just one hundred years, the language and culture of north Wirral would have had a strong Norse flavour, but, ultimately, for the simple pragmatic reason that such a small state was unsustainable, it was absorbed into the wider and stronger English nation. It should be remembered that, despite their apparent aggressive sense of identity, this is what happened to Norse colonies all over Europe, notably in Russia and in France. It is the invasion of England by the descendants of the latter colony which began the period which we call the Middle Ages and is the first subject in our next chapter.

Four

Medieval Wirral 1066~1500

Part One: Conquest to Domesday Book

On Christmas Day 1066 at Westminster, Archbishop Ealdred stood poised with the English crown over the head of William Duke of Normandy. William had beaten the English king Harold at Hastings in October and was now looking forward to getting a firm grip on his new home. Before the crown was placed upon his head, however, he 'gave a pledge on the gospels, and swore an oath besides ... that he would govern this nation according to the best practice of his predecessors if they would be loyal to him'. To William's mind the final clause of his oath obviously justified twenty years of violence, destruction, oppression and theft, because the chronicler went on to say that 'Nevertheless he imposed a very heavy tax on the country and ... [the Normans] harried everywhere they came'.[1]

Every English region can tell its own story of the sufferings which the Normans inflicted on its people, but none more so than the North. In 1069 William punished Yorkshire and Durham by ravaging the countryside—villages were burned to the ground and people massacred. During the winter of that year, he marched across the Pennines and invaded Cheshire. Domesday Book describes many Cheshire villages as still being 'waste' in 1086. They had been so thoroughly ruined by the Normans 17 years earlier that they still had not recovered. The distribution of these wasted manors shows us the route which the Norman army took: they probably entered the county through the 'panhandle' in Cheshire's Pennine north-eastern corner and destroyed Tintwhistle and Hollingworth. They then moved south, attacking Butley and Macclesfield, before they struck westwards across the Cheshire Plain in three prongs, heading for Chester and North Wales. Chester was wrecked. Over 200 houses were destroyed and over a thousand people made homeless. Domesday Book says that, even by 1086, the city was still 'greatly wasted' and that half of its houses were in ruins. Wirral's wasted manors run from east to west roughly through the centre of the peninsula. The furthest east, Mickle Trafford, was probably hit during the original advance on Chester. The other examples—both Mollingtons, Puddington, Hadlow (Willaston), Poulton Lancelyn, Storeton, Noctorum and Little Meols—lie approximately along the alignment of the possible Roman road, the evidence for whose existence was discussed in Chapter Two. Strangely, Barnston is described, without explanation, as having been waste before 1066. Perhaps it had been the victim of some local feuding before the Normans arrived.

William stole the estates from English landowners and gave them to his followers. Many important local families now had no option but to offer themselves up as serfs to the new ruling class. Domesday Book records the Anglo-Saxon and Norse names of 28 men who owned estates in Wirral before 1066. All their lands were now in the hands of Norman nobles and their helpers. The men themselves had either died fighting the invaders or were now peasants on the lands they had once owned. A new era had begun. Of course, many institutions and systems were maintained and adapted, but many more were introduced. In common with the rest of England, as a consequence of being ruled by new masters from a foreign land with different aims and outlooks, Wirral was to experience changes in its society and landscape which were to typify the period we call the Middle Ages. *The Anglo-Saxon Chronicle* makes important points:

> He caused great castles to be built
> Which were a sore burden to the poor.
> A hard man was the king
> And took from his subjects many marks
> In gold and many more hundreds of pounds in silver.
> These sums he took by weight from his people,
> Most unjustly and for little need.
> He was sunk in greed
> And utterly given to avarice.
> He set apart a vast deer preserve and imposed laws concerning it.
> Whoever slew a hart or a hind
> Was to be blinded.
> He forbade the killing of boars
> Even as the killing of harts.
> For he loved the stags as dearly
> As though he had been their father.
> Hares, also, he decreed should go unmolested.
> The rich complained and the poor lamented,
> But he was too relentless to care though all might hate him,
> And they were compelled, if they wanted
> To keep their lives and their lands
> And their goods and the favour of the king,
> To submit themselves wholly to his will.
> Alas! That any man should bear himself so proudly
> And deem himself exalted above all other men!
> May Almighty God show mercy to his soul
> And Pardon him his sins.[2]

By describing events in England as a whole, the chronicler has vividly drawn our attention to some of the themes within the story of medieval Wirral: the over-arching interest of the monarch and his nobles in their lands, especially in the hunting grounds or forests of which Wirral was to become one; the commitment to a social hierarchy; the freedom of the ruling class to exploit everybody else without conscience; and the ultimate, unquestioned and universal belief that all men were accountable to God. In short, the feudal system and its ally the church were the strongest influences on life.

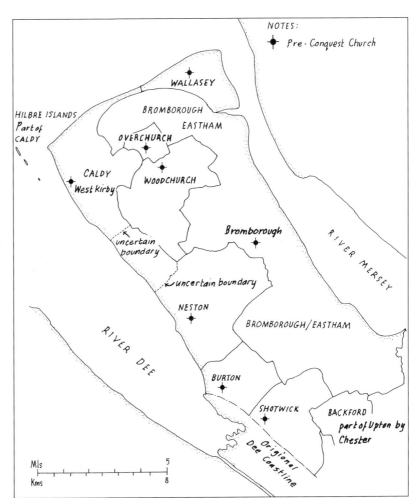

36 A conjectural map of pre-1066 parishes.

In 1085, William the Conqueror made the greatest expression of his belief that England was now his property and that he was going to get what he could from it. He ordered a great survey to be carried out. It was carried out in 1086. William died before its completion. It is known as Domesday Book. Wirral is included in the survey under the name of *Wilaveston* Hundred. As explained in the previous chapter, it was an administrative unit within Cheshire which was named after its central meeting-place at Willaston. There were eight other hundreds in Cheshire. *Wilaveston* was larger than modern Wirral. Its eastern boundaries were the river Gowy and the city of Chester; it contained Guilden Sutton, Wervin, Mickle Trafford, Upton by Chester and Picton, all of which were later incorporated into *Dudestan* (Broxton) Hundred. In all, 45 manors are listed as being within the hundred. Two others were misplaced—Puddington was listed under *Warmundestrou* (Nantwich) Hundred and Burton was under *Risedon* (Eddisbury) Hundred. *Wilaveston* almost literally conformed to its notional qualification for the title of hundred—it contained approximately 100 hides (i.e. units of land area eligible for tax).

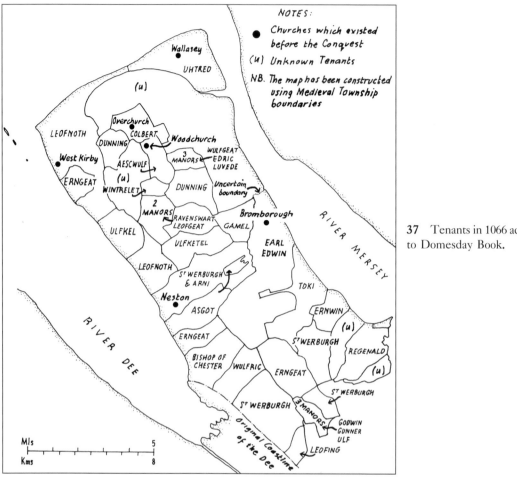

NOTES:

● Churches which existed before the Conquest

(u) Unknown Tenants

NB. The map has been constructed using Medieval Township boundaries

37 Tenants in 1066 according to Domesday Book.

Most readers of Domesday Book look immediately for details of their home town or village. Many Wirralians will, therefore, be disappointed—numerous settlements are not listed. They are, however, accounted for. Eastham was the second largest manor, after Chester, in the whole of Cheshire. Domesday Book says that it encompassed 22 hides— over a fifth of the land area of the hundred—and that it was inhabited by 79 families. It goes on to describe how this large estate was divided into smaller units managed by separate lords. Analysis of the subsequent histories of Wirral townships enables us to suggest that these units were based on the following settlements: the demesne or lord's own portion of land consisted of Eastham itself, Bromborough, Bebington and Childer Thornton; Stoke and Arrowe were the two hides held by Mundret; Brimstage and Oxton were the two hides held by Hugh FitzNorman; Whitby and Tranmere were the one hide held by William Malbank; Netherpool was perhaps the half hide held by Walter Vernon; and Bidston, Claughton, Moreton and Saughall Massie made up the seven hides held by Hamo de Mascy. As discussed in the previous chapter, Eastham was probably the first part of Wirral to be settled by an Anglo-Saxon overlord; it became a royal or noble estate which dominated Wirral's Mersey shore from Wallasey Pool to the Gowy. By 1086, it had been trimmed a little; two of its former townships—Storeton and Poulton Lancelyn—had broken away to become separate manors which Domesday Book lists in their own right. During the years after the Domesday survey, Bidston was probably the next township to break away and become a separate manor.

West Kirby is not listed in Domesday Book. Again, we must recall discussions carried out in the previous chapter. There was a minor hundred based on Caldy which might have been a remnant of the north Wirral Norse enclave and originally have encompassed, amongst other places, Wallasey, Great and Little Meols, Great and Little Caldy, Thurstaston, Heswall, Thornton (Hough), Gayton and Leighton—all of which must have broken away by 1086, because they have their own Domesday entries. West Kirby, however, was still within the manor of Great Caldy. Irby might have formed part either of the same manor or of that of Thurstaston. Woodchurch is not mentioned; it undoubtedly lay within the manor of Landican, which might also have contained Frankby. Liscard and Poulton would have been areas within Wallasey manor and Backford would have been in the manor of Upton By Chester.

Domesday Book offers clues about Wirral people before the arrival of the Normans. Former lords of the manors are named. Twelve out of the 28 bore Norse names—Arni (Capenhurst, Neston and Raby) Gamel (Poulton Lancelyn), Gunner (Mollington), Osgot (Hargrave and Neston), Ragenald (Stanney), Ravenswart (Barnston), Thored (Blacon), Toki (Hooton, Picton and Little Sutton), Ulf (Mollington), Ulfkel (Heswall), Ulfketel (Thornton Hough) and Winterlet (Thingwall). The importance of Scandinavian settlers in Wirral is confirmed, but the distribution of their manors does not particularly support the argument in favour of there being a Norse enclave at the northern end of the peninsula: out of the 17 manors held by men with Norse names, nine were in southern and eastern Wirral, outside the proposed perimeter of the Norse mini-state. Two explanations come to mind: firstly, that Norsemen were quite capable of becoming landlords in areas away from the main concentrations of their countrymen; and secondly, that Norse names might not have been definite indications of Scandinavian ancestry; local Anglo-Saxon and Celtic people could just as easily have borrowed Norse personal names as they did field-names.

38 Warmby, 'the warm settlement'. Possible site of the lost Norse farmstead or small village between Heswall and Thurstaston, just south of the path to Thurstaston Dungeons on the Wirral Way.

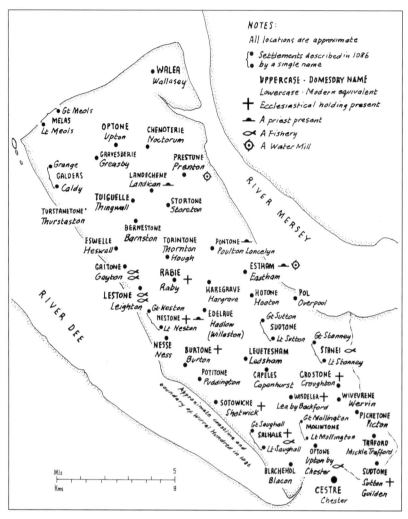

NOTES:

All locations are approximate

{ ● Settlements described in 1086
  ● by a single name

UPPERCASE - DOMESDAY NAME
Lowercase - Modern equivalent
✝ Ecclesiastical holding present
⊸ A priest present
✄ A Fishery
⊙ A Water Mill

WALEA
Wallasey

Gt Meols
MELAS
Lt Meols

OPTONE
Upton

CHENOTERIE
Noctorum

GRAVESBERIE
Greasby

PRESTUNE
Prenton

Grange
GALDERS
Caldy

LANDECHENE
Landican

TUIGUELLE
Thingwall

STORTONE
Storeton

TURSTANETONE
Thurstaston

BERNESTONE
Barnston

ESWELLE
Heswall

TORINTONE
Thornton
Hough

PONTONE
Poulton Loncelyn

GAITONE
Gayton

RABIE
Raby

ESTHAM
Eastham

LESTONE
Leighton

HAREGRAVE
Hargrave

HOTONE
Hooton

POL
Overpool

Gt Neston
NESTONE
Lt Neston

EDELAUE
Hadlow
(Willaston)

Gt Sutton
SUDTONE
Lt Sutton

Gt Stanney
STANEI
Lt Stanney

NESSE
Ness

BURTONE
Burton

LEUETESHAM
Ledsham

POTITONE
Puddington

CAPELES
Capenhurst

CROSTONE
Croughton

WISDELEA
Lea by Backford

WIVEVRENE
Wervin

SOTOWICHE
Shotwick

Gt Mollington
MOLINTONE
Lt Mollington

PICHETONE
Picton

Gt Saughall
SALHALE
Lt Saughall

OPTONE
Upton by
Chester

TRAFORD
Mickle Trafford

BLACHEHOL
Blacon

SUDTONE
Sutton
Guilden

CESTRE
Chester

RIVER MERSEY

RIVER DEE

Approximate coastline and boundary of Wirral Hundred in 1086

Mls ├──┼──┼──┼──┼──┤ 5
Kms   8

39 Domesday settlements in 1086.

Only one pre-Conquest landowner was able to keep its manors—the church, either in the name of the bishop of Chester himself or of Saint Werburgh's Abbey. All the other lands were given to Norman barons and their supporters. To us, the lords' names appear more recognisable than those which went before them. They became and remained popular for all classes of people right up to the 21st century: we have many Roberts, Williams and Nigels, but only the most committed of Wagnerian romantics would today name their sons Ravenswart or Ulfketel. The new earl of Chester, Hugh d'Avranches, nephew of King William (known as *Lupus*, 'The Wolf' or *Gross*, 'The Fat'), gained six Wirral manors with a total area of over forty hides. Robert of Rhuddlan was awarded 11 manors with an area of over fifteen hides and William Malbank received seven manors with an area of about eighteen hides. The other new landlords were William FitzNigel, Nigel de Burcy, Walter de Vernon, Richard de Vernon, Hugh de Delamere, Ranulf, Osbern and Robert Cook. The latter is an interesting example of a nobleman's servant being rewarded with lands and it is tempting to speculate that he might have been the progenitor of the many Cooksons who later flourished in Cheshire and in West Kirby parish in particular, but 1086 was probably too early for the emergence of hereditary surnames amongst non-noble families. It is unlikely that any of these lords would have dwelled in Wirral. Their estates would have been managed by local officials called reeves.

Careful study of the great survey reveals certain details about Wirral's landscape. Cheshire in general appears to have been relatively sparsely populated, under-developed and poor. Wirral, however, was a little more prosperous. It had an approximate population density of 3.7 people per square mile. Neighbouring *Risedon* (Eddisbury) Hundred had a density of approximately 3.3 per square mile and *Dudestan* (Broxton) about 3.2 per square mile. These were the three most densely inhabited hundreds in the county. Wirral's land, with about one ploughteam per square mile of ground, was the second most intensively exploited in the county, after *Dudestan* and *Risedon* hundreds which each had 1.2 ploughteams per square mile. We have seen how the peninsula had already been largely stripped of its tree cover by the time the Romans came. It was still treeless in 1086. Only two manors contained any significant woodland—Prenton had an area one league square and Mollington had two acres. We cannot imagine that there were no other trees in Wirral. There would probably have been a similar distribution to that which can be seen in Wirral's modern countryside—small pockets of woodland here and there, especially in river valleys like Dibbinsdale, as well as lines or stands of trees acting as manorial or parish boundaries. These smaller concentrations of timber would have been deemed unprofitable and would not, therefore, have been taxed; that is why they were not listed in Domesday Book. The land itself, however, would have been quite different. Instead of virtually every piece of ground being cultivated or otherwise exploited, there would have been more heath or waste, perhaps resembling the common recreation lands which today can be seen at Heswall Hills, Thurstaston, Grange, Caldy and Bidston, but situated on the lower-lying and flatter ground. During subsequent centuries, these heaths, firstly, as a result of being turned into an official hunting ground or forest, became more wooded, but were then gradually ploughed up and cultivated, becoming relatively treeless again.

Meadow was a valuable asset of which Wirral was also short: the hundred contained a total of only 25 acres. Meadows usually flourish on the banks of rivers. Clearly, it was the proximity of the flood-plain of the river Gowy which enabled Guilden Sutton, Wervin and Picton to sustain their meadows. Upton by Chester, Croughton, Lea and the Mollingtons lie next to the Broxton Valley or Deva Spillway, which is now occupied by the Shropshire Union Canal. This contained a small stream and was sufficiently low-lying and damp to produce grasslands. Little Sutton had six acres of meadow. Perhaps they lay beside the nameless brook which flows down to Booston Wood through Rivacre Country Park. Shotwick lies in a slight valley caused by a stream which flows into the Dee. This would have formed the heart of its single acre of meadow. Upton (Overchurch) and Caldy's meadows probably lay on the fringes of the northern coastal wetlands.

Fisheries were another economic activity to be recorded. There were two at Gayton, two at Leighton, one at Saughall (opinion is divided over whether this is Great Saughall or Saughall Massie), one at Blacon and one at Stanney. Rather than sending vessels out to sea, they would have operated a system of static traps or fish-yards which were based on the shore. They were set and maintained at low tide, ready for the fish to swim into them on the flood tide. Such methods would produce very few fish today due to the lack of available species, but, in 1086, salmon and trout were abundant both in inland waters and in the sea;

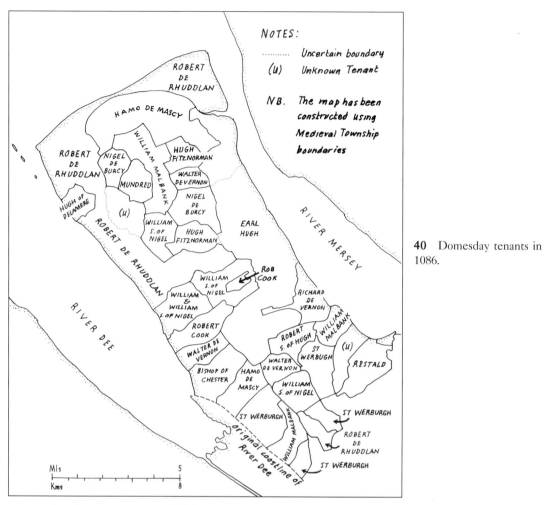

NOTES:

.... Uncertain boundary

(u)   Unknown Tenant

NB.   The map has been constructed using Medieval Township boundaries

ROBERT DE RHUDDLAN

HAMO DE MASCY

WILLIAM MALBANK

ROBERT DE RHUDDLAN

NIGEL DE BURCY

HUGH FITZNORMAN

WALTER DE VERNON

MUNDRED

HUGH OF DELAMERE

(u)

NIGEL DE BURCY

WILLIAM S. OF NIGEL

HUGH FITZNORMAN

EARL HUGH

ROBERT DE RHUDDLAN

RIVER MERSEY

WILLIAM S. OF NIGEL

ROB COOK

WILLIAM & WILLIAM S. OF NIGEL

RICHARD DE VERNON

RIVER DEE

ROBERT COOK

ROBERT S. OF HUGH

WILLIAM MALBANK

WALTER DE VERNON

WALTER DE VERNON

ST WERBUGH

(u)

BISHOP OF CHESTER

HAMO DE MASCY

RESTALD

WILLIAM S. OF NIGEL

ST WERBURGH

ST WERBURGH

WILLIAM MALBANK

ROBERT DE RHUDDLAN

original coastline of River Dee

ST WERBURGH

Mls   5

Kms   8

40   Domesday tenants in 1086.

herring were seasonal visitors; sturgeon were not unknown, although commoners were not allowed to keep them; and all the varieties of estuarine flat fish were commonplace. It is likely that there were many other smaller fisheries based on streams and that some fish were farmed in ponds. Fish were an essential source of protein at a time when all food was locally produced, rigidly seasonal and difficult to preserve.

The only recorded mills in Wirral were in the manors of Eastham, Hadlow (Willaston) and Prenton. They were almost certainly water mills. We are not told how the people from the other manors ground their corn. Perhaps they did it by hand using stone querns, just as had been done in the Bronze and Iron Ages.

So, contrary to the popular view, Wirral was not densely wooded and was not a sparsely inhabited, poverty-stricken no-man's-land. In comparison with the rest of Cheshire, it was economically quite well developed. The reasons for this are not totally clear, but the fact that Wirral is a peninsula must form part of the explanation. Indeed its northern end was endowed with a port, Meols, which had been flourishing since the Iron Age and was an access point for both goods and people from every shore of the Irish Sea—from Wales,

Ireland, the Isle of Man and Scotland. Wirral also lay next to one of the most important settlements and ports in north-west England—the city of Chester—and had a favourable climate, unchallenging terrain and adequate soils. Its coastline and coastal plain themselves were, as we have seen, economic assets. People had been living on the peninsula for at least 8,000 years. In short, it had what people needed, was accessible and known-about.

According to Domesday Book, there were 427 heads of household resident in Wirral in 1086. No names are given, but everybody is listed under titles which denote particular economic roles and social positions. Each head of household is likely to have had a family or other dependents. In order, therefore, to gain a total population figure, we should multiply 427 by five. Thus we can say that there were approximately 2,185 people living in the Hundred of *Wilaveston* in 1086. Let us analyse the separate categories of people in turn.

The two largest groups of people were the villeins or villagers (*villanii* in the original Latin of Domesday Book) who made up nearly 40 per cent of the population and the bordars or smallholders (*bordarii*) who constituted just over 33 per cent of the total. Villeins owned their own houses and were tied to the land upon which they lived. They were perhaps 'semi-free slaves'. Their cattle, tools and chattels belonged to the lord of the manor, who theoretically let them have a portion of land with which to sustain themselves in return for working for a certain number of days per week ('week work') upon his personal land, known as the demesne. In villages where no demesne (or no land 'in lordship') is recorded we must assume that week-work was not carried out. The bordars were probably the brothers and cousins of the villeins and were of slightly lower status and held less land. Their name implies that they were involved with borders—not of a political but of an economic or agricultural nature: they were forced to settle on the outskirts of villages and, in order to survive, had to turn marginal or wastelands into productive fields.

Beneath the latter two categories of person came the ploughmen or oxmen (*bovarii*). They made up nearly nine and a half per cent of Wirral's population and were almost completely enslaved by their lords. The lowest of the low were the slaves themselves (*servii*) who belonged completely to their lords and were required to work solely upon the demesnes. They made up just over seven and a half per cent of the population of Wirral.

Thus, nearly 90 per cent of the population of Wirral were peasants or, in other words, lowly and hardworking farmers of small plots of ground. They were probably always looking for opportunities to gain more land, to hold it more securely and to increase their personal freedoms, while most lords were eager to preserve the status quo and to ensure that their tenants were loyal and productive. The story of the development of feudalism in England is the story of the interaction between these conflicting interests.

Like the rest of Cheshire in 1086, Wirral was home to a number of men who were called riders or radmen (*radmans*). They were common in the border counties and were perhaps a 'superior sort of peasant'.[3] They probably performed personal duties for their lords as messengers, escorts, or bailiffs. They were given shares of the manor's open fields to cultivate for themselves and sometimes employed their own peasants. Eight out of the 16 manors which had resident riders had no demesne land. It is possible that each of these are examples of manors where the rider was acting almost like the lord. Of similar status were the Frenchmen (*francigenae*). There were 12 in Wirral, making up nearly three per cent of the population. Doubtless they were literally men from France who served the Norman nobles as serjeants or military retainers and were rewarded with land. The Frenchman who is listed as living in Caldy in 1086 had a servant (*serviens*).

Finally, there were five priests in Domesday Wirral—in Burton, Eastham, Landican, Neston and Poulton Lancelyn. Their recorded existence enabled discussions in the previous chapter about the location of pre-Conquest churches. It is not known why, when there is good evidence for the existence of ancient churches at West Kirby and Wallasey, they had no recorded priests in 1086. Eastham's priest was probably the one serving at the small chapel in Eastham village itself, which was later to become the parish church. The priest at Poulton Lancelyn was probably the one serving at Bromborough, the head church of the great Eastham/Bromborough estate/manor.

So, in 1086, at the beginning of the Middle Ages, Wirral was populated mainly by peasants. Perhaps this is the way society had evolved throughout the years of Anglo-Saxon and Scandinavian settlement or perhaps the Normans had deliberately reduced a large portion of the population to a servile status in order more effectively to exploit the area for their own gain. Unlike in eastern and central Cheshire, people lived in nucleated villages, in wooden and thatched cottages which huddled together amongst the gentle valleys and on the sandstone outcrops of the peninsula. There were not yet any major buildings; even the churches were made largely out of wood and the communication routes, although based on many ancient ways which had been trod by numerous former generations and perhaps consolidated in Roman times, were rudimentary and rugged. Virtually all work was agricultural. The land meant everything to the people. Production of food and the fabric of the villages were gradually improving after the disruptions of the Norman conquest and the foundations had been laid for a growth in both prosperity and population.

Part Two: Palatinate, Hundred and Forest—Government and Society in Medieval Wirral

Cheshire was a Norman feudal creation. William I gave it to the barons to rule as an earldom. The first earl, Hugh d'Avranches, was appointed in 1071 and reigned until he became a monk of St Werburgh's Abbey three days before his death in July 1101. The succeeding earls were as follows:

> Richard of the White Ship (son of the above) 1101-20;
> Ranulf I de Meschines (nephew of Hugh) 1120-29;
> Ranulf II de Gernons (son of the above) 1129-53;
> Hugh II Gyfylliog or Kevelioc (son of the above) 1153-81;
> Ranulf III de Blundeville (son of the above) 1181-1232;
> John the Scot (nephew of the above) 1132-37.

The earls ruled Cheshire almost like a separate kingdom. It was not regarded as a true part of England. For example, after 1215, when King John signed *Magna Carta* at Runnymede, Ranulf Blundeville issued a separate version for Cheshire. Blundeville was described as 'a prince whose will was law'. The earldom was a threat to royal power, so, when John the Scot died, King Henry III took the opportunity to bring it under control. John the Scot's heiresses were bought off and the rights of the earl were passed to the crown. In the words of Professor Geoffrey Barraclough, Cheshire now became 'a citadel of royal power'.[4] It was given to successive heirs to the throne as a personal domain, a power base and source of income outside the control of parliament. It became a Palatinate, almost an independent kingdom within a kingdom (the word Palatinate echoes the title of the seat of Ancient Rome's palaces—the Palatine Hill). The first three king Edwards were each in turn, before they were crowned, earls of Chester. Edward of Woodstock, the Black Prince, was Earl of Chester between 1333 and 1376. He was succeeded by Richard of Bordeaux, later Richard II (1377-99). When Richard II called himself Prince of Chester and made Cheshire a principality, naturally, its sense of separateness was intensified.

During the Middle Ages, the Hundred of Wirral was, therefore, an integral part of a larger administrative unit which was successively an earldom, a palatinate and a principality—a region with a strong sense of individuality and independence. When a Cheshire man was travelling out of the county he spoke of 'going abroad' and a person could be described as holding lands 'in Cheshire and in England'. Richard II used the county to reinforce his autocratic rule; indeed, he had a personal bodyguard of 400 Cheshire archers (known as the *sagitarii de corona*), some of whom must have come from Wirral. He paid them sixpence a day and used them to bully his opponents. Richard was deposed in 1399 and his successor, Henry IV, curtailed Cheshire's palatine status.

Cheshire played an important role in the military campaigns of the period by supplying much of the necessary finance and a large portion of the king's most warlike military personnel, as well as acting as a base for several of the expeditions. Edward I was probably not that interested in the people of Cheshire, but knew that he needed their support as tax-payers and soldiers in his Welsh campaigns, so he visited Chester and Birkenhead in 1275 and Chester, Birkenhead and Bromborough in August 1277; he came to Chester and Wirral again in 1278, when he stayed at Shotwick Castle in September; in 1283, he visited Bromborough and Stanlow, before moving on to Vale Royal and Macclesfield; and, in 1284, he returned from Wales via Shotwick, where he stayed, once again, in the castle on 17 September. During one of his two Cheshire tours, the Black Prince visited Shotwick, where the houses were cleaned and new furniture made for his office. Shotwick was an important site for the earls of Chester. The manor of Castle Shotwick (distinct from Shotwick village or Church Shotwick, which had different manorial lords—the Shotwick and later the Hockenhull and Bennett families) was, along with Gayton, their personal property. It was a convenient base from which to launch attacks on the Welsh. The castle had been built before 1093. Henry II had camped nearby in 1156.[5] In 1274 the castle's constable was Roger Gille. His successor in 1361 was called a reeve and his name was William Jonet.[6] In 1275, Roger le Strange of Ellesmere, who was granted the royal manor and fishery of Shotwick, as an under-tenant, for life in 1278, was ordered to send two salted stags from the forest of Wirral to the king at Westminster.

Cheshire's peasants were often the mainstay of the king's armies. During the 1277 Welsh campaign, between a third and a half of the foot soldiers were from the county. In 1287 Cheshire supplied 700 of the 11,000 foot soldiers who were used to invade South Wales and 1,000 foot soldiers for a repeat invasion of 1295. It is estimated that, by the early 14th century, some ten to fifteen per cent of Cheshire's adult male population served as soldiers. Of course, a proportion of these warriors would have been from Wirral, but, in 1355, the Black Prince complained that 'there are few archers in Wirral'. By this time, more soldiers were mounted. Horses were extremely expensive both to buy and to maintain. Consequently, in order to go to war, the soldiers were required to be richer. They also needed to be better trained and more committed to soldiering as a profession. It is suggested that there were not as many people of this class in Wirral as in the other hundreds due to the large number of manors which belonged to Chester Abbey, where most peasants had only small land-holdings and were, therefore, unable to accumulate sufficient wealth.[7] In addition, forest laws might have inhibited the Wirral men from owning and using longbows; they were formidably powerful and accurate weapons which could be used both for poaching and for commiting crime. The authorities might, therefore, not have encouraged peasants to indulge in the necessary target practice, although this does not seem to have restricted recruitment from the other Cheshire forests of Delamere and Macclesfield.

Amongst the list of Cheshire archers employed in the Gascony campaign of 1355-7, there are the following names of probable Wirral men: Robert Benet, William Calday, Roger Gille, Peter de Kirkeby, Hugh de Mulyngton, Henry Neston, William de Newton, Thomas de Raby and Randolph de Stoke.[8] In 1400, the Cheshire retinue for the campaign in Scotland consisted of 100 archers from Macclefield and 65 from Eddisbury Hundreds. These are the details of Wirral's contribution:

41 The 'Wirral Stone': a meeting place, mounting stone or 'pissing stone'?

In the hundred of Wyrehal

John de Pulle knight 20 archers
Jacob de Pulle his son
John de Whitemore 10 archers
Gilbert Clegge 6 archers
John de Tildeslegh 4 archers
John de Meols

Total 40 archers.[9]

This was a tiny proportion of the population. Notice how the archers were led by members of local gentry families. It was they who most benefited from war, as success in combat could lead to rewards of land and higher status. In addition, they could expect to get loot from foreign lands and satisfy their natural aggression and lust for adventure.

Government at the local level was carried out by the hundred court, which, in Wirral, as we have seen, was originally based at Willaston. R. Stewart-Brown suggested that, in pre-Conquest days, all such hundred courts met at places which were marked by the existence of special stones.[10] There has been a lot of speculation about the site of the 'Wirral Stone'. A small step-like sandstone feature on the corner of Hadlow Road and the A540 Chester Road is the current bearer of the title, but its antiquity is unknown. In 1909, in his *Perambulation of the Hundred of Wirral*, Young said this about it: 'A learned man might give it a learned name, but the name the villagers, men, women and children, give it is not to be repeated here'.

Willaston's tithe map from the 1840s blandly labels the structure the 'Pissing Stone'. Its unsheltered and open location would have made it an unsuitable site for either a hundred court or a public convenience. It is more likely to have been a mounting block, for passengers boarding the horse-drawn coaches heading either to or from Chester, than a focal point for local government.

Traditionally, the hundred court would have been attended by a reeve (or manorial manager) and four chief men from each township. It was a forum in which new laws were promulgated and local issues discussed. It had the power to elect two serjeants of the peace, who were assisted by bedells. These officers had the authority to arrest criminals and, if necessary, to behead them on the spot. It is not known in what form the hundred court functioned during the years when Wirral was a royal forest, because its jurisdiction was largely supplanted by that of the forest court. However, at the time of the abolition of the forest in 1376, it was the representatives of the hundred court who presented to the government the list of complaints about the forest laws.

Between 1120 and 1123, Randle de Meschines, 4th Earl of Chester, made the Hundred of Wirral into a royal forest. This did not mean that he suddenly ordered the planting of trees, but rather that the district was turned into a hunting ground for the earl and his family and privileged friends. It is not known why Wirral was so designated: the other two Cheshire forests, at Delamere and Macclesfield, are situated on unproductive soils and had small populations. Wirral was quite the opposite. Perhaps, being a peninsula, it was an easy area to define and had obvious boundaries in the form of two rivers and a sea. It was also handy for Chester. Laws were introduced which enforced the protection of the hunters' favourite game: the red, fallow and roe deer and wild boar. The farmers' normal practices of sowing and nurturing crops were inhibited. Deer had to be treated as sacred beasts, whose freedom of movement was never to be prevented: there were serious penalties for chasing them away with dogs or for trying to protect fields of new corn with fences or ditches. Undergrowth and trees were preserved as cover and poaching was punishable by death or blinding. All dogs had to be 'lawed'—their front paws had to be trimmed so that they could not chase game. The environmental effects of the forest laws must have been dramatic. Woodland must have regenerated and a great variety of plants, trees, birds and mammals must have flourished. To us, it would seem like a natural paradise, but the poor folk of Wirral must have gazed with envy at the neighbouring, unforested lands of Broxton Hundred, where there were far fewer restrictions on farming.

Alan Silvester was the first Bailiff or Chief Forester of Wirral. He was given a horn as a symbol of his authority and the manor of Storeton in which to live. Following the death of Alan and his son Ralph, Storeton passed to Alan's grand-daughter, who married one Alexander, a steward or tutor in the household of the Earl of Chester, who assumed the office of Forester. His surviving daughter, Agnes, married Sir Thomas de Bamville, whose family now acquired the manor and its attendant office. Sir Thomas's son, Philip, died without an heir, so the manor of Storeton was divided among his three daughters. On 27 September 1282, his eldest daughter, Joan or Jane, married Sir William Stanley at Astbury church in Staffordshire, where the Stanleys originated. Sir William became the next Forester of Wirral and the office was passed along the male line of his family right untill the forest was abolished, by which time it is clear that they had gained complete ownership of the manor of Storeton.

In 1903, William Fergusson Irvine expressed the widely-held reverence for the Stanley family: 'Thus we have in Storeton the cradle of a race of men, who, throughout the last 500 years, have done much to mould the destiny of England, and to have given us statesmen, scholars, diplomatists, and soldiers.'[11] Elsewhere he described the Stanleys as 'virtual kings in Wirral'. Unfortunately, however, documents from the 14th century do not provide us with much evidence for the prevalence of the qualities which were later to earn the family so much praise. Indeed, far from acting in the manner of great statesmen and wise stewards of office and property, they appear to have behaved more like bullies and extortionists. As a dynasty, they bore a greater resemblance to a branch of the Mafia than to a succession of benevolent monarchs. It is clear that they viewed the forestership as a means of personal enrichment and empowerment, quite to the detriment of the rest of the population. If they had been able to use 21st-century language, doubtless they would have called the office 'a nice little earner'. It is not surprising that, in the 1370s, they bemoaned the dissolution of the forest and demanded compensation for the loss of their special status and privileges.

In 1353, the Black Prince, Earl of Chester, paid a state visit to Cheshire. Ostensibly in order to address many grievances, he held a court known as a General Eyre. In reality, he hoped to impose numerous fines and thereby to raise plenty of money for his campaigns in France. When everyone gathered, it soon became apparent that too many embarrassing details about the misbehaviour of the gentry were about to come to light, so the Prince suspended the Eyre in return for a fine of £3,333 6s. 8d. to be paid over four years. Sessions of Trailbaston were called for instead and, over the coming three weeks, over 130 cases were investigated. The details were shocking. The Jury of the Hundred of Wirral complained that the Foresters, John Lasselles and his servant Richard Knowsley, William Stanley, John Churton, Richard Wayte, Richard Haydock, Henry Molyneux, John Broughton and Ralph son of Patrick of Heswall, 'Have repeatedly oppressed the common people of Wirral by many crimes, to their grave damage. Furthermore, the same men have openly issued threats against the said common people so that none of them dared complain about their behaviour or prosecute them. The accused deny all guilt.' It was also reported that the same men had:

> Commonly gone to the houses of the men of Wirral with horses and grooms to exact their right of puture, that is of hospitality, eating and drinking, although by right, the foresters of Wirral ought not to go around on horseback. As a result, these men have charged the people of Wirral with heavy expenses. Also they have compelled the men of these parts to plough the foresters' own lands and carry their corn and hay, to the great destruction of the rights of the people. The foresters denied all guilt.[12]

The jury found them guilty and they were fined three shillings and fourpence each. William Stanley and John Lasselles acted as pledges for good behaviour.

Many more graphic details about actual crimes were recorded. Henry Bechynton, former Prior of Birkenhead complained that, on 10 April 1346, he had been wrongfully fined £4 by Sir William Stanley Forester of Wirral for cultivating a bit of the forest between Wooton Wood and Birkenhead. Stanley had also been taking 'a great sum of money' from the people of Leighton, Gayton, Greasby, Woodchurch, Bidston, Claughton, Noctorum,

Tranmere, Higher Bebington and Lower Bebington for pasturing their sheep 'in the time of fawning' in the woods. All the priory's lands were supposed to be exempt from the forest laws. William was also accused of taking hens and forced labour at harvest time in the said townships 'against their will, by extortion, to the grave damage of the people of these parts'. The jury found William not guilty of the false fine, but he pleaded guilty to stealing the hens and forcing the labour and was fined one pound. Thomas Hockenhull and John Lasselles acted as his pledges for good behaviour.

John Lasselles was a 'forest under rider' and could be regarded as one of Stanley's 'heavies'. He enjoyed throwing his weight about in the Wallasey area. He was accused of committing six serious crimes against other locals, between 1348 and 1352. He stole a boat belonging to William Coyd and William son of William Alcock at 'Seacombe Pool' in order to carry turves. The boat ended up broken and the anchor and 'other tackle' were lost. When the plaintiffs approached Lasselles, he threatened them so badly that they dared not prosecute him. Two years later he assaulted John the Miller, servant of Henry Litherland of Poulton, and forced him to work for him; he also tied John Tyross to a post in Liscard and forced him to become his servant. In the following year, he assaulted Richard Sampson at Poulton 'shooting arrows at him so that he was forced to leave the country and did not dare return home'. A year later, he assaulted Adam Gray 'boatman at Birkenhead' and, three months later, broke into Matthew Wallasey's house at night and struck his servant 'to the disturbance of the peace'. He was fined one pound. His pledges for good behaviour were Thomas Hockenhull and William Stanley. In 1350, in conjunction with Roger Bechynton and Richard Wooton, he abducted William son of Ralph Meols at Great Meols from the custody of his guardian Ellen, widow of John Meols. With the aim of getting his hands on William's lands and of being able to sell his marriage to the highest bidder, he forced Ellen to give up her wardship of William 'to her grave damage and against the law of the land'. Lasselles and the others denied guilt and were found not guilty.

Another member of the forest mafia, Hugh Forestersman 'of Wirral', was found guilty of raping Ann, a former servant of William Bromborough in Chester. He was fined one pound. His pledges for good behaviour were William Stanley and Ranulf Stoke. Forester John Churton was found guilty of assaulting Roger Tasker and Ellice his wife at Ledsham. He was fined three shillings and sixpence; his pledges were William Stanley and John Lasselles.

It is not surprising that the people of Wirral petitioned for the abolition of the forest. The Black Prince began the process of disafforestation, but died in June 1376. Six weeks later, on 20 July 1376, Edward III granted the Charter of Disafforestation. It refers to the people having 'sustained so much in the way of damage, oppression and loss on account of the forest there'. The Stanleys complained and, in November, their rights of puture were restored. There was then another petition from the people, asking that the Charter of Disafforestation be ratified by Parliament, because forest restrictions were still being imposed and causing the suspension of church services, perhaps because they were forbidden to cut timber for the necessary repairs to the church buildings. The impositions were still not over by 1385 when the king imposed a fine of £400 in lieu of all the forest fines he used to receive. The people of Wirral had to pay it off in instalments. By 1398, William Stanley was still receiving 46 shillings puture rent from several Wirral townships. The disafforestation might have been a charitable deed by the Black Prince to try to get some credit in heaven before he met his maker, but the local gentry and the crown were obviously reluctant to disavow such a lucrative tradition of imposition and extortion.

The crimes of the Stanleys and their henchmen were part of a wider problem which affected the whole of Cheshire. Its isolation and lack of a strong noble family meant that the gentry—knights, esquires and substantial yeomen—were the highest stratum in local society. The lists of pledges to which we have already referred are a sign of the way in which the various strong local families would back each other up. They made it a priority to form alliances by marriage and depended upon each other to protect their manorial rights and to respect each other's estates. By collusion, they made themselves virtually immune to prosecution. The 1353 Trailbaston Proceedings might have raised some revenue and publicised some crime, but they failed to solve the problem of lawlessness. As soon as the Black Prince left the county, the gentry resumed their old ways and even began to 'ride in companies of armed men, or with bows and arrows' in order to attack the neighbouring counties of Lancashire and Staffordshire '... committing felonies, outrages and trespasses in contempt of the prince, against the peace and to the terror of the prince's people'.[13] No doubt the Stanley family's later expansion into south Lancashire by marrying into the Lathom family was part of the same campaign to extend the bounds of their estates and political power. Only at the end of the Middle Ages, when Cheshire was brought more effectively under the rule of London, did the behaviour of the gentry begin to improve.

Part Three: The Monasteries and the Land

In the summer of 1980, a local historian and good friend of the author gave a public lecture about the history of Greasby. Provocatively but wisely, he began by pointing out that Greasby's Domesday Book entry contains no reference either to monks or to the alleged tunnel which they had dug between Greasby Old Hall and Hilbre Island. The intelligent gentleman was dealing with a popular myth which still has currency in Wirral: the half-formed belief that, during the Middle Ages, monks were ubiquitous, pervasive and almost supernaturally ingenious, with a particular enthusiasm for digging tunnels to connect otherwise unrelated surface localities. Either as a result of erroneous school teaching or of playground chatter, the author's mind had already been impregnated with an image of the sweating monk, sandalled and tonsured, hacking his way through the sandstone strata of subterranean Wirral, with no illumination but a dim candle and no refreshment but a jar of Benedictine. It is an image which both the learned lecture and time itself have failed to erase. Like most myths, although it is patently absurd, it does represent the essence of some historical truth: for most of the Middle Ages, only a small minority of people ever became monks, but the effects of monasticism upon both human life and on the landscape were indeed pervasive. Wirral's development was profoundly affected by three monasteries which were based beyond its borders—St Werburgh's Abbey in Chester (with its small cell on Hilbre Island), Basingwerk Abbey in Flintshire and Vale Royal Abbey in Eddisbury Hundred; two monasteries situated on the peninsula itself—Birkenhead Priory and the Abbey of Stanlaw, and three monastic hospitals—one on the border between Thurstaston and Irby, one in Burton and another in Spital.

The Abbey of St Werburgh in Chester had been founded in the 10th century. In 1093 it was reformed as a Benedictine monastery and awarded vast estates by the Earl of Chester. It became the second largest land-owner in Cheshire after the Earl himself. By

42 In 1853 a local artist by the name of J. Butler used his imagination to create this impression of the probable appearance of the Mersey Ferry which was operated by the monks of Birkenhead Priory during the Middle Ages.

the mid-14th century, the abbey owned the following Wirral manors: Bromborough, Childer Thornton, Chorlton, Croughton, Eastham, Greasby, Irby, Lea, Noctorum, Overpoole, Great and Little Sutton and Woodchurch. It had manor houses at Bromborough, Irby, Little Sutton, Saughall and Upton by Chester and rights to wreckage in Bromborough, Eastham, Saughall and Shotwick and to *waif and stray and infangetheof* in Bebington, Frankby, Hargrave, Little Meols, Ness, Neston and Puddington. The abbey also had the advowsons (i.e. the right to appoint the priests and receive the tithes of the parishioners) at Bidston, Neston, Wallasey and West Kirby. It would be tiresome to describe each occasion when the abbey was given more land and privileges, but suffice it to say that it benefited from the desire of numerous barons and gentlemen to earn forgiveness from the Almighty for their sinful lives. They also hoped that the monks would pray for their souls once they had departed.

As early as 1081, Hilbre Island was home to an outlying chapel of Chester Abbey. Robert of Rhuddlan had given it to the abbey of St Ebrulf (or Evroul) in Utica, France. It was too far away from that monastery for the monks to make use of it, so it was passed to St Werburgh's. The island's name derives from its dedication to St Hildeburgh, a Saxon holy woman (her name was joined to *eg*, meaning 'island' and *Hideburgheye* gradually evolved into Hilbre). Hilbre is the home of two monkish legends. The first involves Richard Earl of Chester (1101-21), who, whilst on his way to visit St Winifred's Well in Holywell, was attacked by some Welshmen. A monk prayed to St Werburgh and a new sandbank appeared in the Dee estuary, allowing the Constable of Halton to come to his assistance with a large army. At the back of the island there is a great cavern called the Lady's Cave. This is where a monk is supposed to have found a half-drowned young lady who had jumped from a boat near Point of Ayr because she believed her lover had died. She was the daughter of the constable of Shotwick Castle who had arranged, against her will, for her to marry a Welshman.

Perhaps it was these stories and the island's wild and beautiful setting which made it attractive to pilgrims. We know that they came to Hilbre because many of them dropped some of their souvenirs on the ground in Meols, where perhaps they lodged before either walking across the sands or travelling to Hilbre by boat across the Hoyle Lake. Several of

[81]

Holme Field

Town Field

Brook Field

Heath Field

N

43 Frankby township field patterns from the 1844 tithe map. The long rectangular fields are probably enclosed medieval strips.

these tokens and badges form part of the enormous collection of medieval items which were discovered on the Meols shore during the 19th century. In addition to praying and entertaining religious tourists, the monks maintained a light in their chapel for which the Earl of Chester, perhaps because it acted as a navigational aid, paid ten shillings a year and fished in the *Heye Pol* or Hoyle Lake.

Within thirteen years of the death of Thomas a Becket in 1170, a chapel was built and dedicated to him in Poulton Lancelyn. It was connected to a hospital for lepers. In 1183, Richard, Archbishop of Canterbury confirmed that the chapel owned a ploughland or *carucate*, part of a wood and half a fishery. Between about 1208 and 1226, it is known that divine service was regularly performed by an almoner from Chester Abbey and that masses were enacted for the souls of the earls, abbots and monks of Chester. In return for these offices, the chaplains received most of the revenues of the church at Ince. In 1818,

Ormerod said, 'Of the chapel or its site there are now neither remains nor local traditions'. However, in 1920, James Tait asserted that part of the chapel was by then in use as part of the outbuildings of the house of a Sir Edward Evans.[14] The hospital's former existence was commemorated in the name of the 19th-century railway station, Spital, which is now the name of the suburb which adjoins it.

In 1152, the manor of Great Caldy was given to the Abbey of St Mary at Basingwerk in Flintshire. By 1291 the abbey had lands in Great Caldy or Grange, Newton, Larton, Newbold and somewhere called *Wcton*, all in the parish of West Kirby. They also had the right to pasture sheep in Hoose and were supposed to have the advowson of West Kirby church. Their monastic grange gave its name to the township in which it was situated. Oldfied Manor Barn is believed to be its exact site. The abbey also owned the windmill which stood on the site of Grange Beacon.[15]

Vale Royal Abbey in Eddisbury Hundred (founded 1277) owned Gayton until 1330 when it became the property of the Glegg family.

Sometime in the early 1150s, Hamon de Massie, 3rd Baron of Dunham Massie, founded Birkenhead Priory. It housed 16 monks and was dedicated to St Mary and St James. Massie owned a huge amount of land and had a guilty conscience, so he gave the monks the site for their monastery along with several Wirral manors—Moreton, Claughton, Tranmere, Over Bebington, Saughall Massie and Bidston, as well as a part of Wallasey rectory, the rectories of Backford and Bidston and the vicarage of Bowden outside Wirral. The monks followed the Rule of St Benedict and had the right to elect their own prior. The monastery was exempt from the forest laws and the prior was given rights to hold a manor court in Claughton, where its grange was situated (leading to the modern name, Grange Road) and to fisheries, wreckage and boats for all purposes within the bounds of Claughton from Oxton to the Mersey. The Prior of Birkenhead was one of the most prestigious people in the district: he attended the Earl of Chester's parliament and always rode around his estates accompanied by his servants and senior fellow monks.

Here are the only known biographical details of the Priors of Birkenhead:

> Oliver (during reign of King John 1199-1216);
> Robert de Bechington (died before May 1339);
> Henry de Bechington (elected 1339, mentioned 1342);
> Hugh de Aston (during reign of Edward III 1327-77);
> Roger de Tyddesbury (mentioned 1369 and 1379);
> Robert de Honbrygg (in and before 1408);
> John Wood (from 1408);
> Robert de Urmeston (mentioned 1428);
> Hamo Bostok (from 1435, formerly Prior of Chester Abbey);
> Richard Norman (in and before 1456);
> Hugh Boner or Bover (from 1456);
> Thomas Rainford (confirmed as prior in 1462);
> Hugh Gardener (resigned in 1486);
> Thomas Chestur (from 1486 to 1499);
> Nicholas Stace or Tassy (from 1499);
> Hugh Hyne (elected after death of above);
> John Sharp (confirmed as prior 1519, alive in 1530, probably last prior).

Thomas Rainford's headstone was discovered in 1818 and reads 'Here lies Thomas Rayneford formerly the good vicar of this house who died 20th May 1473'.

In 1818, George Ormerod wrote this description of the site of the priory which is well worth comparing with the modern scene:

> It is beautifully situated near the mouth of the estuary of the Mersey, opposite to the town of Liverpool at the side of Wallasey Pool, a large bay which the Mersey forms at the confluence with the Birken, from which this manor derives the name of Birkenhead, or Birkenheved, as it was antiently called.[16]

In 1178, just before he left to go on a crusade to the Holy Land, John, 6th Baron of Halton and Constable of Cheshire, founded Stanlaw Abbey. It belonged to an order known as the Cistercians—an offshoot of the Benedictines, founded by St Bernard of Cîteaux, who had the intention of returning to an ascetic and isolated lifestyle away from the distractions of luxury and urbanity. Again, Ormerod's words are worth repeating:

> There was not only the absence of the scenery in which the monks so much delighted, the deep valley, the wood , and the shaded stream, but the place was exposed to all the horrors of inundations of the sea, and the greatest difficulties of access. Even at the present day, it is difficult to select in Cheshire a scene of more comfortless desolation, than this cheerless marsh, barely fenced from the waters by embankments on the north, shut out by naked knolls from the fairer country which spreads along the feet of the forest hills on the south-east and approached by one miserable trackway of mud whilst every road that leads to the haunts of men, seems to diverge in its course, as it approaches the 'Locus Benedictus' of Stanlaw.[17]

By 1847 the scene had not improved: William Williams Mortimer described the area as 'one of the most miserable townships in the county' and the site of the abbey as a 'gloomy morass'.[18] For spiritual reasons, this is exactly the kind of territory which the Cistercians favoured, but it caused them serious problems: in 1279 the abbey was flooded and damaged; in 1286 its tower fell down; and in 1289 it was ruined by fire. Enough was enough and most of the monks moved to their allied house at Whalley in Lancashire. By 1294 there were only five monks and the abbot left at Stanlaw; one was based at the monastic grange and another later went to Oxford to complete his doctorate in divinity. The only abbots whose names have been recorded were as follows:

Radulphus;
Osbern (who was given the right to kill beasts of the chase and disafforest his lands in 1209), Charles;
Peter (who gained lands for the abbey in Lancashire);
Simon (sometime before 1259);
Richard de Thornton (for one year in 1269),
Richard Northbury (died 1272);
Robert Haworth (the last abbot).

In 1818 Ormerod noticed that the site of the abbey was occupied by 'a mean farmhouse'. Today it is separated from the rest of Wirral by the Manchester Ship Canal. Its isolated and gloomy character has been maintained by its proximity to the monstrous and forbidding Stanlow oil refineries. Its monastic grange was excavated in the 1960s by R. Brotherton Ratcliffe. Rochester and Ludlow Drives—part of Ellesmere Port's urban growth from the 1970s—now cover its site.

Denhall Hospital of St Andrew was founded in the 1230s. It was given to the church of Burton by Alexander de Savensby, bishop of Lichfield by a charter dated January 1238. Its purpose was to house the poor, the helpless and the shipwrecked. Its masters were also rectors of Burton parish and were as follows:

Simon de Scachell (1302)	William Newhagh (1422)
William de Chanelegh (1319)	Thomas Clerk (1424)
John de Mountsorell (1336)	Robert Dykes (1425)
Nicholas de Heath (1338)	Thomas Wykersley (1427)
John de Charnes (1353)	Roger Wall called Garre (1434)
William de Newhagh (1374)	Edmund Tebbot (1440)
John Lugore (1400)	Roger Wall (1445)
Henry Halsall (1422)	John Bothe (1449, resigned 1495)

Between 1238 and 1293, there is evidence that it housed both male and female chaplains. It declined during the late 15th century and ceased to exist by the 1490s. Part of its structure was later used as the village tithe-barn.

Having become familiar with the essential facts about the relevant monasteries, let us explore the effects they had on life in Wirral. We know very little about the day-to-day lives of the monks because nearly all their records were destroyed when Henry VIII dissolved the monasteries, but we may infer that their teachings must have helped to influence the beliefs and attitudes of the people, not least because every church in Wirral, except Heswall and Woodchurch, was controlled by a monastery. In addition, the hospitals at Denhall, Spital and Thurstaston would have played an essential part in relieving the sufferings of the poor and the sick.

But by far the most important influence of the monasteries was of an economic nature: the abbots and priors were extremely influential landowners and businessmen. The evidence shows that they were always improving and expanding their farms. The Abbot of Chester often felled trees and dug up waste. By the 1290s, he had brought 140 acres of waste in Irby, Greasby, Bromborough and Plymyard (in the parish of Eastham) under the plough. Clearly he felt that, given the financial benefits which would later accrue from such expansion, the inevitable fines levied by the Foresters were worth paying. The prior of Birkenhead was engaged in similar investments: in the late 13th century, he enclosed waste at Wolveton near Birkenhead and cultivated new land in Claughton. At the same time, the Abbot of Whalley (formerly Stanlaw) was fined 6s. 6d. for enclosing a wood near his grange in Stanney and the brethren of the House of Lepers at Spital were given a licence to plough up five acres of the forest. The abbot of Basingerk was also fined for enclosing a piece of waste in Grange. The records often mention monastic rights of pasturing animals in various manors and of allowing pigs to feed (*pannage*) in certain woods.

Marling was a significant form of investment. In the late 13th century, the abbot of Stanlaw made two marlpits in the waste at Backford and three others 'half in the waste and half in the cultivated land'. In the late 1340s, the Abbot of Chester was in trouble for digging 35 marlpits in Greasby and 65 in Irby. It is estimated that an acre of Wirral land required 100 loads of marl at three shillings a load.[19] This was indeed an expensive practice, but obviously one which was worth carrying out.

Legal records from the 13th and 14th centuries contain numerous examples of disputes between the monasteries and other landowners. For example, at the County Court in Chester in 1282, the Prior of Birkenhead disputed the ownership of some land with Ysabel Lady of Oxton; in 1288, the Abbot of Chester argued with William de Hunkelawe over some oaks in Little Saughall; and, in 1289, the Abbot of Stanlaw entered into litigation with the delightfully named Tangumstell (or Tanguistell) de Staney. Chester Abbey's book of charters (*chartulary*) contains details of a satisfyingly pragmatic agreement between the Abbot of Chester and a lady called Agnes de Arderne over a portion of heath between their two manors near Eastham—they decided to leave it untilled, but, if the abbot did plough it up, Agnes was to be allowed one acre for every two acres which he took. Linguistic evidence locates this former heath to the area around Street Hey Lane near Willaston, where there are several fields with names containing the word heath. Little brotherly love was displayed when two monasteries disagreed over land rights; this was the case in 1288 between Chester and Stanlaw.

The monasteries were also happy to engage in non-agricultural businesses. In 1332, Birkenhead Priory was given the right to operate the ferry to Liverpool. An inquiry of 1354 found that it charged 2d. for a man and a horse, laden and unladen and ¼d. for a man on foot. On Liverpool's market day, a man was to be charged ½d. and a man and his baggage 1d. These sums were judged to be excessive. It also sold a lot of its produce in Liverpool and had a granary in what is now called Water Street.

Denwall Hospital's brethren had rights to:

> ... Fish in the water of Dee, as far as the thread of the same water, through the whole of the bounds of the aforesaid priory or hospital, with all fisheries, fishings, nets, ships, boats etc., and at every time of the year and all fishes take to their own uses; and that no ship or boat, shall lie within the bounds aforesaid.[20]

It also had a right to all wrecks and of transferring cargoes from incoming vessels to Chester, either by boat or by cart for a fee of 16d. per ton.

Chester Abbey perhaps made the largest contribution to Wirral's developing economy when, as a result of a charter of Edward I, in February 1278, it gained the right to hold a weekly market and annual three-day fair (10-12 June) in Bromborough.

Mainly due to the destruction of the monasteries which occurred in the 16th century, we have very few details about the monks themselves. But one way in which they did get themselves mentioned in the records was by breaking the law. So, for example, the Calendar of Trailbaston Proceedings mentions a monk of Birkenhead Priory, called Thomas Wallasey, who assaulted Richard Jolibrid in Moreton in May 1353 and a 'chaplain' (probably from Denhall Hospital) named Thomas Hopwell, who stole a sale from a ship at Burton in July 1353. Wallasey pleaded guilty and was fined 1s. 6d. Hopwell was fined 13s. 4d. Ranulf de Chaddesden was a monk from the cell on Hilbre Island. In 1360 he was charged with having struck William del Bache with his fist in West Kirby two years earlier. John Lancaster was one of his successors; he also was charged with hitting someone with his fist in both 1491 and 1498. He was in trouble in 1492 for catching a *thirlpoll* (porpoise), which was royal property, and not handing it over. In 1425, before he became Prior of Birkenhead, Robert de Urmeston and his then Prior, John Wood, were indicted for breach of the peace. Thomas Chestur was Prior when he was ordered to keep the peace towards Edward

44 This is how the ruins of Birkenhead Priory appeared during the 1780s. The building on the left is believed to be the Ferry House.

Jankyn in 1499. It seems that monks were just as prone to violence and crime as were the rest of the population of medieval Wirral.

In all, the evidence certainly supports the idea that the monasteries were a powerful force in Wirral's economy and society in the Middle Ages. Unfortunately, there are very few extant records which help us to perceive either the spiritual beliefs and doctrines of the religious communities or the degree to which, each day, they were put into practice. The few existing references to individual monks do, however, imply that, far from being either totally other-worldly or even supernaturally exceptional, monks were disappointingly similar to the rest of the population.

Part Four: The Life of the People

Burton has attracted the attention of some excellent scholars who have found that, between Domesday Book in 1086 and a manorial extent (survey) which was carried out in 1296, the village's population increased by 300 per cent. This was partly due to Burton's rise as a Deeside port, but other evidence—particularly the details of agricultural expansion—strongly imply that, between the 11th and 14th centuries, Wirral's population was growing at a faster rate than was ever witnessed again until the 19th century. Furthermore, the population was increasing in complexity: Domesday Book recorded only a rider, a priest and a series of peasants as living in Burton, but, 211 years later, the manorial extent mentioned Richard the

[87]

Cobbler, William the Cobbler, Alexander the Smith and Gilbert the Cutter as well as a merchant. A greater variety of trades was obviously being pursued because the economy was diversifying. Of course, not every settlement's population would have reflected this development, but we may suppose that it was a general trend throughout the district and that at least the market town of Bromborough and the maritime settlement at Meols would have contained similar populations.

Part of the explanation for the population increase must be the existence of avowries, the result of the official policy of allowing runaway peasants and criminals from other counties to settle in Cheshire. The extent from the manor of Shotwick Park in 1280 lists eight such people: Hugh Grount, Richard son of John, Richard Berie, Roger Brun, Hamo son of Peter, Hawisa de Moleton, Richard le Counte and Nicholas Rotel. There are other examples of known immigrants; during the 13th century, Robert and Nik Cook moved to Shotwick from the Isle of Man and married local girls.[21] Their descendants flourished throughout the district; perhaps they were the antecedents of the Cooksons, who were to become important in north Wirral later on. The appearance of Lancashire place-names as surnames shows that immigrants were arriving from across the Mersey as well: there were Aspinalls, Newbolds and Litherlands in Wallasey, an Orrel in Tranmere and a Preston in Higher Bebington. The presence of Welshmen is shown by variants of the name Walsh (eg. *Walens* and *Walensis*). In contrast, there is evidence of people who must still have preserved some sense of Norse identity and were, therefore, the descendants of a much earlier group of immigrants: a charter from 1280 mentions a lady land-owner called Seurydzis (Sigrithr) in Wallasey; and a rental of 1398, for St Werburgh's Abbey, mentions an Agnes and a Johanne Hondesdoghter in Great Sutton and a Mabilla Raynaldesdoghter in Thornton.[22] This method of naming a female child as 'daughter' of the parent is still practised in Iceland.

Surnames evolved during the Middle Ages. Twenty-seven of the 36 tenants mentioned on the Shotwick Park extent of 1280 were listed as being 'the son of' somebody else. Examples include the bondsmen, Roger son of Richard, Stephen son of Robert and Thomas son of John. It is not known whether these names were inherited by the next generation, giving the common surnames Richards, Roberts and Jones, but, clearly, several of the other tenants had inherited ancestral names. For example, there is a Daykin Owen, a William Hog and a Roger Gille (Constable of Shotwick Castle and possible forefather of the Guile families which flourished in early modern Wirral). The Shotwick Park extent certainly gives us a sample of one of the early stages in the evolution of a regular system of personal naming. By 1356, all the Wirral people who appeared at the Trailbaston Court seem to have been using hereditary surnames. Unsurprisingly, many of them were also local place-names, indicating the origins of the bearers' forefathers, but there is also an interesting range of descriptive and occupation names.

We must now consider the society in which these people lived. Feudalism dominated social and economic relationships. Domesday Book showed us how most Wirral people were semi-free or unfree peasants. By 1296, there were more free tenants who paid rent instead of performing services for their lords. The Burton extent names the manor's leading tenant; he was as a man called Baty. He paid five shillings a year for his 24 acres of land and could be viewed as the descendant of the 1086 rider or radman. Other tenants held less land, but there were more freemen than there were villeins. However, in nearby Gayton, all the tenants were villeins or bondmen, completely servile to the manorial lord, the Abbey of Vale Royal. Shotwick Park's 1280 extent lists four freemen. Their leader paid no rent, but was obliged to act as summoner for the manor court and as a carrier of the manor's official letters. The other three paid rents of between 10 pence and 20 shillings per year. Twenty-five bondsmen and their lands are listed; they paid rents of a shilling per acre (i.e. three shillings per *bovate*) per year. They also had to perform services for the lord of the manor: a day's ploughing on his land at their own expense, using their own ploughs and oxen, a day's ploughing in Lent at the lord's expense and three days' ploughing in the autumn. In addition, the men of Saughall were required to collect a cartload of rushes for the lord (the Earl of Chester) in order to furnish the castle when he was resident. So, it is clear that, in Wirral, there was a complex mix of manorial systems which combined payments and services. In general, however, many people were still viewed as the property of their manorial lords: following their deaths, a third of their property was given to their lord; girls were not allowed to marry out of the manor without the lord's permission; peasants were not allowed to work for other lords or to move away; fines were imposed for sexual relations outside marriage; sons were prevented from becoming priests; and there were tight controls on business activities.

In 1349 the Black Death hit Cheshire. It killed between a fifth and a half of the population. Local economies were ruined: the port of Meols and the markets at Burton and Bromborough seem to have gone into decline. But the surviving peasants and their descendants benefited from the catastrophe: due to the lack of manpower and in order to attract peasants from neighbouring estates, landlords offered higher wages. Peasants themselves began to demand better pay and conditions; the tramels of feudalism were being eroded. The Statute of Labourers of 1351 tried to restrict wages to their pre-1349 levels, but the peasants already had too much power. This was shown in Wirral when, in 1368, at the sheriff's court in Woodchurch, one Joan Getegod 'webster' refused to work with the men of Neston and sought higher pay. During the summer of 1381, peasants in Kent and Essex rebelled against their lords and rioted in London. On 23 July, a royal proclamation, warning of the consequences of rebellion, was read out in Chester and later at Eastham parish church. On 29 July, Hugh Hervy and 15 other peasants from the Abbey of Chester's manor at Lea by Backford gathered together and then went to Chester Castle to demand improvements in their lot. Later, they were allowed to go home in peace, but they were summoned to attend the next county court.[23]

The latter episode must be viewed in context: Cheshire was a notoriously violent and lawless region. Of course, the sources have a bias towards recording the exceptional rather than the routine, but they still give us the impression of a troubled society. Property was a major cause of conflict. In June 1260, Cheshire Crown Court heard an appeal by Adam de Witeby that John de Albo Monasterio (Whitchurch) had taken his mare from Whitby's common pasture. A trial by combat was ordered. Adam defeated and killed John, whose body was then hanged. In August 1287, the County Court heard the case of Roger de Haselwall and Robert Bernard who stole an ox in Oxton, belonging to Hugh son of Cecily of Oxton. There are numerous other accounts of disputes over animals and land boundaries. There were many cases of assault and several of rape. In June 1292, Chester City Court heard that Nicholas the Scrivein raped Matilda daughter of Simon Gyrkoke on 'Gruggeworth Heath near Mollington'. He was found guilty and imprisoned.[24]

We will now carry out some detective work in order to find out how the land was used. Firstly, we know that farming was mixed: the peasants tended both crops and

45 An evocative print showing Eastham village in the early 19th century. It shows the traditional buildings and rural way of life which predominated throughout Wirral during the 18th and early 19th centuries and had changed little since the Middle Ages.

animals. The evidence for this comes in the form of lists of property. For example, in 1315, Stephen Gofyry fled justice after murdering Bertram the Miller of Denhall. His listed goods included an ox, a bullock and three bushells of barley. Barnaby Greaves murdered a Shotwick woman in 1310; his property was seized and included 10 cattle, 22 sheep, seven pigs, and measures of wheat, oats and peas. In 1336, John de Waley of Larton in the parish of West Kirby killed Robert Hondesson in Newton. He fled and his seized goods included an ox, a horse, three cows, two young oxen, two heifers, three *stirks* (bullocks), six sheep and two *piglings*. We have also seen how the population was growing and how more and more land was being ploughed up and improved. Burton's manorial extent of 1298 indicates that over 720 acres were being cultivated, 300 more than were in use in 1813. There was only one medieval agricultural system would enable such mixed and intensive use—that which relied upon the annual rotation of crops on strips of land situated in three open fields.

The three-course rotation system is the classic form of agriculture which marked the landscape of large areas of England. The signs of its former importance can clearly be seen in the form of ridges and furrows which often run contrary to the alignments of hedges and fences on the beautiful rolling fields of Leicestershire, Warwickshire and Northamptonshire.

Wirral does not contain such obvious archaeological evidence, but there are other clues. Before we consider them, we must first grasp the principles of open field agriculture. Each manor contained three large, open fields. Each open field was divided into strips, which were also known as selions. Selions were grouped into furlongs. Strips were demarcated by the way in which they were ploughed; the soil was pushed into a long mound in the centre of the strip, so that there were hollows on either side, forming boundaries with neighbouring strips. An individual peasant would own several strips in each open field. This enabled the different types of soil to be shared out equally. In any one year, all the peasants in one open field would be growing the same crop. During the following year, that same field would either be sown with a different crop or left fallow; this enabled the soil to remain healthy. Everybody was responsible for ensuring that the system worked. By early modern times, most open fields had been divided up into square, enclosed fields and the three-course rotation system had been abandoned.

Post-medieval maps contain references to the old strips. Estate maps from Neston (1732) and Burton (1768-92) depict several unenclosed strips.[25] Tithe maps from the 1840s hold similar clues. In the words of Gill Chitty, Frankby's example, dated 1844, shows us that the village is '... surrounded by one of the best preserved open field enclosure patterns that remain in the district'. It displays the outlines of four large open fields, called Heath, Holme, Town and Brook Fields and the way in which they have been divided into separate rectangular fields which clearly follow the alignments of the old strips.[26] Most Wirral townships owned examples of this kind of field arrangement and words which were used to describe the old strips, such as *land, lawnd, loon, loont, loom, shoot, shutt, flatt, platt, dale, butt, gore* and *pingle* and other attendant features, such as *baulks* (the unploughed areas between groups of strips) and *headlands* (the areas at either end of the strips, where the ploughs turned around), appear as later field-name elements. Charters record the ownership and giving of land and often mention strip names. An example is that of William son of Adam son of Geofrey de Lisnecarte, dated 1300-10. It mentions strips, all in Liscard, called Le Knot, Le Gatebut and Le Houe (which itself was divided into Le Scheuelbrod and Merebut).[27]

Unlike in other parts of England, Wirral's open fields were not enclosed by formal acts of parliament, but were removed by a series of largely unrecorded agreements between local landlords. A Wallasey charter from 1280 gives us a rare glimpse into this process: with the apparent aim of consolidating their holdings, Alice and John, offspring of William de Hanewood, exchanged some strips with Henry de Bechinton. The strips' names included Magna and Parva Croke, Twafeting, Half Hadlant and Havinardishathir. In modern urban Wirral, those who are interested in the siting of former open fields should look for road names which contain the element 'townfield'; at least seven are listed in a current street atlas.[28] Sensitive developers might, in these cases, have commemorated the names of the fields upon which they built their new estates.

Trees were another important product of the land. Domesday Book mentioned only one large area of Woodland (in Prenton), but, by the 14th century, there was an important concentration of timber at Saughall which belonged to the Earl of Chester. It was partly the product of the creation of Shotwick Park by Edward III in 1327, a deer park within the forest of Wirral which was surrounded by a pale fence, deer-leaps and wolf-traps. But there had been a mention of the wood's existence in 1260, when its boundary with Blacon was demarcated by marked oaks and ditches.[29] The infamous William Stanley was made keeper of the park in 1351. Between 1347 and 1349, 10,000 faggots of cut wood were sold to John Calle, a baker in Chester, for 60 shillings; they were obviously for fuelling his ovens. There are also records of Saughall timber being used in repairs to the nearby fisheries and to the Dee Mills.

Other economic activities included fisheries all around the coast, especially at Wallasey, in the Hoyle Lake and at Shotwick. There were windmills for grinding corn at Grange in West Kirby, Great Meols, Neston and Stanney. In 1299, Burton received a charter for a weekly market and annual fair in July and it operated as an outlying port for Chester.

For details of domestic life we must look to archaeology. The bulk of Meols' huge collection of antiquities, which were exposed by sea erosion during the 19th century, date from the Middle Ages. In the words of archaeologist Dr Rob Philpott, 'It is the largest collection of Medieval domestic items to have come from any single site outside London'.[30] There are objects which represent virtually every domestic and agricultural routine, as well as many luxury items. The many medieval coins seem to have been dropped at a regular rate up until the middle of the 14th century, when either sea erosion or the Black Death destroyed the town. It is not yet clear whether, if other Wirral settlements had met such sudden ends, they would have produced a similar quantity of archaeology or whether Meols was unique.

During the 1890s, Edward Cox was extremely fortunate to witness the erosion of the coast and to see evidence of the old settlement:

> ... The remains of medieval and older houses are continually washed out, together with ploughs, spades, and other agricultural implements; showing that this was arable land. The houses are mostly built on rough stone foundations set in clay, with clay floors, and the walls of the upper part of rough stakes and wattled work. These seem to have lined an irregular village. On one occasion in 1890, traces of wheels of carts, horses' feet with round shoes, and the footsteps of cattle and of men, who wore pointed shoes, were for a short time visible on ground below the level of high tide; by the side of the road were refuse heaps, containing bones, shellfish, fragments of iron, coal, cloth and shoes similar to the footmarks.[31]

We can imagine that this scene at least was representative of the appearance of most Wirral townships in the Middle Ages.

Documentary references to domestic property only really appear in the 1353 Trailbaston records. They say that Henry Cherleton stole a coverlet worth 6s. 8d. from Robert Poole's house in Neston; Robert Prenton 'and others' broke into Thomas Buck's house in Higher Bebington, where they assaulted Henry Ball and then stole a belt, a pouch and some silver and gold with a value of five pounds; and that William son of William Alcock stole 22 ells of linen cloth from William Morley in Seacombe and sold it. There is not enough detail here upon which to build a hypothesis, but we are at least beginning to see that the residents of other townships apart from Meols also owned valuable goods.

In 1485, Henry Tudor became king of England. He was the first of a dynasty whose reigns were to see England transformed: the monasteries were dissolved and the feudal system weakened and ultimately expunged; the country became a Protestant nation state and the dominant member within the alliance which was to become the United Kingdom. We will see how these developments affected Wirral in the next chapter.

Five

Early Modern Wirral 1500-1800

Introduction: The Beginnings of Modernity

After defeating Richard III at the Battle of Bosworth in 1485, Henry Tudor became king. He is regarded as England's first modern monarch, but it was the reign of his second son, Henry VIII between 1509 and 1547, which transformed English society. He was remarkably similar to the monarch whose reign began the last chapter: he showed the same desire to know, to control and to exploit his kingdom. He changed the country's religion and reformed its local and national government. Feudalism disappeared and England became a nation state. The other Tudor monarchs and the Stuarts who succeeded them after 1603 had to cope with the consequences of the great religious, economic and social forces which Henry had, largely unwittingly, stirred up. This chapter attempts to explore the ways in which the people of Wirral were affected by these great changes as well as generally to discuss developments in the local economy and landscape.

Part One: End of the Monasteries and Change and Continuity in Local Government

When, during the 1530s, the once powerful monasteries of Wirral were suddenly dissolved, everybody felt the effects. The government confiscated all monastic lands and properties and then sold them to secular landlords. Birkenhead Priory was in government hands until 1545, when it was sold to Ralph Worsley of Lancashire and described as 'a house and site; church, belfry, churchyard, house, edifices, mills, barns, yards, a dove house, mill, fishyards, two acres of meadow, 78 acres of arable; a parcel of land where flax used to grow; Hagge Coppice; Bidston and Wallasey'.[1] We can imagine how these assets would have boosted Worsley's prosperity and prestige. Space will not allow a description of every post-dissolution land transfer, but suffice it to say that some existing gentry families were able to increase their holdings and that certain newcomers were able to gain footholds in Wirral for the first time. For example, in December 1548, John Gryce sold the manor of Bromborough to a member of an important gentry family, Sir Rowland Stanley of Hooton. The relevant document listed: '... all lands, tenements medose ... also th'arbage and pannage of one wood called Willanryce and one lease or Deide indented ... made for term of LXI yeres p'sently enduring by Thomas late Abbot of the late dissolved monastery of Chester ...'[2]

The tiny township of Hoose had emerged as coastal grazing land between Little and Great Meols. Its story is a fascinating example of how monastic landownership has influenced the modern landscape. It had become the property of Basingwerk Abbey, upon whose dissolution it was passed to the crown, where it remained until 1579, when two citizens of London, Edmund Downyng and John Walker, bought it. They must have viewed it as a little investment, but certainly never lived there. Subsequently their tenant, Ralph Proby, bought it and then, in 1585, sold it in two lots to Miles Fells and John Roberts. Hoose's neighbouring manors continued to be the property of sole landlords. Being so small, Hoose seems not to have been viable as a manor and was gradually divided into many more smaller plots which were purchased by lower-class but prosperous people, such as the fisherman John Eccles. By the 19th century, when Hoylake began to grow due to fishing and then to the rail link with Liverpool, Hoose was developed as a working-class residential area. This had not occurred in neighbouring Great and Little Meols because their lands had not been divided into smaller plots at such an early date. They remained largely agricultural villages until the late 19th and early 20th centuries when they were developed as much more middle-class neighbourhoods for commuters to Liverpool. Thus, today we see that the area of densest housing in Hoylake lies between Deneshey and Alderley Roads—the old boundaries of Hoose, which were in turn the product of both monastic land-holding and post-dissolution land deals.

Documentation from the dissolved monasteries is rare, but there is an inventory of goods found at the cell at Stanlaw in 1537. It contains important details about the old monastic life. There were numerous religious clothes and artifacts including 'a vestment of rede sylke bawdykyn with all thynges thereunto belongyng for the prest', 'an alter table of allybaster with a blewe clothe hangyng before the same' and 'On image of our Lady of Grace old gylte with playtes of sylv'r opon the ffeyte and xv pens naylled abowte the tabernacle'. The latter reference is to pennies which had been stuck to the image as offerings and is an example of the kind of idolatry and superstition which Protestants were so keen to expunge from the life of the church. A list of agricultural property follows on:

> Item. Cattell xxii whearof iiii of on yere olde; v of ii yers hold; v of iii yers olde; and other iii of iii yers hold called effers and v kyen.
> Itm' ii oxen claymed by Antony Derwent.
> Itm' on horse ii mares and on colt, wyche mares and colte are claymed by Antony Derwent and John Whyttacar.   Sold for xxxiis iiiid
> Itm' v score sheype and xxxii lambes.
> Itm' vii swyne.
> Itm' in the Berne by estymacyon vi thrayf (a measure of 12 or 24 sheaves) of unthrashen barleycorne.
> Itm' in the Garner by Estymacyon iii hopers of barly and peyse together.
> Itm' on bushell of grene peyse claymed by William Whyttell.
> Itm' on bushell of whete.
> Itm' xvi busshells of barly by Estymacyon.[3]

It is evidence that local farming was mixed, based on both the rearing of animals and on the growing of crops. Additionally, the crops themselves were typical of those which were grown in Wirral right up to the 18th century. The three named men who were claiming these goods were probably either former monastic tenants or employees. The document finishes by telling us that William Whyttell was 'admitted to the possessyon, custody, and kepyng of the sayd sell with the appurtenaunces and all the gudds and cattalls

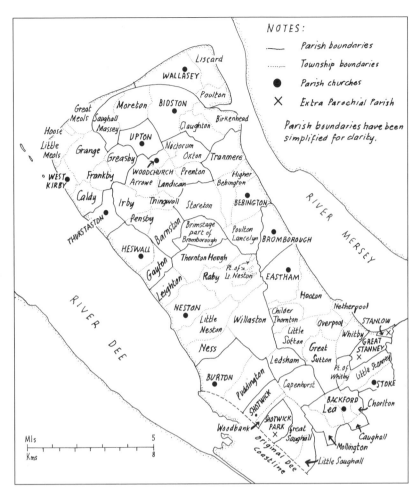

46 Medieval parishes of Wirral which were in existence by the time that parish registers were coming into use in the 16th and 17th centuries.

aforesayd, to the Kynges use until the Kynges pleasor be further knowen'. He was clearly acting as an interim estate manager until the properties were sold off. It was, perhaps, the beginning of Whytell's new life as a secular tenant farmer with prospects for raising his status and for increasing his wealth. In this respect, he is representative of many people in England at that time.

The exact fate of every single former monk is unknown, but the few details which have survived indicate that they were not as badly off as we often like to imagine. Older brethren were given pensions. John Sharpe, the last prior of Birkenhead, got an annual pension of £12 and died in Neston in 1543. Others found employment as clergymen in parish churches. John Gostilowe was a former monk from St Werburgh's Abbey who became rector of Wallasey in 1549. He received an annual pension of £5 and was buried in Wallasey in January 1580. He was served by two other former monks—Thomas Tassey from Birkenhead Priory, who was described as a 'chappeleyn' in 1549 and who died in 1582 aged 75 and John Bird, an ex-friar from Chester, who, between 1548 and 1554, was described as 'curate of Wallasey'. Brothers from other Cheshire houses found employment in Wirral: William Wright came from Vale Royal Abbey and was rector of Woodchurch between 1549 and 1571;

and William Dycunson came from Grey Friars in Chester and was clerk in Heswall in 1542. Traditional monastic skills often enabled former monks to gain secular employment; thus the Corporation of Liverpool account books for 1541 mention the payment of 'ii shillings to a monke of Birket, for byndynge a boke'.[4]

Details about the dissolution of the Hilbre cell are fascinating. In 1575, depositions were taken from local people concerning the practices of the former monks. John Diall, aged 70, of West Kirby said that he remembered how the two monks of the cell used to say services in the chapel and to catch herring and other fish from a boat. John Brassie of Tiverton said that, 45 years earlier, he had been 'one of the boys of the chamber' and had known the last monks, Robert Harden and John Smith. The latter said that he had gone to live on Hilbre some 50 years previously and had stayed there for 14 years. His uncle, John Smith, had been a monk. He said that their fishing boat was called the *Jack Rice*. No monks had paid tithes to the rector of West Kirby. The last monk was called Robert Wigan (also known as Wingham, Harden or Hawarden). He was well off. His will, which was proved in 1550 and in which he is described as a 'Clerk of Hilbre', mentions a boat called the *Michael of Hilbre* which he left along with an 'ambling filly' to Edward Smarley, a sailing boat called a 'counter' which he left to Mr Rowland Stanley Esq. and a 'red heifer that goeth upon the island' to Alice Davy. He had been in receipt of an annual pension of £6.[5]

Such retrospective insights into the internal life and the local effects of monasteries are rare, but they do convey a poignant sense of an end of an era. When we look at the ways in which local government was being reformed we see an important feature of the succeeding era.

In 1536, the government observed that Cheshire still had a reputation for lawlessness 'by reason that common justice had not been indifferently ministered there like and in such form as in other places in the realm'. An act was, therefore, passed which gave the Lord Chancellor and the Lord Keeper the right to appoint justices of the peace. They were to be people with local knowledge who were to administer the law in an impartial and responsible fashion and to be accountable to central government. In order to deal regularly with all matters of civil order and to enable maximum attendance, the courts (or quarter sessions) were to meet four times a year in Chester, Nantwich, Northwich and Knutsford. On the one hand, things were now very different to what they had been during the Middle Ages; Cheshire's isolation and the ability of certain people to exploit local government for their own benefit had been removed, but, on the other hand, the justices of the peace came mainly from from the gentry. By the middle of the 16th century, local government in Wirral had become more efficient, but society was still rigidly hierarchical; the gentry were still in charge. A list of gentry made in 1578 tells us the names of the most powerful families in early modern Wirral:

> Sir Rowland Stanley Esquire (*c*.1517-1614) Hooton
> John Poole Esquire (1524-1613) Poole
> William Massie Esquire (1516-1579) Puddington
> John Whitmore Esquire (1539-?) Thurstaston
> Robert Fletcher Esquire (of Morley and Chester; Wirral estates unknown)
> John Hockenhall Esquire (1540-1590) Prenton
> Thomas Bunbury Esquire (1542-1601) Stanney
> Richard Hough Esquire (died *c*.1574) Thornton Hough and Leighton
> Edward Stanley, Poulton Spital

William Glegg (died 1629) Gayton
Robert Parr (*c*.1535-1582) Backford
Peter Bold (died 1605) Upton
John Meols Gent. (*c*.1531-1592) Meols
Thomas Doe, Saughall
Richard Sheppard, Greasby
William Bennett (1506-90) Carnsdale, Barnston
William Prenton, Heswall
John Wirral, 'de Eade', either Heswall or Ledsham (?)
Richard Linacre, Grange, West Kirby
Edward Burgess, Eastham
John Martin, Saughall Massey (?)
Edward Swallow (?)
Henry Glover, Eastham (?)
John Younge, Neston;
Edward Dallamere, Thingwall
Robert Radcliffe, Greasby
Richard Coventry, Newhouse in Newton, West Kirby

Notice that the list describes a hierarchy. Unsurprisingly, a Stanley is at the top. By this time, the family had effectively become noble. In fact, as a result of strategic marriages, their main interests were now in Lancashire. The seven persons beneath Sir Rowland were officially described as gentry by virtue of their titles, but those below them could just as easily be described as yeomen: they did not have titles, but qualified for inclusion on the list by virtue of their property, manners and dress. It is a good introduction to the names of Wirral's most influential families.

Part Two: People, Names and Places

Just as William I's obsession with information about his property created the most useful local historical source of the Middle Ages, Henry VIII's desire both to know and to exploit his kingdom led to the most comprehensive list of local residents until the national censuses of the 19th century. It was carried out in 1545 and is called the Subsidy Roll; it reveals much detail about the people of Wirral at the beginning of the early modern age and bears the names of Wirral householders who owned property to the value of at least 20 shillings and were thus eligible for taxation at a flat rate of a penny in the pound. This low financial qualification for the tax implies that most householders in Wirral probably owned property of at least this value and, therefore, would have been listed. Sixty of Wirral's townships are mentioned and nine missed out (Arrowe, Blacon, Heswall, Hooton, Pensby, Great and Little Sutton, Childer Thornton and Woodbank). We are able to compute approximate sizes of population by multiplying the number of heads of household by five, giving us the figures which are laid out in Tables 4 and 5 on page 98.

The figures are approximations. Naturally, some populations appear great because the townships themselves are large. Shotwick had the highest population density, about nineteen people per 100 acres.[6] West Kirby had a population of about seventy, but a density of about fifteen people per 100 acres, making it the second most populous district in Wirral. Great Neston and Liscard had the same population density of about thirteen people per 100 acres, while Tranmere had about twelve people per 100 acres. Eastham had

Table 4: The Largest Townships of Wirral in 1545

Township	Heads of Household	Approximate Population
Great Neston	37	185
Burton	33	165
Wallasey	28	140
Tranmere	26	130
Liscard	25	125
Shotwick	21	105
Eastham	20	100

Table 5: The Smallest Townships of Wirral in 1545

Township	Heads of Household	Approximate Population
Netherpool	1	5
Mollington Banastre	2	10
Croughton	2	10
Great Stanney	2	10
Noctorum	3	15
Crabwall	4	20
Thingwall	4	20
Woodchurch	5	25

eleven people per 100 acres whilst Burton and Wallasey had about nine each, making their population densities a little above average for the Hundred. Clearly, in the cases of West Kirby, Neston and Shotwick, maritime trade along the Dee estuary was the main cause of their relative prosperity and ability to sustain larger populations. The apparent importance of the other townships should not be exaggerated, but is probably due to relative soil qualities and the suitability of sites for settlement. This can be seen in the cases of Wallasey and Liscard, where there are good sandstone outcrops upon which to build, a mixture of sandy soils and clay and a mild local climate.

According to the Rolls there were 770 heads of households in Wirral implying a possible total of 3,850 people. If we say that the population of each of the missing townships was 11, equivalent to the average for the whole of Wirral, this gives us a further 440 people and a grand total of 4,290. Modern Wirral has 'villages' (e.g., Greasby, Irby and Pensby) with larger populations than that. We are again reminded that the land was comparatively empty.

Population figures are interesting, but impersonal. Most of us will, in fact, peruse the Subsidy Rolls in pursuit of ancestral names, especially as they offer the chance of pushing back a lineage beyond the commencement of most extant parish registers. In our quest for the next generation, do we perceive the value of all those other surnames which we impatiently discard like severed foliage from the trail we are hacking through the archival jungle? Surnames are like little envelopes, containing bequests from previous generations, which we have dismissed as being too insignificant to be opened. In one sense we are right: if you open your envelope, you will only find that your surname was probably acquired by some anonymous medieval ancestor, who began to find it necessary to distinguish himself from his neighbours by acquiring an extra title and that this title would come from one of four categories—a nickname, a relationship name, an occupation name or a place name. But, consider the possibilities for extending our understanding of the origins of Wirral people in the 16th century if we pile up all the envelopes from the Subsidy Rolls, open them up, study them, list and categorise them and use them to test out our preconceptions or pet theories about Wirral's past.

One of the most vehemently held beliefs about Wirral's past is that the district has contained an isolated population; it is after all a semi-island: the Irish Sea and the rivers Dee and Mersey have acted as deterrents to both emigration and immigration. It is thought that people simply could not travel either outwards or inwards until the Mersey Ferries became steam powered in the early 19th century. The raging waters of the mighty Mersey are regarded with particular awe and that famous river has acted as the boundary between Cheshire and Lancashire for over a thousand years; indeed, Mersey means 'boundary river'. It is believed, therefore, that the people of Early Modern Wirral must have been uniformly descended from the people who had settled there some 20 to 30 generations previously, during the Early Middle or Dark Ages. If there was any dilution of this ancient family, it would only be due to immigration from, at the furthest, other parts of Cheshire. The contents of our pile of envelopes tell us a different story.

Now for the surnames which are also place-names: during the Middle Ages, as the population grew and became more mobile, those who moved away from their native villages and registered themselves in new ones acquired surnames in order to ease identification. Often, the most obvious surname for a clerk to bestow upon a peasant would be the name of his home village. Thus a man who moved from Newton might become known as John de Newton; the 'de' would eventually be dropped and future generations would bear the same name. Doubtless, it would not be many generations before John's descendants would cease to know or even care about the origins of their family name, but of one thing we can be sure: at some time in the middle of the Middle Ages, one of their ancestors must have moved from a village called Newton to somewhere else. Newton is one of the most common names in England and so we are unable to be sure about the precise medieval origins of modern bearers of that name. Other names are, however, singular. For example, there is only one Burscough in Britain; it is in south-west Lancashire, as are Scarisbrick and Sefton. We can say of each bearer of these names that, at some stage in the Middle Ages, one of their ancestors, who lived in those villages, moved away and settled somewhere else.

There are 298 surnames listed on the Wirral Subsidy Rolls for 1545. Eighty of these are identifiable place-names. Remarkably, 40 of the 80, or 50 per cent of them (or 32, if we withdraw the ambiguous and doubtful ones, making 40 per cent) are from Lancashire. They constitute the largest category and appear in Table 6 on page 100.

It would be mischievous to project the proportion of Lancashire place-names within the geographical surname category onto the other three surname categories (i.e. descriptive or nicknames and occupation and relationship names) and thereby assert that some 50 per cent of Wirral heads of households must either have come from or were descended from

Table 6: Lancashire Place-names Appearing as Wirral Surnames in 1545

Surname	Lancashire place-names in modern form (if different)	Wirral townships in which they appeared as surnames in 1545
Angleshargh/Inglesarghe	Anglezarke	Eastham
Assheton	Ashton (In Makerfield, Under Lyne)*	Eastham
Aynsdale	Ainsdale	Liscard, Great Meols, Great Neston, Wallasey
Barrow*	Barrow and Barrow in Furness (unlikely)	Mollington Tarrant
Blackborne	Blackburn	Bidston
Boland	Bowland	Poulton Cum Spittal, Storeton
Bolton		Wallasey
Brusco	Burscough	Little Neston, Poulton Cum Spittal, Little Stanney, Storeton
Byllynge	Billing	Moreton
Charnocke	Charnock Richard	Brimstage, Claughton, Little Neston, Willaston
Fazackerley		Barnston, Landican, West Kirby
Hale		Gayton, Stoke
Hesketh/Hesky	Hesketh Bank	Capenhurst, Prenton
Hollande	Up Holland	Bidston, Little Caldy
Home/Holme/Hulme	Hulme	Over Bebington, Tranmere
Knowsley		Over Bebington, Whitby
Ley	Leigh#	Raby, Saughall Massey, Storeton, Thingwall
Lynnacre/Linakar	Linacre	Caldy Grange, Greasby, Great Meols, Moreton
Lunt		Over Bebington
Myddleton	Middleton	Great Neston
Nelston	*Nelson (doubtful)*	*Burton*
Newton	Newton le Willows#	Backford, Tranmere
Parbott/Parbolt	Parbold	Bidston, Claughton
Pemberton		Little Caldy, Liscard, Moreton, Prenton, Saughall Massey, Thingwall, Upton
Pendleton		Wallasey
Penkythe/Penket	Penketh	Claughton, Raby
Pynnyngton	Pennington	Gayton, Tranmere
Radcliffe		West Kirby
Scarysbricke	Scarisbrick	Lower Bebington
Sefton		Burton, Mollington Tarrant, Puddington, Stoke, Whitby
Tarleton		Great Neston
Trafford	Trafford Park *	Capenhurst, Chorlton, Eastham
Troughton	*Trawden (doubtful)*	*Little Saughall*
Tyldesley		Brimstage
Urmiston/Ormeston	Urmston	Irby, Moreton, Little Saughall
Walley	Whalley	Great Neston
Walton		Little Stanney, Upton
Warrhenton/Wayrington/	Warrington	Caldy Grange,
Werynton		West Kirby
Wauton	Warton	Little Caldy, Greasby, Oxton, Thurstaston,
Whyttfield/Whytfeld	Whitefield	Shotwick, Oxton

(* It would be unsafe to assert that these three are definitely Lancashire surnames, due to their frequency as place-names throughout England, including Cheshire, i.e. Ashton-Upon-Mersey, Great Barrow and Bridge and Mickle Trafford, but there are no examples of these place-names in Wirral.)
(# These place-names are also common throughout England, including examples in Wirral, i.e. Newton Cum Larton near West Kirby and Lea in the parish of Backford.)

people who had moved to Wirral from Lancashire, because, of course, location names were, by their very nature, only bestowed upon people who moved away from home; and the numbers of other sorts of name being bestowed upon immigrants would, consequently, be proportionally smaller. But, surely, the least we are able to say is that between 12 and 40 per cent of Wirral people in the 16th century were so descended. It is reasonable to suggest that our estimate should be nearer the top than the bottom of the range. A brief survey of several smaller documents from the same period, printed in *Wirral Notes and Queries*, yields further examples of Lancashire place-names acting as Wirral surnames: Robert Hausted (Halstead) appears on a Brimstage Rent Roll for 1557; the Litherland family had flourished in Wallasey since the Middle Ages; and a William Formbie (Formby) appears on the will, which was proved in 1605, of John Penketh of *Birkett alias Birkened*. The same documents also produce many repeats of the names from the tables.

Tables 7 to 9 show the other identifiable place-names which acted as surnames for Wirral people.

Five surnames are not synonymous with geographical locations, but give a very good idea of their bearers' ancestral origins: Irrysheman (Great Neston) and Welchmann (Overpoole) speak for themselves. The other three are Welsh surnames: ap Ithell (Burton)

Table 7: Cheshire Place-names from Outside Wirral Appearing as Wirral Surnames in 1545

Surname	Place-name in Modern Form (if different)	Wirral Townships in which they Appeared as Surnames in 1545
Barrow*	Great Barrow	Mollington Tarrant
Braderton	*Barterton (doubtful)*	*Eastham*
Bunbury		Backford
Crewe		Great Neston
Delamore	Delamere	Thingwall
Hoole/Hole		Tranmere
Hough		Oxton
Huntynton	Huntington	Lower Bebington, Lea, Tranmere
Kelsall		Backford
Kynderton	Kinderton	Little Stanney
Moston		Whitby
Spursto	Spurstow	Overpool
Warmyncham		Storeton, Wallasey
Waverton	(possibly Warton not Waverton)	Shotwick
Werburton	Warburton	Claughton

(*This name has also been included in Table 6; please see the note above.)

Table 8: Wirral Place-names Appearing as Wirral Surnames in 1545

Surname	Place-name in Modern Form (if different)	Wirral Townships in which they Appeared as Surnames in 1545
Blacon		Great and Little Neston
Brumburgh	Bromborough	Tranmere
Cawday	Caldy	Great Neston
Denwall		Lea
Grevesby	Greasby	Great Neston
Irreby	Irby	Moreton
Ledsham		Little Caldy
Leighton		Irby
Ley	Lea*	Raby, Saughall Massey, Storeton, Thingwall
Meols		Burton
Newton*		Backford, Tranmere
Prenton		Gayton
Whitby		Whitby
Willaston		Mollington Tarrant
Wirrehall	Wirral	Brimstage

(* These two have also been included in Table 6; please see the relevant note there.)

Table 9: Other Place-names Appearing as Wirral Surnames in 1545

Surname	Place-name in Modern (if different)	Where Found (Historic Counties)	Wirral Townships in which they appeared as surnames in 1545
Brabon	*Barbon* *Brabourne (doubtful)*	*Westmorland* *Kent*	*Little Caldy* *West Kirby*
Carleyll	Carlisle	Cumberland	Little Saughall
Colton		Norfolk, Yorkshire etc.	Thornton Hough
Coventre	Coventry	Warwickshire	Greasby, Knocktorum, Great Meols, West Kirby, Woodchurch
Hampton		Shropshire, Worcestershire etc.	Nesse
Hoggeston/ Hoggleston		Buckinghamshire	Lower and Over Bebington, Oxton, Willaston
Irland	Ireland		Storeton
Newbott*	Newbold	Derbyshire, Leicestershire	Frankby, Greasby, Newton Cum Larton
Radley		Oxfordshire	Brimstage
Stanton/Stoneton		Gloucestershire, Suffolk etc.	Brimstage, Thurstaston
Washington		County Durham	Capenhurst
Wyllibye	Willoughby	Lincolnshire	Whitby

(* Possibly also from farm of that name in Great Caldy.)

NOTES:

UPPERCASE : FAMILIES
Lowercase : Family Seats

Wallasey
Wheatland House
Leasowe Castle   WILSON
STANLEY (E. of DERBY)
EGERTON, BOODE, CUST   Wallasey
MEOLS

Ancient Meols
MEOLS   Bidston

Grange. Newhouse   Upton   STANLEY (E of DERBY)
COVENTRY   BOLD   STEELE, LORD KINGSTON
BENNETT   VYNER

Grange. GLEGG   Greasby Old Hall   Tranmere MASSEY
SHAW·LEIGH   RADCLIFF, GLEGG, WARTON

Grange Old Manor Farm   Prenton. PRENTON,
COVENTRY. BENNETT   GLEAVE, HOCKENHULL

Thurstaston   Irby: HARPER,   Storeton. STANLEY
THURSTASTON,   LEIGH, GLEGG,
HESWALL, WHITMORE   Brimstage   Bromborough
Oldfield Hall, Heswall   DOMVILLE, HULSE   Hall: MAINWARING
STANLEY   TROUTBECK, TALBOT   Courthouse: HARDWARE

Poulton Lancelyn
LANCELYN, LANCELYN-GREEN

Gayton. GLEGG

Leighton.   Hooton: STANLEY
HOUGH, WHITMORE,
SAVAGE, MOSTYN   Willaston: TRUSSEL   Netherpool
BENNETT   Pool Hall: POOL

Puddington MASSEY

Shotwick HOCKENHULL

Mls   5
Kms   8

47 Family seats of the gentry in early modern Wirral.

means 'Son of Ithell' and is more familiar in its anglicised form, Bithell; Annyon (recorded in Crabwall, Ledsham, Neston and Puddington; and often written as Ennion or Onion) comes from the Old Welsh *Enniaun* and ultimately the Latin *Annianus*; the name transcribed as *Beynyn* (Claughton) is probably Beynon, the anglicised form of *ap Ennion*.

There are 12 unidentified names which resemble place-names, but whose locations or meanings have not yet been discovered: Bachdale, Bawley, Daneham, Dunsterfield, Godelston, Gyrtrey, Swynnley, Weyley and Yoxton. For the purposes of this study they have not been included in the place-name category of surnames.

Wirral was not as insular or as isolated during this pre-industrial era as many of us have liked to suppose. We have overestimated the ability of the two great rivers and the Irish Sea to keep people out and underestimated both the desire and the ability of people to travel away from home and to settle elsewhere. Many of the immigrants came from villages located in counties which are not even coterminous with Cheshire, at distances from Wirral which would have necessitated many days' travel, either on foot or on horseback. We will probably never know how or why each family made such moves. Some people came from semi-foreign countries—Ireland and Wales—with their distinctive languages and cultures, but most incomers originated from Cheshire and Lancashire. Surprisingly, far more came from the latter county than the former. This has implications for the social and cultural history of Wirral.

Wirral was administratively and politically a part of Cheshire, but perhaps, socially and culturally, in the minds of many people, especially at the northern end of the peninsula, it had more in common with south Lancashire. The reasons for this partnership might, in fact, lie in pre-Conquest times, when the Norsemen conquered Wirral and Lancashire. A glance at settlement names in the area just north of Liverpool shows a similar proportion of Norse names to that which can be found in Wirral. Medieval Lancashire people might have felt inclined to move to Wirral because of ancient kinship ties. Of course, the two districts are not far apart; it is simply the River Mersey which acts as a barrier between them. Compare the relationship with that between Wirral and the rest of Cheshire: there is no physical boundary equal to that which the River Mersey presents, but it would appear that the number of immigrants from the villages of the Cheshire Plain was much smaller, possibly because the kinship ties were not as strong.

This cultural and genetic explanation for the migration of Lancastrians into Wirral does not, however, take any account of the motivations behind our proposed population movement: perhaps there was more of an economic need to move out of Lancashire to pastures new than there was to move away from the Cheshire Plain. The latter might have been either less overcrowded or more prosperous than the former during the Middle Ages, creating less of a need for emigration. It is also possible that the Black Death of the middle of the 14th century so denuded the population of Wirral that Lancashire peasants were tempted, by higher wages, to move in to revive the economy. Perhaps, between the 14th and 16th centuries Wirral offered better economic prospects.

Do any of the other documents from the 16th and early 17th centuries reveal current or thriving relationships between the people of Wirral and South Lancashire? *Wirral Notes and Queries* contains transcriptions of 16 wills made by people from north Wirral at this time. They contain references to many people, who were not only the testators' family and friends, but also debtors and creditors. Lands and properties are also described. Despite the frequency of Lancashire names amongst the testators, there are only two references to any personal, family or business connections with Lancashire: Thomas Mollineux bequeathed his 'ambling nagge and a colt named Wyllie' to his 'cozen John Molenyx of Melling' and William Fells referrs to his lands in Liverpool. Amongst the many other human connections the testators mention, there are only two people who did not reside in Wirral: 'Mr Pemberton of the City of' Chester, who received Margaret Harrison's 'nagge and Mr. Edward Vawdrey' of The Riddings in Timperley, Cheshire, who was to act as Jane Penketh's overseer.

We do not conclude that the society and economy of Wirral were intimately involved with those of Lancashire any more than they were with the rest of Cheshire. Rather, we gain the impression that Wirral, especially at the northern end, was, in a current, day-to-day sense, quite self-contained and distinctive. Many residents had ancestral roots in Lancashire and elsewhere, but they were fundamentally Wirralians. By this stage, they had probably ceased to be interested in the heritage which their surnames implied. Indeed, we could say that names like Linacre, Pemberton and Urmston are typical and quintessential Wirral names of the period.

Table 10: The Most Common Names in Wirral in 1545

Rank	Name	No. of heads of household for each	Townships in which they were found in 1545
1	Robinson/Robenson	19	Brimstage, Burton, Leighton, Liscard, Moreton, Oxton, Prenton, Poulton Seacombe, Raby, Saughall Massie, Shotwick, Tranmere, Upton, Wallasey
2	Smythe/Smith	17	Landican, Liscard, Puddington, Saughall Massey, Little Stanney, West Kirby
3	Bennett	16	Barnston, Nesse, Great Neston, Newton Cum Larton, Puddington, Raby, Saughall Massey, Willaston
4	Pemberton	12	Little Caldy, Liscard, Moreton, Prenton, Saughall Massey, Thingwall, Upton
5	Coke/Cok	9	Lower Bebington, Chorlton, Eastham, Mollington Banastre, Ness, Shotwick, Thornton Hough
	Shurleacre/Sherlock	9	Bidston, Liscard, Little Meols, Oxton
	Forshaw	9	Backford, Chorlton, Mollington Tarrant, Great Neston, Willaston
6	Goodecar/Goodacre	8	Barnston, Brimstage, Little Neston
	Hylle/Hyll	8	Poulton Seacombe, Raby, Tranmere, Wallasey
	Johnson	8	Liscard, Mollington Tarrant, Poulton Seacombe, Storeton, West Kirby
7	Williamson	8	Poulton Seacombe, Poulton Spittal, Tranmere, Upton, Wallasey
	Brydde/Bird	8	Knoctorum, Liscard, Poulton Seacombe, Thurstaston
8	Hancocke	7	Bidston, Moreton, Nesse, Great Neston, Newton Cum Larton, Oxton
	Hiccocke	7	Claughton, Little Stanney, Tranmere
	Home/Holme	7	Over Bebington, Tranmere
	Linacre	7	Caldy Grange, Greasby, Great Meols, Moreton
	Taylyar/Taylor	7	Bidston, Ledsham, Great Neston, Raby, Shotwick, Storeton
9	Barrow	6	Mollington Tarrant
	Brusco/Burscough	6	Little Neston, Poulton Cum Spittal, Little Stanney, Storeton
	Coventre	6	Greasby, Knocktorum, Great Meols, West Kirby, Woodchurch
	Deynson/Deanson	6	Little Neston, Storeton, Whitby, Willaston
	Gyll/Gyle	6	Burton, Moreton, Poulton Seacombe, Upton, Newton Cum Larton
	Ley/Lea	6	Raby, Saughall Massey, Storeton, Thingwall

Table 10 lists the most common Wirral surnames of 1545.

Smith has always been a common surname in England. Robinson is popular in the North of England. Bennett, although more common in the North than in the South, is a strong Wirral surname. It is interesting to note certain other names which have remained strong in the peninsula: Bird and Sherlock; the reader will notice their frequency in subsequent chapters of this book.

To summarise the above discussion: the Subsidy Rolls have revealed that Wirral's population was still tiny in comparison with what it was to become after the Industrial Revolution. They have shown that, during the period 1300-1500, there must have been considerable migration into the peninsula and that more people came from Lancashire

48 The geographical origins of Wirral surnames.

than anywhere else, even from Cheshire. This might have affected the culture and economy of Wirral, but, in fact, other evidence shows that, by the 16th century, Wirral was quite self-contained. The Mersey had not made it as demographically isolated as was once thought, but Wirral's identity was unique; it was neither a simple extension of Cheshire nor of Lancashire. Certain names were common and typically Wirralian.

Part Three: 'Confessing with Holy David'—Religion

During recent decades it has been deeply unfashionable to speak about religion as anything other than the product of social and economic forces. Historians have attempted to explain both the Reformation and the English Civil War in broadly Marxist terms as the products of class political conflict. Although these accounts have been stimulating and valuable, they have, perhaps, failed seriously to consider the effects of human belief in the transcendent and the supernatural. The early modern age was a time when people, for the sake of their religion, were prepared to kill and die, imprison and be imprisoned and receive and inflict torture. Between about 1500 and 1690, religion was probably the most important single influence on social relationships, individual behaviour and political events and thereafter, until the end of the 19th century, at least continued to act as one of the most potent forces in national life.

In 1535, by the Act of Supremacy, Henry VIII made himself the head of the English Church. During the following year, he began to suppress the monasteries. Doctrinally, Henry was still a Catholic, but, between 1547 and 1553, his son, Edward VI, ruled as a Protestant monarch: the Catholic mass book was banned and the first English prayer book introduced. Edward's sister, Mary, ruled between 1553 and 1558. She attempted to return the country to Catholicism, but was succeeded by Elizabeth I who, by means of the Second Act of Supremacy and the Act of Uniformity of 1559, made England Protestant again. Use of the prayer book and attendance at church were enforced by law. Those who broke the law were fined one shilling and became known as recusants. Let us see how these changes affected life in Wirral.

Comparison between the preambles of two wills from the period illustrates some differences between Catholic and Protestant beliefs. The first is Catholic and runs like this:

> In the name of God Amen xi Aug. 1549 I Thomas Molenix clearke, p'son of the moitye or one halffe of the p'ish of Wallasey doe leave my soule to God and our Ladye Seynt Marye and to the holie companye of heaven, and my bodie to be buried in the High Chancel of the Parish Church of Wallesey.

John Goodicar of Eastham expressed the Protestant beliefs which, by his time (1623), were more conventional: 'Firstly and chiefly I bequeath my soul into the hands of Almighty God trusting in the merits and mediation of Jesus Christ, my Saviour, etc. Secondly I leave my bodie to be buried in decent Christian burial in the Churchyard of Eastham.'

We can see how Goodicar eschewed reference to any mediator between man and God but Christ, while Molenix still clung to the Catholic belief in the intervention of the saints. The many more differences in doctrine and in ritual are too numerous to describe, but it is clear that, between the 16th and 18th centuries, Wirral was home to a small number of people who refused both to renounce Catholicism and to accept the doctrines and practices of the new Church of England. They were a constant headache to the authorities and, consequently, their names appear in contemporary records. Table 11 (p. 109) lists known 16th-century Wirral Recusants and shows how most of them either came from or worked for gentry families.

The government persecuted the Catholics because it wanted everybody to conform. It also feared that they might assist Catholic Spain to invade England. Several suspected Catholics, therefore, demonstrated their loyalty to the homeland. During the Spanish Armada crisis of 1588, Sir Rowland Stanley took enthusiastic charge of the Wirral militia and George Massey contributed £25 to the national defence. The two families remained Catholic throughout the next two centuries. Puddington Hall, the Masseys' home, witnessed several dramas caused by the recusancy of its owners. During the Civil War, Sir William Massey supported the King and took part in the defence of Chester. In his absence, Roundheads burned down part of his home and he was fined £1,414 for opposing Parliament. His son, Sir Edward Massey maintained his own priest, John Pleasington, who was implicated in the 1678 Popish Plot and executed in 1679. In 1715, the attempt to put James Francis Edward Stewart on the throne, known as the first Jacobite Rising, came to an ignominious end at the battle of Preston. Legend has it that the 60-year-old William, son of Sir Edward Massey, left the battlefield on horseback and galloped the 45 miles home to Puddington, riding through the Mersey between Speke and Hooton. His horse is supposed to have died as soon as it got home. Massey himself died, a prisoner in Chester Castle, the following year. Puddington Hall passed to a branch of the Stanleys of Hooton, who then changed their name to Massey-Stanley.

By the 18th century, the Hooton Stanleys were still Catholic. In 1778 Archdeacon Travis of Chester inquired into the state of religion in Eastham parish, which included Hooton. He asked the vicar about dissenters from the established church and was told that there were 49 'papists' and that 'the only persons of rank ... are Sir William Stanley ... and his sister. Few or none of the parishioners have been perverted to Popery during my incumbency which began in 1766.' He went on to describe how the Catholics were served by the Stanleys' domestic chaplain. The Papists did not have their own school and no 'Popish bishop' had performed any confirmations or even visited the district. It is clear that, by this time, Roman Catholics were few in number and posed absolutely no threat to the establishment. We gain the impression that they never actually had done: after all, they were members of the social elite and had nothing to gain from insurrection. It was only during times of civil war that they overtly took up arms for their faith and even then it was in support either of the King or someone they believed to be the rightful heir to the throne.

Records which describe the unexceptional people—those who were neither deviants nor were rich—are rare. In this regard, the records from the Consistory Court for the diocese of Chester are invaluable: amidst their routine descriptions of infringements of laws about local parish ritual and administration, there are glimpses into the lives of the common people of Wirral.

They contain evidence for the way in which the church attempted to control the people's morals. Numerous men and women were indicted for sexual liberality. In Wallasey in 1602, John Crisley, Ellen Hodgson, Henry Bird, Jane Smith, Alice Richardson, Richard Aynsdale and Elizabeth Sherlocke were all told to attend the court on suspicion of fornication. Only Henry Bird turned up, but the chancellor 'enjoined Aynsdale to do public penance for three Lords Days or Feast Days in the Church of Wallesie'. The penance involved standing, attired in white robes, at the front of the church throughout both Sunday services. In Woodchurch parish in 1605, Lawrence Pemberton and Alice Robinson were accused of adultery but had not done any penance. During 1606, Pemberton confessed and he and Alice were 'ordered to abstain therefrom' and to perform public penance in the churches at Heswall, Wallasey and Woodchurch by 25 June. In 1605, Hugh ap Jones of Shotwick was accused of 'keeping a howse of Bawdrie in suffering David Norris and Shayne ap Roberts to lye together in the howse sometymes for the space of a weeke together'. For the churchwardens who made this complaint, the suspicion of homosexuality was doubtless of more concern than the implication of sloth. No verdict was recorded.

Other people were in trouble for their irreverent or indifferent attitudes to state religion. In 1592 George Pemberton of Moreton was indicted for 'sitting uppon the Crosse at service and would not come in at the Churchwardens request'. Six years later, Arthur Keiric and Thomas Younge of Bidston were in trouble for 'bowlinge uppon the sabbath daie' but replied that they 'never dyd boule butt once and then nott att prayer'. In 1605 Robert Forshawe of Shotwicke was described as a 'common disturber of his

Table 11: Elizabethan Recusants in Wirral
(from K.R. Wark, *Elizabethan Recusancy in Cheshire*)

Name	Condition	Place	Dates
Elizabeth Andrew		Woodchurch	1582
Richard Cawley	Yeoman or Husbandman	Bebington	1582-5
Richard Cawley	Yeoman	Woodchurch	1582
Elena Cooke	Servant	Thurstaston	1601
Thomas Dowra	Yeoman	Neston	1600
Robert Foster	Miller	New House, West Kirby	1587-90
Elisabeth Glasier	Wife of William Glasier; Son Hugh was Catholic Mayor of Chester, 1603	Lea by Backford	16th century
William Glasier	Husband of above; Vice-Chamberlain of Chester, suspected of recusancy due to wife and children	Lea by Backford	16th century
Thomas Hesketh	Gentleman	Thurstaston	1593-1600
Elizabeth Hesketh	Wife of above	Thurstaston	1593-1604
Roger Higginson	Yeoman	Woodchurch	1582
John Hocknell	Gentleman	Prenton	1581-90
Margaret Hocknell (Later Ravenscroft)	Wife of above	Prenton	1591-8
Jane Hough	Wife of William Hough	Leighton and Thornton	1578
William Hough	Gentleman, Husband of above	Leighton and Thornton	1577-86
John Langton		Thurstaston	1598
George Litherland	Weaver	Woodchurch	1582
Joan Maddocks	Wife of Thomas Maddocks	Thurstaston	1576-92
Thomas Maddocks	Yeoman, Husband of above	Thurstaston	1571-92
Anne Mallam,	Widow	Grange, West Kirby	1587-1600
George Massey	Son of William Massey who died in 1579; J.P. in 1587; suspected Recusant only	Puddington	1587
Edward Stanley	Son of Sir Rowland Stanley, Priest and Jesuit	Hooton	In England from 1612
John Stanley	Brother of above, Priest	Hooton	
Lady Elizabeth Stanley	Wife of Sir William Stanley	Hooton	1587-1600
Jane Stanley	Daughter of above	Hooton	1592
Sir Rowland Stanley	Knight; Sheriff of Chester in 1576, Special Commissioner for Musters in 1579, J.P. at least until 1603; suspected of being a recusant only	Hooton	died 1612
Alice Whitmore	Wife of William Whitmore	Leighton	1581-1600
Christina, Eleanor and Jane Whitmore	Daughters of above	Thurstaston	1598-1605
Elen Whitmore	first Wife of John Whitmore	Thurstaston	1576-84
Jane Whitmore	second wife of John Whitmore	Thurstaston	1587-1600
John Whitmore	Gentleman	Thurstaston	1571-97
John Whitmore	Son of Above, Gentleman	Thurstaston	1599-1600

neigbors and a conteumer of the Minister in tyme of Catechizinge'. In the same year Anne 'fforbeck' of Woodchurch was found to have 'absented herself from the Church this half yeare at least and hath not been purified after childbirth'. The story of Richard Richardson, John Barrowe and John Tottie of Eastham in 1605 reminds us of the universal problem of trying to impose piety upon persons who are preoccupied with more mundane matters: the three men were caught arguing over their 'pewes' during the service so the chancellor 'enjoyned them to continue quiett and not disturbe the service and because ytt appeareth they were nott disturbers butt spake ii or three words the chancellor dismissed the case'.

Other people annoyed the authorities by retaining Catholic practices or by indulging in folk religion. Joan Goodicer of Woodchurch was in trouble in 1605 because she 'Useth bie reporte to praie on beads'. When she appeared in court, she said that she had 'bourned her beades and thereupon tooke her othe and hath promised not to use anie'. Margery Hare of Bidston seems to have been a local 'wise-woman' of the type which used to exist in rural areas right up until the 20th century. The record for 1598 says that she 'Doth use to blesse thinges ... and ytt is reported that shee is an honest poore woman ... that shee blesse noe more anie cattell'.

Women seem to have received particular attention for their supposedly anti-social behaviour. In 1605 Margaret, wife of John Dannatt was described as 'A common scold and disturber of the neighbors. She is ordered to do penance one Sundaie in Shotwick Church' and at Eastham in the same year Margaret Elcocke, Jane Mercer and Elizabethe Swifte were similarly accused and ordered 'to confesse their falte and certifie before Easter under the Churchwardens hands'.

When we remember that the churchwardens were all male and from the gentry or yeoman class, it seems evident that the role of the consistory court was to try to make the mass of the population conform to the norms of society's elite minority. This is an argument which has been well rehearsed in the historiography of recent times and arises from the reluctance to see religion as a social force in its own right. An alternative view would be to see the apparent conflict as one which subsisted between those who were serious about the Christian religion and who tried to implement its moral implications and those who were indifferent to it and were either happy to wander through life clinging to a quaint mix of superstition, folklore and half-understood Bible stories or without bothering even to think about anything spiritual all. It just so happens that, in Tudor and Stuart days, the position of what might be called the 'godly' group was stronger because it was also the official position of the state.

By the 18th century the division was still evident. But local records imply that, now that church attendance and public morality were no longer so rigidly enforced, a smaller proportion of the population actually went to church for anything other than a baptism, wedding or funeral and that the people were as 'immoral' (i.e. their behaviour did not conform to classic Christian expectations) as they had been 200 years previously. The most obvious evidence which corroborates this assertion appears in the form of the large number of illegitimate children whose baptisms are recorded in the parish registers. Between 1759 and 1812, 17 illegitimate children from Hoose, Great and Little Meols were baptised in West Kirby. Jane Guile had four children christened between 1774 and 1789 and on each occasion she was described as a 'single woman'. Every Wirral register contains its own version of the same story. People did not change their behaviour simply because the established church told them to. It was necessary for people to make their own decisions.

49 Poulton Hall, one of Wirral's many manor houses. It was the home of the Lancelyn and Lancelyn-Green families. Nathaniel Hawthorne visited it in 1853 and admired its innovatory methods of fertilising the gardens.

Each decision would only conform to Christian values if the individual believed in and was committed to the doctrines of the Bible. When exploring the life of people during this time, the power of individual faith must not be ignored. There could be many sources of this faith, but one of the most important was, of course, the teaching and witness of individual clergymen.

During the 17th century, the clergymen who tried hardest to spread the Protestant Christian message were called Puritans. They wanted to remove every last vestige of Catholicism from the Church of England and to encourage more people to find individual salvation. Samuel Clarke became vicar of Shotwick in 1624; his story reveals important details about the beliefs and practices of Wirral Puritans. He had been ejected from the parish of Thornton-le-Moors for refusing to wear a surplice or to use a cross during baptisms or rings at weddings. At Shotwick he became 'an instrument for converting many souls to God'. He arranged discussion and study groups in the homes of his parishioners. In his own words:

> I was never acquainted with more understanding Christians in all my life, though the best of them went in russet coats and followed husbandry. Hereby holy affections were kindled and kept alive. Mutual love was promoted; so that all the professors of the gospel living ten or twelve miles asunder were as intimate as if they had been of one household. The necessities of the poor being known and provided for. The weak were strengthened, the mourning comforted, the erring reclaimed, the dejected raised, and all mutually edified in their holy faith. Moreover they hereby enjoyed opportunities for private fasts and days of thanksgiving as there was occasion.

As a result of his faith and enthusiasm, Clarke developed a local following. This was true for several other Wirral Puritan ministers. Henry Tottie became a curate at Thurstaston in 1597. Upon the retirement of the incumbent, Thomas Sharpe (a Neston man and probable relative of the last prior of Birkenhead), in 1601, he became vicar. Twenty-nine of his parishioners and followers from neighbouring parishes had submitted a petition recommending him for the post in which they said that in their 'opynions' he was 'sound in religion and in profession zealous' and had 'discharged his dutie therein diligentlie and carefullie by often preachinge the worde unto us to our good lykeinges and to his owne comendacion and credicte'. Some of the signatories were members of local gentry families: William Glegge Esquire of Caldey Grange, Thomas second son of Arthur Glegge Esquire of Gayton and Christopher Bennett Gentleman of Greasby.

Tottie died within a year and was succeeded by Hugh Burches, who was not warmly received by Tottie's former flock. The ensuing story is truly representative of the religious conflict which occurred throughout England during the following half century. Burches was not a local man; he came from a privileged background and was a pluralist, meaning that he was nominal incumbent for several parishes at the same time and lived in a substantial house in Chester some twelve miles away. He must rarely have taught or visited his flock and seems to have been fonder of literature and of book collecting than of ministering. In his will of 1614, he hints at the opposition which he had received from the disgruntled parishioners:

> ... I have lived an unfayned protestant and faithfull maintayner of the faith and forme of servinge that this church of England doth hold, soe to ende I continue a sincere worshipper of the God of my Fathers and die within the unity of the church, nothing altering my profession nor doubtinge of a glorious resurrection of my bodie to life everlastinge. My wants in the discharge of my dutie and especially that I did not with more zeale beate down the subtill proceedinges of the novelists, [Puritans] seekinge or privily labouringe an overthrow of the reverend church, and although some pretende an upright intente and carriage, I proteste that by my continuall molestation they are better known to mee for ... [a] Preumptuous and spitefull crue of schismatics ...

Burches articulated the big question of the day: were people going to continue to support a state church with its official semi-Catholic rituals and numerous apparently 'ungodly' clergymen or was it to be further reformed by the simplification of its rituals, the dismissal of bishops and the appointment of 'zealous' pastors? Those, in Burches' words, with the apparent 'upright intent and carriage' were probably the gentry who were just as important in the sponsorship of Puritanism as were other members of the same class for the patronage of Catholicism. Puritan families formed alliances by means of strategic marriage. Richard Adams was parson of Woodchurch between 1588 and 1615; he also was supported by a branch of the Bennett family and was married to a member of one of Cheshire's leading Puritan families, the Bruens of Tarvin.

Religion was the main cause of the English Civil War. Broadly, the Puritans supported Parliament. Catholics and Anglicans supported the King. Many people wanted to be left alone and supported neither. The siege of Chester occurred between November 1644 and February 1646. Parliamentarian troops occupied Puddington and the ferry house in Birkenhead. Some men must have gone away to fight, but there were no battles in Wirral. From 1649 the life of the local churches was thrown into ferment by Parliamentiary rule, but both the Church of England and the monarch were restored in 1660.

After the restoration, many people with Puritanical inclinations became non-conformists. By 1672, Edward Litherland was holding religious meetings in his Wallasey home. The 1689 Act of Toleration permitted Nonconformists to have their own places of worship; a chapel was opened in Bromborough and another in Upton. Thomas Lea became the minister at Upton in 1690. He was supported by members of the Glegg, Hardware,

50 A very interesting view of one of Wirral's most famous and attractive manor houses, Bidston Hall, painted by Edward Goodall in 1816.

Ball, Day Urmston, Pemberton and Wilson families. Indeed, the will of Robert Wilson of Bidston Hall of 1697 instructs his sons to pay £5 yearly to Thomas Lea 'if he continue to preach to that people to which he now stands related'. By 1715 the two chapels had about 180 members, but after the death of their last minister, Thomas Woodcock, in 1728, they seem to have closed down and Nonconformity became virtually unknown in Wirral until an Independent Chapel was opened in Parkgate in 1809.

Throughout the 18th and 19th centuries, the character of local religion was largely dictated by the personalities of the clergymen. Honoratus Lebeg was vicar of Eastham between 1728 and 1766. His ancestors were probably European Protestant refugees, but he is chiefly remembered for his eccentricity. Over a hundred years after his death, people still had their favourite vicar stories. He punished the congregation for not paying their tithes by not filling in the parish register for 20 years. One day, he was strolling along the shore having forgotten about a couple who were waiting to be married in church. Upon his return, he was told that they were going to leave because the vicar was too late. 'Too late!' he replied, 'Not a bit of it; why I have not had my dinner yet and it is never afternoon in Eastham until the Vicar has dined'; and then he married them. At another time, a batch of local gentry had been made into J.P.'s. One of them saw Honoratus trudging along a lane near Poole Hall, asked him why he always walked and suggested that, if he could not afford a horse, he should have bought an ass. The vicar replied, 'I have been wishing to do so, but the fact is that all the asses in these parts have lately been turned into Justices of the Peace, so that I am so far unable to realise my wish.'

It is hoped that the reader now has a better appreciation of the importance of religion in the lives of people in early modern Wirral and that this understanding will underpin the analysis of life, work and the economy which appears in the next two sections of this chapter.

51 Greasby Old Hall was the home of a branch of the Bennett family.

Part Four: 'The World we Have Lost'—Land and People

When we study the social history of early modern Wirral we enter the last days of pre-industrial and pre-urban England. It was a time when the the fastest form of land transport was a galloping horse; the largest gatherings of people (apart from battles) occurred in the parish churches, which were in turn the largest buildings which most people ever saw. Most homes were single-storey thatched cottages, which seemed to be growing out of the soil upon which they stood. All food was grown either at home or at least in the neighbourhood and nearly everybody worked on the land. Medical care was rudimentary, expensive and rare and disease and poverty common. Life was hard, but, even though they were unaware of it, people had riches which we have lost and which many of us long to rediscover—pure air, open space, a flourishing natural world, organic local produce and an unhurried routine.

It was a time when everybody had his or her place. The nobility and gentry were at the top; then came the prosperous famers—the yeomen and husbandmen; beneath them were the labourers; the poor and the destitute lay at the bottom. Hierarchy was enforced at every gathering, especially in church. In 1634, upon the orders of Chester consistory court, a seating plan was devised for Wallasey church. The chancel was 'inclosed' and the local gentry, Litherland and Gill, instructed to pay for 'decent seats' for themselves and their 'husbands and wives'. Below them, seats were provided for Thomas Meoles Esquire and then for the servants of the three families. The rest of the population were allocated seating areas according to their relative status. The churchwardens were also told to accommodate a range of people who had not yet been listed: freeholders came first; 'amongst tennantes of the same valuation they bee p'ferred whoe have more worthier landlordes'; 'auntient Cottagers' were similarly positioned. Penalties were to be imposed for breaches of 'decencie and order and p'suminge to sitt above their betters'.

Every class of person had one thing in common—dependency on the land. Most of the people who left wills called themselves either yeomen or husbandmen or both. There were also people who called themselves widows, gentlemen, mariners, fishermen, weavers and clergymen, but virtually every will from 17th-century Wirral contains evidence of farming. Robert Fletcher, husbandman of Burton, died in 1634; his will is typical; it mentions 260 measures of barley, wheat and rye, 'green pease', 'gray pease', 'peas, beans and vetches, nine bushells of oats, four oxen, 14 cows, seven pigs and four lambs'. John Goodicar died in 1623 and called himself 'Clarke' of Eastham. He left 'one cowe, two sheep and two lambs', 'geese and poultry' and 'corn and hay'. John Eaton was 'Clerk of Bidston' and died in 1696. He had a similar range of agricultural produce and equipment: 'beasts young and old', 'corn and hay', 'Two swine' and 'a cheese press'.

Farms in modern Wirral concentrate mainly upon dairying. Before 1700 it is clear that they both grew crops and raised animals. Indeed, it has been calculated that Wirral grew 20 per cent of Cheshire's barley, 40 per cent of its corn, 33 per cent of its wheat and a small amount of oats.[7] The subject requires further research, but it seems that dairy farming began to be more important during the 18th century, when wills contain more references to cheese. Simon Croft of Hoose died in 1752. A list of receipts from the sale of his goods includes £5 5s. for some cheese. This was a substantial sum of money, equivalent to a year's wages for a farm labourer. Simon's inventory was the first one in the Hoylake area to mention potatoes: they fetched a price of £1 12s. 6d. By the 19th century, the district was famous for the quality of this particular crop.

Most of the agricultural tools and methods of the 17th century would have been quite familiar to the people of the Middle Ages, but, as was described in the previous chapter, the way in which the land itself was divided up was changing: by the 16th century, many open fields and strips had already been enclosed, but others were still in use during the 18th century. For example, Burton's manor court records contain an instruction to one Margaret Williams to 'ditch her ditch' between her 'Fidlestone' and Samuel Meoals' 'Fidlestone'. In other words, she was being reminded to keep her portion of the open field in order. By the 19th century, virtually all remnants of the open field system had been removed.

The wills contain evidence of the second most important economic activity of the district: the production of yarn for textiles. Flax for making linen and hemp for turning into coarse cloth, sacking and rope were grown throughout Wirral. The stems of these plants are fibrous and can be beaten, cleaned and spun into threads. The majority of wills and inventories mention spinning wheels. They were operated by the female members of the family.Yarn was sold to specialist weavers.

Other local resources included gorse, which was grown for hedging and harvested as horse fodder and as a domestic fuel, and turf, which also acted as fuel. The harvesting of these commodities was usually controlled by local manor courts and communal agreements. In some places, bracken was collected and turned into potash by being burned. Some wills refer to piles of wood found lying in the testators' yards. In the coastal districts these could have been the remains of wrecked vessels. We are reminded of the importance of wood for building and for repair and of the fact that timber was, by this time, quite rare in Wirral.

Many wills allude to the greatest social evil of the day—the inequitable distribution of wealth and the dependence of far too many people upon the charity of the better-off. Wallasey parish produced typical examples of yeomen with a social conscience: in 1646, Thomas Gleave bequeathed the annual rent of £2 16s. 0d. on one of his pieces of land to be used for buying bread for the local poor; John Hill's will of 1795 ordered the investment of £100 of his estate and the use of the interest to feed the poor people who attended

52 Saughall Massie village: still a rural scene in the early 20th century.

church on Sundays; John Hough's will of 1797 invested £6 and the interest was to be used for buying bread for the poor.

Cow charities were another way of providing for the poor. The one in Woodchurch was established, originally as a bullock charity (they were for pulling the ploughs of those who could not afford their own beasts) by James Goodyker of Barnston in 1525. By 1670, the charity had been augmented by two bequests of £50 each from Thomas Gleave of London and the Reverend Richard Sherlock, formerly of Oxton and then of Winwick. The cows were hired by poor people for 2s. 8d. per year so that they could use the milk. William Hulme set up a cow charity in Bebington in 1620 which was similarly augmented by subsequent bequests, including another one of £50 from the generous Thomas Gleave.

Such spontaneous acts of benevolence are sure to have played an essential role in saving a great many people from premature death, but, in addition, central government required local parishes to carry out poor relief. The Poor Law Acts of 1601 and 1662 created the poor law which operated in England until the 19th century. Burton's records show how the system was working in the 18th century. They speak of a pauper called Robert Basnett. Between 1751 and 1752, the overseers of the poor paid his 5s. rent, spent 22s. on 'clothes and trimmings' and 1s. 10d. for corn for him and his wife. Between 1755 and 1756 they bought him 7s. worth of coal. By the following year it is clear that he was totally dependent upon poor relief. The unfortunate fellow was typical of so many Wirral people at that time.

Richard Hough was a landowner and churchwarden in Wallasey during the middle of the 18th century. He kept a journal which, nearly 200 years later, passed through the hands of the town's two great historians, E.C. Woods and P.C. Brown, before being lodged in the Picton Library, Liverpool, where it was destroyed during a German air-raid. Fortunately, Mr Woods had transcribed sections of this invaluable source. A large portion of the transcripts refer to a man called 'Rough Dick'. His proper name was Richard Perry; he was a pauper. Hough's terse diary entries hint at a relationship with Rough Dick which was a bit more than merely perfunctory. Rough Dick was clearly totally dependent upon parish relief in exactly the same way as was Robert Basnett in Burton, but there is touch of warmth in such comments as:

1755 Jan. 19 Dick at Deane's came to Liscard.
Feb 20 21 One shilling paid for to diet himself.
Thos. Wilson tabled Dick at Deanes for me.
June 14 John Hough (paid) ... Thos. Wilson for tabling Rough Dick
2 dayes 1s
Nov. 10 Pd. To Samuel Cotton 1s 8d on Rough Dick's Account.

1757 Jany. 3 The Township agreed with Wm. Evans for Richd. Perry's meat, drink, washing, and lodging at £7 10s 0d per year.
July 1 Pd. To Geo. Mulls & Wm. Evans upon Bellisses' a/c for buying Rough Dick some cloaths.[8]

53 An old lane in Woodchurch, another rural scene.

Rough Dick would appear to have belonged to that perennial and ubiquitous category of homeless person whom we might call the 'local character'—a man who is pitied, but also liked, sometimes respected and even revered as a kind of wise man (known in India as a *Sadhu*), the subject of local gossip and folklore and whose predicament seems sometimes to prick the conscience of the conventional citizen and remind him that 'the son of man had nowhere to lay his head'.

Hough employed servants. If they had not been accommodated by their master, they would have been paupers themselves. A maid was paid 30 shillings per year. These entries show that she often relied upon advances:

> 1756   Feb. 28. Lent Jane Jones 6s 6d towards buying stays and is for
> mending her shoes, which is her first quarter's wages.
> Apl. 23. Pd. To Thos. Bellison for Jane Jones for one pair of shoes
> and soaling and heel tapping.
> Aug. 6. Lent Jane Jones 4d for mending her shoes.
> Aug. 21 Lent Jane Jones 1s 9d for weaving her gown.[9]

Further details about 18th-century life are contained in some farm account books which came into the hands of Canon Abraham Hume during the 19th century.[10] They were compiled by members of the Wharton family who cultivated lands in Upton, Moreton and Bidston. Again we see the humble maid being given loans to pay for her clothing:

> 1784   Agreed with Ann Peers for £300 for Dying your stockings   3d
> for to bye some Binding for your coat   6d
> For to pay for a pair of Buckels   10d
> Etc...

Other entries give details about local customs and leisure activities. The employees looked forward to Upton Fair which was held on the last Friday in April and before Michaelmas. There are numerous references to payments to the workers so that they could attend; Thomas Ellobe was given five shillings for that purpose in 1761 and Ann Peers one shilling in 1784. Ellobe enjoyed dancing. He was paid five shillings for 'the dancing master', one shilling for 'the dancing' and five shillings for 'a pair of pumps'. Seasonal customs included 'cake plays' when the poorer people were able to glean the remainder of the harvest and make cakes out of the resulting flour, which they then sold. 'Gutut' or Shrove Tuesday was celebrated with feasting; 'rushbearing' was carried out during July and August and the 'neck-cutting' or harvest home was celebrated later in the year. The people enjoyed cock-fighting and bull-baiting. Horse and foot races were popular sports. The main team game was called the 'Prison Bar Play' and required the representatives of two townships to form two rings, one inside the other, which then revolved in opposite directions. Opponents would then 'tick' each other and race off. The winners received a half-barrel of ale and everybody shared a meal of roasted sheep and potatoes.

Some general observations made in 1762 by a gentleman who signed himself 'Benevolus' provide us with a little more detail about the local people of the time. He said that Bromborough folk were 'a hardy race' who lived upon 'the coarsest fare, as the inhabitants of these parts chiefly do'. In Eastham he noted that the people

54 A cottage on Sidney Road in Tranmere in 1866. This is one of the many local scenes painted by the Liverpool artist W.G. Herdman. It captures a moment in the history of Wirral when the landscape was changing: a traditional rural cottage stands next to the Mersey, a river whose commercial trade was causing the area to become increasingly urban.

were 'robust' and that the 'poorer sort' lived chiefly off barley-bread, potatoes and butter-milk. He further recorded a peculiarity of local speech which has long since disappeared; everybody seemed to replace their *q*'s with *w*'s, causing them to say *quick* as though it was spelled *wick*. Words which ended in *ll* were pronounced as though they were spelt with *au*.

All the sources point to some conclusions: in 18th-century Wirral, farming was the most important activity; landowners and prosperous tenant farmers lived the most comfortable lives and employed and housed the majority of the rest of the population as servants or labourers. The 'lower classes' received little pay, but were protected from destitution by living as part of their masters' extended families. Some people became incapable of supporting themselves and were either helped by a series of informal local charities or supported by parish poor relief. Food was coarse, simple but usually adequate. A number of local diversions in the form of fairs, games and sports helped to alleviate the drudgery of an agricultural routine in a quiet and unremarkable district of northern England which had developed both a unique accent and a distinctive culture.

Part Five 'Wizard Stream'—Shipping on the Dee Estuary

After farming, the second most important occupation in early modern Wirral was seafaring. Between 1600 and 1800, 280 wills were made out by Wirral people who called themselves mariners. Most of them lived close to the Dee estuary (see Table 12). The Dee was Chester's river, but, even though it had enabled the city firstly to come into being and then to flourish as a port, it was becoming increasingly unreliable as a shipping route.

The Dee estuary has a shape which makes it silt up very easily. Its mouth, between Red Rocks and Point of Ayr, is five miles wide. At ebb tide, therefore, the water flows slowly out into the Irish Sea. During the 1950s it was observed that, at the spring tides at Hilbre Island, the ebb tide lasted three hours longer and was, therefore, much weaker than the flood tide. Consequently, flood tides tended to bring in the silt from the Liverpool Bay, but the ebb tides were not powerful enough to flush it out again. These conditions are the exact reverse of those which pertain in the Mersey estuary, where a huge volume of water is squeezed through a narrow channel and constantly flushes out the silt, keeping the channel deep. Man's intervention has not helped the situation: during the 11th century, the earls of Chester built the Dee Mills which inhibited the river's flow; in 1732 the New Cut was dug between Chester and Wepre Gutter on the Welsh side of the river; this forced the Dee to flow towards Pentre Rock, where it was deflected towards Parkgate, creating a navigable channel but encouraging further siltation and salt marsh development upstream or behind the main flow, beween Neston and Blacon. In 1819 the New Cut's embankment was extended further along the Welsh coast to Mostyn Deep. This took all the rapidly flowing water completely away from the Wirral shore. Sealand was created in 1840 when five miles of the upper part of the estuary were reclaimed. In 1875, the area was 'inned' when a new embankment was built between Shotton and Connah's Quay. All this new land was consolidated when John Summers' Iron Works and the Neston to Hawarden Railway were built in 1898.[11]

Even during the Middle Ages, the merchants of Chester viewed the Dee estuary almost as their property; when records mention the landing of goods at Chester they could be referring to anywhere between the city itself and the Hoyle Lake. Indeed, by the 16th

Table 12: Wirral Mariners who had Wills Proved at Chester 1600-1800

Deeside		Merseyside	
Place	Number of mariners	Place	Number of mariners
Neston	69	Wallasey	9
Parkgate	44	Eastham	5
West Kirby	17		4
Heswall	16	Liscard	7
Caldy	15	Tranmere	1
Great Meols, Leighton	10	Arrowe, Birkenhead, Brimstage, Bromborough, Caughall, Claughton, Moreton, Oxton, Poulton Lancelyn, Poulton cum Seacombe, Saughall Massie, 'Sutton'	
Burton	9		
Little Neston	8		
Little Meols, Thurstaston	6		
Grange, Ness, Shotwick	4		
Barnston, Raby, Willaston	3		
Irby, 'Thornton', Hoose/Hoylake,	2		
Denhall, Frankby, Greasby, Ness, Puddington	1		
Total Number of Mariners on Deeside	242	**Total Number of Mariners on Merseyside**	38

55 A view of the banks of the Dee estuary and colliery buildings at Neston, painted by Arthur Suker in about 1875.

century, the latter area was in constant use; we find references to mariners living in West Kirby and to vessels being registered at West Kirby and Hilbre. The Hilbre boats are interesting: it seems unlikely that their owners lived on the island because it was too small to accommodate them all, but it must have been surrounded by channels which were filled with enough water to keep vessels afloat and which were protected from the south-westerly gales by the island itself. Even today a reasonable channel is visible on Hilbre's eastern side (i.e. the side which faces Red Rocks and Hoylake) which sometimes accommodates pleasure craft. This is effectively an extension of the old Hoyle Lake and is probably the successor of the ancient haven or sea road which in 1544 acted as an anchorage for the following vessels:

Vessel	Master
Nottocke	Richard Lyttill
Michaelle	Thomas Lyttill
?	Robert Radcliffe (of Greasby)
Peter	Richard Sheppard
Christopher	John Wright

The following vessels might have used the same haven or anchorages closer to shore:

	Vessel	Master
West Kirby:	*Trinitie*	Peter Warrington
	Rose	Thomas Wright
	Pride	John Coventrye
Caldy:	*Goodlocke*	Thomas Hogg

Their cargoes were various combinations of herrings, sheepskins, wool and corn and their displacements were recorded as between five and 16 tons. Records from 1571 make further mention of some of the above, but also list vessels from 'Much Meols', Heswall and Neston.

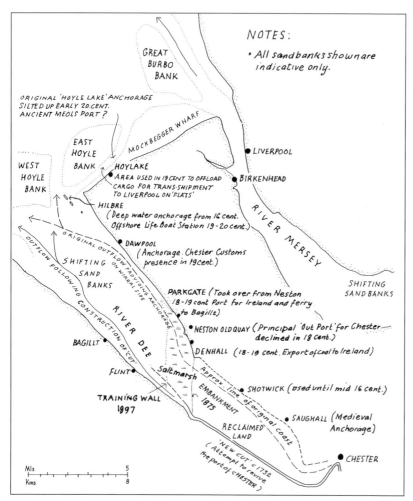

NOTES:
- All sandbanks shown are indicative only.

GREAT BURBO BANK

ORIGINAL 'HOYLE LAKE' ANCHORAGE SILTED UP EARLY 20. CENT. ANCIENT MEOLS PORT?

MOCKBEGGER WHARF

EAST HOYLE BANK

WEST HOYLE BANK

LIVERPOOL

HOYLAKE
AREA USED IN 19 CENT TO OFFLOAD CARGO FOR TRANS-SHIPMENT TO LIVERPOOL ON 'FLATS'

BIRKENHEAD

HILBRE
(Deep water anchorage from 16 cent. Offshore Life Boat Station 19-20 cent.)

RIVER MERSEY

OUTFLOW FOLLOWING CONSTRUCTION OF CUT

ORIGINAL OUTFLOW PROVIDING ANCHORAGE ON WIRRAL SIDE

SHIFTING SAND BANKS

DAWPOOL
(Anchorage. Chester Customs presence in 19 cent.)

SHIFTING SAND BANKS

PARKGATE (Took over from Neston 18-19 cent. Port for Ireland and ferry to Bagillt)

NESTON OLD QUAY (Principal 'Out Port' for Chester declined in 18 cent.)

RIVER DEE

BAGILLT

DENHALL (18-19 cent. Export of coal to Ireland)

FLINT

Saltmarsh

Approx line of original coast

SHOTWICK (used until mid 16 cent.)

EMBANKMENT 1875

TRAINING WALL 1897

RECLAIMED LAND

SAUGHALL (Medieval Anchorage)

'NEW CUT' c.1732 (Attempt to revive the Port of CHESTER)

CHESTER

Mls 5
Kms 8

56   The Dee estuary.

The Radcliffe family appear in both lists. In 1566 Robert Radcliffe of Greasby owned a 'barke' called the *Sunday* which was used to transport some of the Earl of Sussex's troops to Ireland. Robert was typical of all the mariners of the period in that he combined seafaring with farming. His will of 1569 listed his lands in West Kirby parish and mentions that he held the lease of Grange Mill.

There has been a tendency to imagine that the effective port of Chester migrated at a steady rate along the Wirral shore, starting at Shotwick and finishing up in the Hoyle Lake. The fact that shipping was using anchorages at the northern end of the estuary at the same time as it was using more southerly locations, such as Heswall and Neston, shows that the idea is a myth. The truth is that there was a number of different ports and anchorages situated along the shore of Wirral. In deciding which one to use, ships' masters and merchants had to consider variables such as wind speeds and directions, the draft of their vessels, the availability of accommodation on shore and the ease with which they could transport goods to Chester. Furthermore, sandbanks were always shifting; a haven that was useful one day was liable to become dangerous the next.

Evidence indicates that, throughout the early modern period, to varying degrees, all Wirral's Dee ports were in use. The Hoyle Lake was used in the salt and cattle trades and was an embarkation point for the armies of William III in 1689 and 1690; John Wesley landed there in 1773 on his return from Ireland. Dawpool, between Thurstaston and Caldy, was formerly known as Redbank and had been in constant use between 1353 and 1492. Dean Swift, the Irish man of letters, landed there in November 1707; he sailed from Dawpool on his return journey in June 1709. The haven was also used in the cheese and lead trades. Denhall, which straddles the boundary between Ness and Burton, was still in use at the same time. Even Great Saughall was used as late as 1808, when a 'storm-blown' ship anchored there. The decision to build Neston's stone jetty—the New Key—was

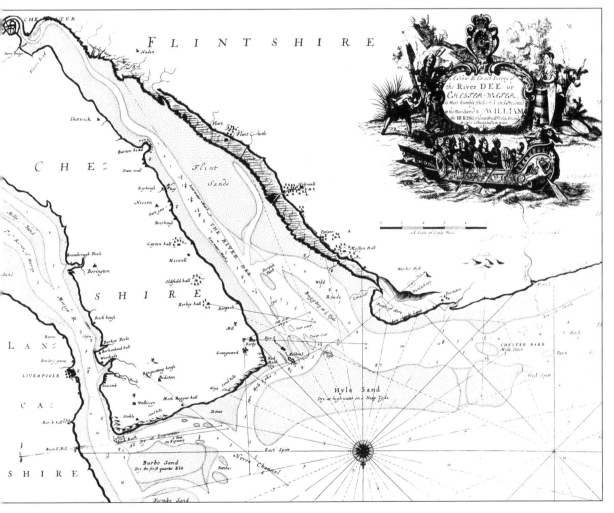

57 The River Dee drawn by Captain Grenville Collins in 1689, an important source for understanding developments in Wirral's coast. Notice denotion of anchorages by small anchor symbols and their distribution between the Hyle (Hoyle) Lake, Hilbre, Dawpool, Parkgate, Neston and Burton. Features on the shore of the Mersey are also well represented, notably Wallasey Pool and Birkenhead's own little peninsula.

58 Haven in the Lee of Hilbre, taken from the eastern side of Hilbre. Middle Eye is visible on the right and Caldy Hill on the mainland in the distance. The sea here is protected from the south-westerly winds by Hilbre itself and is relatively calm. It was probably the haven in which the merchant ships lay at anchor during the 16th century.

made in 1541; it straddles the boundary between Great and Little Neston and is ten miles down river from Chester. It had an inadequate road link with Chester and no money was spent on it after 1604. It was used until the 1690s, after which time it became known as the 'Old Key'. Clearly, however, it was the Neston water front, which included Parkgate, which was the main focus of Wirral's nautical activity: Table 12 shows that this is where most mariners lived.

The name Parkgate was first recorded in 1610 and referred to the coastal section of the township of Leighton, which had been turned into a deer park in about 1260. There are no records of anybody living there until the 1680s, but, during the following century, it became a significant port for sailings to Ireland. The original anchorage was called Beer House Hole and lay offshore from the modern public house called *The Boat House* at the bottom of Boathouse Lane. Naturally, as more passengers used the town, so more buildings were erected both for their accommodation and their entertainment. All kinds of travellers, including the Lord Lieutenant of Ireland, John Wesley, G.F. Handel and a multitude of ordinary English and Irish people passed through the town. It also thrived as a sea-bathing resort. By 1815, the Dee no longer flowed along the shore of Wirral and soon there was insufficient depth of water for either ships or swimmers. Parkgate then functioned as an inshore fishing village and, following the arrival of the railway in 1866, started to become a dormitory town for Liverpool. In 1973, Cheshire County Council recognised the town's unique heritage and designated it a Conservation Area.[12]

Unlike other regions of England, by 1800 the landscape of Wirral had not been affected by the development of industry or the growth of towns. The population earned its living mainly from the land and at sea. Most residents viewed Chester as their most important regional centre and the Dee as their main nautical highway, but all of this was about to change. Wirral's population was about to explode and some tiny clusters of buildings on the banks of the Mersey were about to become three of the most dynamic and diverse economic centres in the north of England: Ellesmere Port, Birkenhead and Wallasey.

Six

1800-1914

Part One: From Ormerod to Young—Changes in the Wirral Landscape

In 1819 *The History of the County Palatine and City of Chester* was published in three volumes. It was and is a seminal and monumental work of local history and genealogy. Its author was George Ormerod, who was 34 years of age by the time he completed it. He had begun it in 1813, two years after moving into Chorlton Hall in the parish of Backford. The work has been treated as the reliable starting point for most histories and descriptions of Cheshire, justifiably so: it contains a dizzyingly vast amount of information about the county, much of it in the form of transcriptions of ancient documents, which most people would find too difficult to obtain and read for themselves. Whilst he was engaged in the work, he was a Wirral resident and his account of the Hundred can be found in Volume Two, where he presents us with much primary historical information which still has vast potential for exploitation by family and local historians. For the purposes of this chapter, however, we will study Ormerod's observations of Wirral primarily as those of a contemporary resident and visitor rather than those of an antiquary. Let us see what he had to say about the area in order to try to build a mental image of Wirral as it must have been at the beginning of the 19th century. In doing so, we will have to consider what kind of a man Ormerod was: what were his beliefs, prejudices and aims and what does an understanding of these reveal about the nature of the scenes he described? This exercise will help us to understand how concepts of Wirral as a place evolved and encourage objective assessment of the relationship between the people and the landscape at that time.

Wirral was one of Ormerod's least favourite places; his unflattering assessment of the district has often been quoted:

> The general appearance of the Hundred is a bare uninteresting flat; but exceptions may be found in the valley which separates Wirral from Broxton, and in a beautiful, and sequestered dingle below Poulton Lancelyn. Many noble sea-views occur, particularly those from Bebington, Burton, and Bromborough ... The communications by road are excellent, as far as respects the turnpike roads, which are all reduced under one act. The others, where no spirited proprietor has exerted himself, are proportionably bad, and indeed must necessarily be so, from the manner in which the farm-houses are grouped in villages, and the cattle driven along the lanes, which are rarely composed of any material but natural clay. No higher praise can be given to the hovels, or the appearance of the lower orders, which are in general extremely squalid. This class of the population from its contiguity to the Principality, is mostly Welsh, or of immediate Welsh origin; and the patronymics of that country have nearly superseded the Cheshire names.

The great man is introducing us to some of his likes and dislikes. We can see that he did not like flat or treeless landscapes; he preferred to see either undulating, wooded scenery or a landscape which spoke of good human management and displayed the fruits of a functioning social hierarchy. Ormerod was a man of his times and of his class. He believed that the great land-owning families had a responsibility to manage the countryside for the benefit of both the landscape and the people. He disapproved of landlords who did not reside on their estates (absentees) and neglected their duties. He admired the great dynasties who, for generations, had maintained the peace, order and prosperity of their properties. He believed in the old idea of aristocracy: 'rule by the best'. Indeed, he had pretensions to aristocracy himself: he was fascinated by genealogy and, during the period 1806 to 1808, began work on his own family tree, pursuing noble and royal connections and coats of arms. He received allowance for his coat of arms in 1814. Ormerod was not an aristocrat, but a gentleman, who had no need to work in trade or business, as he was in receipt of funds and inheritances from his own and his wife's families. He had enjoyed a traditional, classical education at The King's School in Chester, from private tutors and at Brasenose College, Oxford. He was a loyal member of the Church of England and regular attender at Backford parish church, where he kept a private pew. His daughter Eleanor recorded a memorable event in 1815: 'My father, when living near Chester (Chorlton Hall), had the first news on a Sunday morning before church time, of the Duke of Wellington's success, and that the Battle of Waterloo had been fought and won. After service he mounted on a tombstone and announced the glorious news to the assembled congregation.'[1]

Here was a man who was largely uninterested in the lives of those whom he called the 'lower orders'. George Ormerod was a man of great intellect and of keen powers of observation and description; but these talents were underemployed when it came to considering the majority of the population. He did, however, in the introduction to his great work, demonstrate an almost poetic ability to capture the atmosphere of country life. The following example is relevant to Wirral, for we know that marling (extracting marl from the subsoil for use as a fertiliser) was an important local activity, which has left its mark on the countryside:

> The ceremonies of the Marlers are probably peculiar to Cheshire. In the Western Hundreds they elect a lord of the pit, demand money from the neighbouring landowners whom they see passing near the pit, and proclaim their acquisitions daily, and at the end of the week; previous to which proclamation, and subsequent to it, they form a ring joining their hands and inclining their heads to the centre, shouting repeatedly, and finishing with a lengthened cadence. The words vary between the shouts, but are generally to this effect 'Oyez, Oyez Oyez! Mr. _____ of _____ has been with us today, and given my lord and his men part of a hundred pounds'; but if the donation is more than 6d, it is part of a thousand pounds. The same ceremony is repeated at the village alehouse, where they spend their acquisitions on Saturday, and the sound of the prolonged shout, as it dies gradually away, may be heard for miles in a still summer's evening.

Thanks to Ormerod's brief excursion into social observation, that 'prolonged shout' echoes even now in our ears, as strongly as the reddening western sky of those still summer evenings lingers in the eyes of our imagination. How we wish he had described more such scenes, which were, to him, so commonplace and banal, but are to us are so evocative and haunting. He demonstrated a similar poetic ability, almost in spite of himself, when he described Oxton:

> ... is mean and small, composed of wretched, straggling huts, amongst roads only not impassable. The township occupies an eminence which commands a full view of the buildings and shipping of Liverpool, exhibiting a picture resembling metropolitan bustle and splendour, almost immediately below the eye; but no degree of civilisation or improvement has reached this part of the opposite shore, which is a scene of solitude, broken in upon only with the voice of the cowherd, or cry of the plover. Bleak and barren moors stretch round it in every direction, and exhibit an unmixed scene of poverty and desolation.

The description freezes a moment in time—a critical point in the history of England, particularly in the north west and especially on Merseyside. The great maritime city of Liverpool could be seen across the Mersey. Its buildings must have seemed awesome to the farming people of Wirral, the greatest edifices that any of them were ever going to see. The water front was growing: churches, factories, workshops, the Customs House, the Town Hall and six man-made docks earned Liverpool the sobriquet 'The Venice of the North'. It handled over 5,000 ships each year. Some travellers said that it was more impressive and more promising than London. But, back here in Wirral's hinterland, the people still lived on a bleak and barren landscape, in poor and 'dirty' houses. The prosperity and urbanisation, which are attendant upon commercial growth, had not penetrated the remoteness of the peninsula. But, as Liverpool spilled over the river and engulfed Wirral's acres, all of this was soon to change. Ormerod did not speculate upon such matters. He had made it clear, in other parts of his work, that he did not consider it part of his role to comment on commercial and industrial development. The commercial activity of the great port was merely viewed like a point of interest in a great landscape painting. Apparently, he was equally uninterested in the concerns of ordinary rural folk: how we wish Ormerod had written one more line about that cowherd; what did he actually call to his cows and in what dialect? How many cows did he own? What was his name? What was he wearing? What did he eat that evening upon his return to his humble home?

That 'cry of the plover' stirs a deeply-seated fragment of memory in our souls: we have heard it before, probably in some of the few remaining rural portions of Wirral or in other parts of the country to which we have travelled in pursuit of solace and peace in an ugly world. We realise that such qualities were universally available to Ormerod and his contemporaries, so much so that they found them personally disturbing and repellent. To them, an untamed, empty landscape felt like a threat; it reminded them of mankind's frailty. To us, who have not only tamed, but virtually annihilated nature, that landscape and that world seem deeply desirable, unutterably beautiful and, saddest of all, totally unobtainable: we have made our choice and traded the clay for the concrete and the moors for the metropolis.

Ormerod travelled around Wirral, on horseback, in an anti-clockwise direction, during the summer months whilst he was resident at Chorlton Hall, visiting every settlement at least once. In addition to Oxton, Lower Bebington's dismal scenery was improved by views of Liverpool: '... the port and shipping of which, joined to the view of the estuary, the Lancashire shore, and the Eddisbury Hills, give a character to the prospect which amply atones for the insipidity of the foreground'.

Upton was similarly redeemed: 'The town stands on a knoll, about a mile from Woodchurch, in which parish the buildings are partly situated. The surrounding country is bare and desolate, but the prospect is enlivened by a view of the Irish Sea, and the numerous sails passing and repassing the port of Liverpool.'

Several other townships were deemed to be as unattractive as Oxton. This is how he described ...

Stoke: The village is a collection of ragged and filthy hovels, scattered round the church without the least attention to arrangement, on a small elevation adjacent to the marshes through which the Gowy (flows) ... Of the roads it may be sufficient to say, that they are not worse than could be expected ... The soil is deep clay ... The landlord an absentee, and the tenants of a description peculiarly apt to neglect their duty in this respect ...

Great Stanney is nearby: Cheshire presents few districts more eminently unblest in situation than the present township, bounded on one side by the waters of the Mersey, which have worked their way to it, by the destruction of lands deemed unworthy of the expense of preservation; on another by stagnant brooks and morasses, and approached on the third of roads of deep clay, almost inaccessible in the midst of summer.

Overpool: The village consists of a few ragged huts and farmhouses, situated near the shore of the Mersey ...

Netherpool: The township has ... Suffered much from the ravages of the waters ...

Little Sutton: The present appearance of this township is destitute of anything to attract the eye, or excite curiosity of the traveller: it contains merely a group of ordinary farmhouses, forming an inconsiderable village on the road from Chester to the Liverpool Ferries, in one of the most flat and monotonous parts of the Hundred.

Brimstage: The appearance of the township is bleak and moorish. It is watered by a small rivulet, which flows through the collection of straggling huts which compose the village.

Storeton: The Little villages of Great and Little Storeton are both comprehended within this township, which is situated immediately south west of Lower Bebington. Both are composed of straggling huts, scattered along the edge of a bleak and barren moor.

Noctorum: The village consists merely of two or three farmhouses, situated on an elevation opposite Woodchurch, in a very dreary part of Wirral.

Heswall: Haselwall [*sic*] and Gayton are both situated on the shore of the Dee, along which they present a fertile tract of meadow ground, which gradually changes to a dreary and barren flat as it advances inwards; to the north east this rises into a wild and rocky moor, immediately under which the parish church is situated commanding the estuary and environed by huts and farms mostly of stone, rude in their structure, and placed in great disorder.

Thingwall: ... composed of a few straggling huts, and (contained) no object of the slightest curiosity or interest.

Barnston: ... stands high on a yellowish rocky soil, among bleak and desolate moors two miles south west of Woodchurch. No remains of the antient hall are now in existence.

Neston: The general aspect of the parish, from the flatness of its surface, and its exposure to the sea-breeze, which prevents the growth of timber, is extremely naked and cheerless. With one sole exception it is deserted by considerable landholders and manerial proprietors; and one antient hall only, ruinous and abandoned to farmers is now standing within the district.

Pensby [was on]: ...a moorish flat ...

Parkgate [had a]: Forsaken and melancholy aspect ...

Raby: The early connection of this township with the serjeancy of the Bridge Gate of Chester, gives a degree of interest to as dreary and unpromising a district as any which this country can furnish, and which, since the extinction of its local lords since the 14thC has been altogether abandoned to the residence of farmers.

Bear the above scenes in mind, concentrating upon the qualities which Ormerod despised, while you consider the following accounts of villages which he found more pleasing:

The village of Backford stands pleasantly, on an eminence adjoining to the principal road from Chester into Wirral, which, immediately below the village, crosses the deep valley which separates the hundreds of Wirral and Broxton, from which circumstances the parish undoubtedly derives its name. The old hall is mostly taken down. A part of its site is occupied by a handsome brick mansion, built by the father of the present proprietor... The grounds from the contiguity of the turnpike road, are very confined, but most judiciously laid out by Webb, the tower of the parish church grouping remarkably well with the plantations, and the boundaries being successfully concealed.

His home village came next:

Chorlton: The greatest part of the township occupies an elevated situation, commanding the fine range of the forest and the Frodsham Hills. The ground which slopes from this part to the canal is reputed to be some of the richest land in this part of the country.

Then *Mollington Tarrant*: The present mansion, a handsome and spacious brick building, well screened with timber, was erected in 1756, in a flat situation, but in a point which commands interesting views of the city of Chester, and the Eddisbury and Broxton hills.

Croughton: ... A very romantic dingle, called the Dungeons, branches from the valley which forms the line of the Chester Canal in this township, and extends upwards nearly half a mile, the sides being uniformly over-spread with almost impervious thickets ...

Eastham [was]: ... in a situation which derives no inconsiderable degree of beauty from the contiguity of the broad estuary of the Mersey and the views of the Lancashire shore ... The hall above the ferry house from the combination of the rich woods of Hooton with the grand expanse of water backed by the Eddisbury hills, commands by far the most beautiful view which the Hundred can boast of.

Hooton: In one of the most delightful situations which the banks of the estuary can boast, lies the interesting town of Hooton, commanding a peculiarly beautiful view of the Forest Hills, the bend of the Mersey and the opposite shore of Hale, and shaded with venerable oaks of a growth which the Wirral breezes have elsewhere rarely suffered. These claims to attention are, however, of a very secondary nature when compared with those which it possesses from having continued, during a lapse of five centuries, the seat of the eldest branch of the noble house of Stanley.

[129]

Whitby was described as a 'pretty port' at the mouth of the Ellesmere or Chester Canal.

Bromborough: ... an antient respectable village chiefly built with red stone ... [the hall's] grounds command an interesting view of the port of Liverpool, and terminate in a steep declivity and rich woods overhanging the ferry house of Eastham, beyond which opens by far the most delightful prospect which Wirral Hundred can boast, consisting of the broad expanse of the Mersey, seen over the woods of Hooton, and backed by the Lancashire shore and by the Eddisbury Hills.

Poulton Lancelyn: The township ... [is] ... on the bank of a deep and richly wooded dingle, presenting a scene of sequestered beauty, totally different from anything in this part of the county ... Poulton Hall and the grounds adjacent are situated above the most romantic part of the valley, sheltered by respectable timber and commanding a delightful prospect of the Clwydian mountains .

Birkenhead: It is beautifully situated near the mouth of the estuary of the Mersey, opposite the town of Liverpool, at the side of Wallasey Pool, a large bay which the Mersey forms at its confluence with the Birken.

Thurstaston: ... occupies high ground, overhanging a slip of meadows, which runs along the edge of the Dee. Immediately north of the township this tract of valley bends inwards, and sweeps, in a bold semicircle, between rocky elevations, to the flat district in the centre of the end of the peninsula, which adjoins the shore of the Irish Sea ... The village of Thurstaston, seated at the western termination of the valley immediately above the estuary, forms a wild and pleasing accompaniment to the brown moors and abrupt precipices with which it is environed.

Prenton: ... [had] a respectable stone built farmhouse, situated in a warm sequestered dingle, somewhat better sheltered with trees than the rest of the surrounding country.

Willaston: ... situated some eighteen miles north of Chester, is very sequestered and chiefly composed of antient and substantial farmhouses. It is environed by timber of a better growth than most of the Wirral townships can boast, which adds much to the respectability of its appearance.

Burton: ... Is situated on a rocky eminence, screened from the north by a superior elevation, under which the little promontory called Burton Point juts out into the estuary at a short distance from the village. Burton Hall, the residence of the Congreves is a modern building in a situation somewhat exposed and bare, but commanding a noble view of the Dee sands, the Welsh mountains and the richer scenery which stretches from their base to the water edge.

And finally,

Capenhurst: The township is in a flat part of the hundred, but is judiciously broken by plantations; and one of the best cross-roads in this part of Cheshire has been formed between the Parkgate and Liverpool turnpikes, by the present proprietor, through the centre of the township'.

We conclude that George Ormerod was choosy about his landscapes: if woodlands and valleys were not present, then he would hope to find evidence of the landowners having improved the scenery by planting trees and tidying up the buildings and amenities.

Landscapes are, in one sense, a creation of the mind, for if there are no people to look at them, ponder and describe them, then they do not become known. Ormerod is our only detailed observer from that time. For him, a large part of Wirral's landscape was repugnant; but would observers from the 21st century find it so? Almost certainly not. Just imagine what must have flourished on those many 'moorish flats' and 'desolate tracts' of land; all kinds of wild flowers, birds and animals, of many species which, today, are rare or extinct. Imagine also the atmosphere, pure and unbreathed, and the silence broken only, as Ormerod himself hinted, by the cries of birds or the wind sighing through the grass. If such landscapes existed today in Wirral, there would be campaigns for their protection, perhaps by turning the entire district into a national park or nature reserve. Responses to the environment have changed: the people of Ormerod's day would never have contemplated such developments, because nature was unthreatened, raw and even dangerous. In our day, it is rare, fragile and distant; we long to find and commune with it; that is why so many of us spend much of our leisure time visiting the few remaining open spaces.

For Ormerod, the countryside was attractive when it conformed to classically derived notions of the picturesque. Much of Wirral failed to conform to such notions. Unfortunately, we have no accounts of what the dwellers in those 'huts' and 'hovels' felt about their environment. They are unlikely to have indulged in much abstract contemplation of the aesthetics of their land, because the need to make a living on it consumed all their energy. They must, however, have been unwitting beneficiaries of the attributes of that lost world: fresh air, organic produce and abundance of wildlife.

It is possible that Ormerod's opinions about Wirral were not shared by his contemporaries, but we have no way of telling because there are no other surviving descriptions. Fortunately, however, some 34 years after the publication of Ormerod's work, an observant and sensitive literary man came to live in Wirral. His observations were recorded in two works: *Our Old Home* (1863) and *Passages From the English Notebooks* (1867).[2] They reveal a different side to local life and scenery. He was Nathaniel Hawthorne, American Consul in Liverpool between 1853 and 1857. While he was living in Wirral, he took every opportunity to tour the country and to get to know the people. Chester was his favourite place, but he also described the villages nearer his doorstep. On 29 August 1853 he passed through Higher Bebington and saw 'narrow streets, and mean houses, all of brick or stone ... There was an immense alms house in the midst; at least I took it to be so.' So far he is sounding like Ormerod, but the description takes an interesting turn when he sees an unusual house:

> ... Built in imitation of a castle, with a tower and turret, in which an upper and an under row of small cannon were mounted, and now green with moss ... At the end of the house opposite the turret, we peeped through the bars of an iron gateway, and beheld a little paved courtyard, and at the farther side of it a small piazza, beneath which seemed to stand the figure of a man. He appeared well advanced in years, and was dressed in blue coat and buff breeches, with a white straw hat upon his head. Behold, too, in a kennel beside the porch, a large dog sitting upon his hinder legs chained! Also, close beside the gate-way, another man seated under a kind of arbor! All these were wooden images, and the whole castellated, small, village dwelling, with the inscriptions and this queer statuary, was probably the whim of some half crazy person, who has now, no doubt, been long asleep in Bebington churchyard.

59 This painting is believed to have been made by Charles Eyes in about 1780 and shows the beautiful scene at the 'Headland with the Birches'—the site of the future Birkenhead. This is how it would have appeared to George Ormerod during the early 19th century.

This was the home of Bebington's famous eccentric, Thomas Francis, who is noted for sometimes having invited guests to dine at his home and then serving them with roast sparrow or a few cockles. Hawthorne's obvious amusement at this scene tells us that he was a little less formal and decorous than the great Ormerod and implies that we can expect more 'human interest' in his accounts. He loved the sight of St Andrew's church in Lower Bebington, describing it as 'old, old, old' and 'the fulfilment of my ideal of an old country church'. This is his account of a visit to an inn in Eastham:

> A girl peeped out of the window at us, and let us in, ushering us into a very neat parlour. There was a cheerful fire in the grate, a straw carpet on the floor, a mahogany sideboard, a mahogany table in the middle of the room; and on the walls the portraits of mine host, no doubt, and his wife and daughters ... This village is too far from Liverpool to have been much injured, as yet, by the novelty of cockney residences which have grown up almost everywhere else, so far as I have visited.

Hawthorne shows us that there is another way of looking at old Wirral: rather than being an under-developed and featureless plain inhabited by listless peasants, it was a quaint piece of rural England, of the fragility of whose assets Hawthorne was clearly aware. Of course, it is possible that Wirral had improved a little since 1819, but Hawthorne must also have been pinpointing some of the attractions which Ormerod had missed.

In 1882 Thomas Helsby's edition of Ormerod's *History* was published. It contains numerous comments about the changes which had occurred since 1819. Regarding Wirral, he noticed that there had been 'a revolution in the habits and mode of life of the whole population of this Hundred, to a greater extent, perhaps, than in any other Hundred in the county'. In brackets after Ormerod's description of squalid cottages, Helsby wrote: 'But these have partaken of the general improvement of the last half-century; and a degree of comfort exists, so far as the dwellings of the peasantry are concerned, which has not been the lot of the poorer inhabitants for many generations'. Following the gloomy portrayal of Oxton, he inserted these words:

All this is now changed. Within comparatively short period Oxton has been transformed almost into a town, principally consisting of moderate-sized villas. Building operations, however, being incomplete, the broken-up pastures scarcely add more attractive features to the scenery of [1819].

Helsby's remarks about Childer Thornton are typical of those made about many other Wirral villages: 'The population here has much increased, and villa residences been built by, and for the accommodation of Liverpool gentlemen, among which may be mentioned Brook Lea and Thornton Lodge'.

A revolution was in progress: the population was growing and wealthy Liverpool businessmen were coming to live in Wirral. The landscape was being transformed; apparently, overall, for the better, but the threat of excessive urbanisation was also there. Wirral's countryside was now being viewed as a desirable place to visit or in which to live.

In 1909 Harold Edgar Young in the introduction to his *Perambulation of the Hundred of Wirral* described the area as follows: 'Few large centres of population can, like Liverpool, boast of such delightful and such unspoilt country lying at the very door; country, moreover, that has historical associations so full of interesting and picturesque incident.'

His account of the Overpool area is worth comparing with that which was penned by Ormerod:

The Mersey here takes a wide sweep to the south west, so that at high tide the river Gowy seems to fall into a beautiful lake, and the view over to the prettily wooded shores on the Lancashire side ... When the tide is out the mud flats are tenanted by numerous sheldrakes—or, as the Wirral people call them, burrow-ducks, on account of their nesting in the rabbit burrows—whilst wild geese and other water-fowl are scattered over the mud flats, and in the winter the place is visited by numerous swans.

We can conclude that the Wirral of Ormerod's day *was* under-developed and parts of it *were* squalid, but that he failed to describe its charms. Some of these charms were still in existence nearly a hundred years later, by which time, due to increased urbanisation, more people were aware of them. The fact that it was being developed made people more acutely aware of the attractions of its under-development. In addition, due to better management and greater investment, Wirral's countryside *had* actually been improved, such that even Ormerod might have been impressed. We will explore the details of these developments in the next part of the chapter.

Part Two: A New Gentry and a New Land

Liverpool was growing. Overseas trade and its attendant industries and services were enabling many people to become very rich. There had been ferry services between Liverpool and Wirral for a long time, but, in 1817, they were greatly improved when *Etna* the first steam ferry boat was introduced: it both reduced crossing times and made the service more reliable. Rich businessmen began to see Wirral as a desirable place in which to live. Birkenhead's waterfront was the obvious place to set up home; it was rural, quiet and offered stunning views across the estuary. In 1801 in Birkenhead there were 110 people living in 16 houses. Twenty years later there were 200 residents and ten years after that, 2,569. There was a new church and, in Mortimer's words, 'several piles of houses' and the new *Birkenhead Hotel*, where people could board coaches in order to travel to

60 Rock Park was a residential estate built for wealthy Liverpool businessmen between 1837 and 1850. All the houses are now listed buildings.

Chester. As Birkenhead's waterfront became industrialised, the wealthy people moved inland, settling in Oxton and Claughton.

Nathaniel Hawthorne lived at Rock Park, a specially designed housing estate for wealthy commuters. He described it as follows:

> Rock Park ... Is private property, and is now nearly covered with residences for professional people, merchants, and others of upper middling class; the houses being mostly built, I suppose, on speculation, and let to those who occupy them. It is the quietest place imaginable; there being a police station at the entrance; and the officer on duty admits no ragged or ill-looking person to pass. There being a toll, it precludes all unnecessary passage of carriages; and there never were more noiseless streets than those that give access to these pretty residences. On either side there is thick shrubbery, with glimpses through it at the ornamental portals, or into the trim gardens, with smooth shaven lawns, of no large extent, but still affording reasonable breathing space. They are really an improvement on anything save what the very rich can enjoy in America.

Rock Ferry had been developed in the 1820s. The hotel and ferry had been improved during the 1830s. The land for Rock Park was purchased in 1836 and building began during the following year. Nearly all the houses were complete by 1850. It is a fine example of a type of urban development which came out of the 18th-century fashion for landscape parks. Informal layouts and the inclusion of trees helped the houses and roads to blend into the scenery. It has long been recognised as one of Wirral's architectural treasures, but perhaps we should contemplate its economic importance: it was home to a lot of wealthy people whose incomes were derived from Liverpool. The money they spent on food, servants, services and leisure must have provided extra incomes for their neighbours and, thereby, boosted the local economy.

Rock Park's residents were not, however, the richest newcomers. Extremely wealthy shipping magnates made a huge impact upon Wirral's landscape and society. John Shaw was a Liverpool ship-owner whose vessels were used in the slave trade. In 1807 he bought Arrowe House Farm and much of the surrounding land. He died in 1829 and was succeeded by his nephew John Ralph Nicholson Shaw, who built Arrowe Hall in 1835. Surrounding fields were turned into a country estate; trees were planted and Arrowe Brook was diverted and dammed to form a boating lake. The hall was extended in 1840, 1870 and 1880 and attendant workers' lodges and cottages were built around the estate. Shaw had got his money from trade and he used it to buy himself the lifestyle of a minor country aristocrat. Birkenhead Borough Council bought the estate in 1927, creating Arrowe Park. The words of local historian Greg Dawson are worthy of contemplation: 'The evidence suggests that without the money made from ships used in the Slave Trade, John Shaw might never have bought the Arrowe Estate, and the people of Wirral may never have inherited the beautiful Arrowe park—but at what cost?'[3]

James Harrison was born in Cockerham near Lancaster in 1820. He entered the shipping trade with his brother in Liverpool and eventually founded the Harrison Line. He moved to New Brighton in 1851 and lived at 'Quarry Bank' on Rake Lane. His family donated Harrison Park to the people of Wallasey in 1896. Harrison Drive was opened in June 1901.

William Inman was born in Leicester in 1825. He moved to Liverpool and set up the Inman Shipping Line which specialised in using iron steamers to carry mail and emigrants to America. He built Upton Manor in 1857 and paid for the building of Moreton church where he is buried.

Thomas Henry Ismay was one of the greatest ship-owners of the 19th century. He had humble beginnings in Maryport, Cumberland and moved to Liverpool in 1853. When he was in his 30s, he bought the White Star Flag and, in 1869, founded the Oceanic Steam Navigation Company which provided first-class steamship travel to America. In 1877 he moved to Thurstaston and bought a house called 'Dawpool' and 350 acres. He demolished the original house and had a new 'Dawpool' built in its place. His sensibilities influenced the location of two transport routes—the West Kirby to Hooton railway, which he insisted be placed nearer the coast, and the Chester High Road, which he had sunk within a cutting so that he could not hear the horse-drawn carts going past his house. He incorporated much of the village into his estate, demolished several cottages and closed down the local pub. His wife paid for the building of Thurstaton's village school and made sure it was placed on the other side of Thurstaston Common—well away from 'Dawpool'. He died in 1899 and 'Dawpool' was later demolished. Thomas's son Bruce took over the White Star Line and escaped from the sinking *Titanic* in April 1912.[4]

Owners of other Liverpool industries were equally important. Robert Macfie was a sugar refiner and settled in Ashfield Hall in Neston in 1857. Following his departure, the local people felt the effects of the withdrawal of his spending power and support of local charities. The Bushell family came along in his place and fortunes were revived. Christopher Bushell was on 15 local committees and boards. Reginald Haigh was a cotton-broker who moved to Neston in about 1880. He founded the cricket club and opened up his grounds for navvies' recreations. The wives of these magnates were noted for their charitable and educational work.

Carlett Park was a mansion house and estate which was built and laid out between 1859 and 1860 for John Torr, a cotton-broker and Liverpool M.P. Because it was convenient for the Eastham Ferry, it had originally been bought from Sir Thomas Stanley by William Laird, who wanted to establish a residential estate along the lines of Rock Park. Torr made it into a single residence with surrounding parkland, gardens, lodges and cottages. He died in 1880 and was succeeded by his High Church son, the Rev. Edward Torr, who had a private chapel built in 1884. The house later became a Roman Catholic seminary and then a college of further education, which was attended by this author between 1975 and 1978. At that time the chapel functioned as a staff room.

'The Lydiate' in Willaston was the home of Liverpool merchant, Duncan Graham. He paid for the village water supply to be piped in from Hinderton and for the vicarage; he also sponsored the church and the village school. He became a local magistrate in 1861 and the first chairman of Cheshire County Council in 1889.

Without the presence of Joseph Mayer, the story of Victorian Wirral would have been totally different. He was one of the leading lights of the Historic Society of Lancashire and Cheshire, a collector and philanthropist. He made his fortune as a jeweller and goldsmith in Liverpool. In 1864 he came to live in Bebington at 'Pennant House', which subsequently became the Municipal Offices. Two years later he purchased Thomas Francis's old house and converted it into a free public library which, four years later, he transferred to a converted farmhouse. Outbuildings were made into a lecture hall which was demolished in 1878 and turned into 'Mayer Hall'. The adjoining fields were turned into a park which was opened to the public in 1869. Norman Ellison said 'that whilst [Mayer] resided in Bebington, a spirit of good fellowship prevailed, greater than ever before or since'. He also records part of his obituary notice: 'He was a tradesman by choice, a gentleman by nature, a ripe scholar by study, a wealthy man by industry, and a modest philanthropist by instinct.'

61 'Pennant House', in 1869 the home of Joseph Mayer, businessman, antiquarian and philanthropist, who did so much to enrich the lives of the people of Bebington. The buildings now house council offices. Painting by W.G. Herdman.

Incomers from other parts of the industrial north were also responsible for rebuilding local villages. Richard Watson Barton was a Manchester businessman. He bought Caldy Manor in 1832 and soon rebuilt the entire village. Joseph Hirst was a Yorkshire textile manufacturer who settled in Thornton Hough in the 1860s. He paid for a new church and had a fifth clock face attached to the tower so that he could see it from his home. He also built the vicarage and a row of shops and cottages called Wilshaw Terrace.

During the middle and later years of the 19th century every part of the peninsula became accessible by railway. It was now possible for many more people whose work was in Liverpool to reside in Wirral. Most townships had their 'Millionaires' Rows' and well-known locations where the 'toffs' lived. Older Wirralians can relate stories which reveal the importance of these wealthy local families in establishing churches, funding local clubs and charities, providing employment for domestic servants and gardeners and stimulating the retail trade. At the beginning of the 19th century, George Ormerod lamented the departure of the old gentry families—the Stanleys, the Massies and the Pools—from Wirral; according to Helsby, by 1882, even the Gleggs had gone. The wealthy incomers whose stories we have just reviewed were the new gentry. A whole new range of surnames became associated with Wirral. The economy was stimulated and the landscape transformed. There were now many more big houses, adorned with parks and gardens filled with rhododendrons and scots pines and sealed off from the common people by forbidding

62 'Mayer Hall', Bebington. Another of Joseph Mayer's bequests to the village in which he settled—originally a lecture hall and library, in common with 'Pennant House', it now houses council offices.

sandstone walls. During the 20th century, many of them became public buildings—council offices, schools and care homes. It seems that, even if Wirral had not experienced economic development in its own right, this influx of wealthy people by itself would have been enough to transform the peninsula. But the truth is that, in tandem with the economic growth which was the result of colonisation by Liverpool's upper classes, Wirral developed in its own right as well.

63 Shrimpers at Heswall on the Dee estuary, *c.*1917, evidence that the sea still provided an income for some people at the beginning of the 20th century.

Before we discuss the role of agricultural improvement in changing Wirral's landscape, it is necessary to consider the continuing importance of the sea. The Dee had ceased to be a commercial thoroughfare, but, during the 19th century, it continued to provide an income for small numbers of fishermen. Between 1841 and 1871, Parkgate was home to between 13 and 25 fishermen. They caught shrimps and flat fish from their nobbies (inshore sailing boats) and raked up shellfish from the shore. Before the coming of the railway in 1866, most of the catch had to be taken on foot to Birkenhead and sold on the streets. By 1910 there were 36 fishing boats moored between Parkgate and Heswall.[5]

At the northern end of the peninsula, the Hoyle Lake formed a natural anchorage which had been home to a small number of fishing boats since the 17th century. During the 19th century, Little Meols and Hoose gradually merged to create a town which took its name from the adjoining stretch of sea. As Britain's population and the associated need for protein increased, so did the number of Hoylake fishing boats. By the 1860s, there were about 50 smacks employing a total of some 250 men and boys. They fished all over the Irish Sea and could be away for months at a time. Later in the century, the Hoyle Lake silted up and some of the fleet was forced to use Liverpool's Albert Dock. Eventually, fish stocks declined and the smacks disappeared, to be replaced by a fleet of inshore nobbies similar to those on the Dee.

Fishing was a precarious occupation. Fishermen suffered particularly badly during the great storm of 1889, which wrecked 22 Parkgate vessels and damaged at least 12 from Hoylake. Hoylake's worst year was 1894 when two smacks, the *Ellen and Ann* and the *Stag*, and both sets of crew were lost. In addition, incomes were unstable: inclement weather or the absence of fish would always lead to the cancellation of wages and inevitable hardship.

North Wirral bears much evidence of the importance of the relationship between land and sea. There are lighthouses at Hoylake, Leasowe and New Brighton and a beacon on Grange Hill. Leasowe Embankment protects the area from erosion and flooding. Its original construction was enabled by an act of parliament in 1829. After 1864 all those who lived within the 5,828 acres of land which it protected were required to pay a special tax to cover its upkeep.

The people who lived on Wirral's Irish Sea coast had always made use of the flotsam and jetsam which could easily be picked up from the shore. Indeed, several 17th-century inventories from the Meols area mention the existence of piles of timber and barrels in the testators' yards, but, by the 1830s, this understandable enthusiasm for recycling had made the inevitable transition into a far less excusable activity—wrecking. At best it involved collecting valuable goods from the shore and hiding them from customs and excise officials; at worst the sight of a foundering ship would draw hundreds of Wallaseyans to the beach, equipped with carts, barrows, horses, asses or oxen—not for the rescue of mariners, but for the theft of cargoes. Indeed, in many cases, when half-drowned sailors did appear in the surf, begging for assistance, they were murdered, robbed and thrown back in. In 1820 the *Mary Betsy* of Wexford lay foundering on a sandbank for five and a half hours, while 100 people, equipped with horses and carts, made ready to collect the loot, but ignored the drowning sailors. Only Mrs Boode of Leasowe Castle showed any compassion and rescued the ship's master. In 1866 the *Elizabeth Buckham* was wrecked and her cargo of coconuts and rum was distributed over the sands. Many wreckers became so drunk that they collapsed and were only saved from drowning by the customs officers and constables who dragged them away from the incoming tide. On another occasion people could be seen sucking sand on the beach—they were extracting the sugar which had spilled out of another stricken vessel. It was reported that the locals were fond of uttering the prayer, 'God bless feyther, and God bless muther and God send us a wreck afore

64 The foundation of the New Brighton lighthouse was laid on 8 June 1827 by Thomas Littledale, Mayor of Liverpool. It is built of Anglesey Granite and coated in *Puzellani*, a volcanic substance from Mount Etna. It was first lit on 1 March 1830 and is proof of the great efforts which were made to protect the Mersey's shipping during the early 19th century.

morning'. Upon news of one wreck, the vicar of Wallasey is alleged to have said, 'Now friends wait till I get down from my pulpit and doff my gown, and then we all start fair'.[6]

The story of wrecking is merely a sinister interlude in the account of Wirral's economic development. It died out as the number of shipwrecks declined due to improved navigation and ship construction and because of the increased vigilance of the authorities. In addition, it is important to record that the wreckers did not represent the feelings of the majority of the coastal population towards mariners in distress. Hoylake Lifeboat was in place by 1803 and that of the Magazine Station at Wallasey was operational by the 1820s. Hilbre Island had a station between 1848 and 1938 and New Brighton's Lifeboat began work in 1863. Between them, the vessels saved hundreds of lives and the crews received numerous medals in recognition of their heroism and self-sacrifice. Many other people, including lighthouse-keepers, pilots, coast-guards and members of the public are also known to have helped during nautical emergencies.

The land itself was a much more important employer than the sea. It would seem, however, that in 1819 Wirral's agriculture did not make many people rich. Most of it was still designed only to provide sustenance to the local population. Practices were inefficient and profits and investment were low. Markets were distant and scarce, providing little incentive for expansion and improvement. The Napoleonic Wars of 1793-1815 encouraged a brief boom in arable farming which has left a tiny mark on the face of Wirral. The conflict increased the demand for grain and, throughout the country, lands which had either been pasture or had been lying dormant were ploughed up. In many areas of the north west of England the evidence for this activity is still visible in the form of long, narrow ridge and furrow patterns in the fields. Interestingly, such patterns are visible in Arrowe Park and at the Wirral Country Park in Thurstaston. In the former case, the effects of the ploughings were fossilised when the Shaw family emparked the old fields; in the latter case the land was probably turned back into pasture or rough grazing land soon after the price of corn went down again; the subsequent use of the site for public recreation has sealed its preservation. By the middle of the 19th century, Wirral's agriculture was being transformed. The heritage of that time is much more visible and ubiquitous than a few ridges and furrows; it is the tidiness and regularity of the fields and the solidity and cleanliness of the farm buildings.

65 Harvesting in Greasby during the 1920s. Farming was still a substantial source of employment at this stage, but after the Second World War most of Greasby's fields were buried under bricks and mortar.

By the early 19th century, the population of England was growing and towns were expanding. By 1841, 223,003 people were living in Liverpool; ten years later it had 376,065 residents. Birkenhead was growing at a phenomenal rate. The people were hungry and formed a growing and increasingly accessible market for farm produce, which encouraged local farmers to improve their lands and methods. New fertilisers were employed. Nathaniel Hawthorne visited Poulton Hall in 1853 and observed:

> By means of a steam engine, and subterranean pipes, and hydrants, the liquid manure from the barnyard is distributed wherever it is wanted, over the estate—being spouted in rich and filthy showers from the hydrants. Under this influence, the meadow at the bottom of the valley had already been made to produce three crops of grass during the present season.

This was a spectacular version of the growing practice of spreading animal dung on the fields, which, in turn, was facilitated

66 Joe Smith, a Greasby farmer, at work on his fields during the 1920s when farming was still important.

by the increasing use of barns. Other fertilisers included Peruvian guano (imported via Wallasey Docks), bones and soap waste. Marling fell out of fashion due to the comparative ease with which the new manures could be brought in by train. More complex patterns of field rotation were used and some farmers experimented with soil mixing. In addition, land-holdings were consolidated, creating larger, more efficient farms, which employed some of the old smallholders as labourers. Certain farmers were picked out for public praise: during the 1860s Messrs Jackson of Noctorum, Russell of Brimstage Hall and Wright of Spital were acclaimed for having doubled their yields within ten years.[7]

Wirral's farming had always been mixed, with a strong emphasis upon producing grain. It now began to concentrate upon dairy produce. Former corn fields and marginal lands were turned into grassland and many farms acquired new dairies for the production of cheese and butter for which the city-dwellers had an insatiable appetite. It is estimated that, by 1823, Cheshire as a whole was producing 9,700 tons of cheese per year, much of which was being sent to London. As Merseyside and the northern industrial towns grew, the destination of Cheshire cheese changed accordingly. John Byram was dairy manager of a successful farm in Overpool. He kept detailed records which have survived. Before 1840, most of his cheeses were sent to London. His 1843 accounts mention the sale of 104 cheeses, worth £148, to Wilson and Company of Newcastle Upon Tyne. His records for the period 1844 to 1853 mention purchasers in Bradford, Manchester, Stockport, Dewsbury, Birmingham and Liverpool. After 1854, all of his cheese was sent to Bells of St John's Market in Liverpool.

By the end of the 19th century, few places were further than four miles away from a railway station. It had, therefore, become possible to send fresh milk straight to the urban consumer. By 1915, 60 per cent of Liverpool's daily milk supply (between 10 and 11,000 gallons) was coming from Cheshire. As well as contributing to this supply, many Wirral farms supplied milk to their own neighbourhoods. Littledale's Farm in Seacombe had been supplying the Wallasey area since 1850. By 1882, a farm in Noctorum was paying a man one pound a week to deliver milk locally at 16d. a gallon.

Fruit and vegetables were also grown. The soil of the north Wirral coastal plain contains sand and clay. It is, therefore, suitable for market gardening. Wallasey had been supplying potatoes to Liverpool since the 1790s; it was not long before Hoylake and West Kirby did likewise. Early radishes were sent to Yorkshire and Manchester.[8] Damsons were another local speciality. The author grew up next to a derelict market garden in Greasby. The overgrown damson trees of late August provided enough fruit for many a jar of jam.

67 Willaston windmill was an important part of the rural economy in central Wirral in the late 19th and early 20th centuries.

68 Irby windmill, seen here in a ruinous condition at the end of the 19th century, not long before it had to be demolished.

Random perusal of Victorian local newspapers confirms the continuing importance of agriculture. For example, the *Birkenhead and Cheshire Advertiser and Wallasey Guardian* for 16 and 23 March 1895 recorded ploughing matches at Raby and Leasowe which had been well attended. The lists of competitors act like directories of some of the most important north Wirral farming families—Wilson of Moreton, Fairclough of Arrowe, Broster of Saughall Massie, Dodd of Greasby and Sherlock of Liscard. The *Chester Chronicle* of 13 April hinted at the inherent dangers of agriculture—a young employee of Home Farm in Great Saughall, called Edward Rosedale, 'was attacked in a most savage manner by a bull, which dashed him violently against some railings, inflicting serious injuries to his side and arms, and bruising him very severely'.

Even by the beginning of the 20th century, agriculture was still a major source of employment for the people of Wirral. During his 'Perambulation' of 1909 William Edgar Young often recorded his conversations with local farmworkers. He noted approvingly that, both in Willaston and Woodchurch, the land showed signs of 'hard work and investment' and that employees could expect to earn between 18 and 20 shillings per week; cottages could be rented for about two shillings and sixpence per week and land for about two pounds per acre per year. He observed that 'large families are brought up in some hardship, but in most cases in great respectability'. Ormerod might now have found Wirral more attractive— its transformation was complete; it had not happened in the way in which he could have imagined, but it was displaying the fruits of a resident and enthusiastic 'gentry' and of an industrious and imaginative agricultural community. This was not, however, the full story: the peninsula was also home to a veritable explosion of industrial and urban expansion.

Part Three: Wirral's Industrial Revolution

The Industrial Revolution began in areas which were well endowed with raw materials and sources of power. Wirral was not, therefore, one of the first areas to witness the great changes of that dramatic era. There was coal at Neston, but not enough to make Wirral into another Rhondda Valley or Wigan. Sandstone and clay were abundant, but they did not, in their own right, stimulate the growth of local industry. Indeed, quarrying and brick-making increased because the economy of Merseyside was expanding due to trade. By the middle of the 19th century there were probably 30 quarries in north Wirral and a growing number of brickfields which must have encouraged immigration into Wirral and enabled some people to become rich. For example, in 1828 Mr Brassey was contracted to supply millions of bricks from Birkenhead for the new Liverpool Customs Houses and, in 1845, the Birkenhead brickfields employed 2,000 men to make 85 million bricks for the building of the new docks.[9] On their own, brickfields would never have made the Wirral shores of the Mersey into the great centre of industry and population which they subsequently became. In fact, it was the Mersey itself which caused Wirral's 'industrial revolution'. The conditions which enabled the growth of Liverpool also caused the expansion of Birkenhead, Wallasey and Ellesmere Port. They did not flourish because of a local abundance of raw materials, but due to the ease with which they were able to transport, house and process raw materials and finished products from elsewhere. Liverpool was able to become Britain's second greatest port because of the navigability of the Mersey, its proximity to the Atlantic Ocean and Britain's overseas empire, and its closeness to the industrial hinterlands of the North and Midlands. Wirral shared these advantages and expanded in parallel with its great neighbour.

By the end of the 18th century, the trade routes from which Wirral was to benefit were being laid down. Due to the first Wirral Turnpike Act of 1787, there were fairly good roads between Chester and the Eastham and Woodside ferry stations. Horse-drawn passenger coaches passed through the villages of Whitby, Little Stanney, Stoke, Childer Thornton and Little and Great Sutton. During the 1920s, Eric Rideout observed how many of the buildings of the latter township seemed to date from the Georgian period, revealing how passing trade had stimulated some pre-industrial local prosperity. It was further developments in transport which ultimately transformed the entire district and led to the creation of the new settlement known as Ellesmere Port.

Canals were an innovation which enabled huge loads to be transported cheaply overland. The first one ran from the Duke of Bridgewater's coalmines at Worsley to Stretford in Manchester. Coal prices were halved. The 1790s were a time of 'Canal Mania'—51 new canal companies were created with a combined capital of over £7½ million. The Act of Parliament which enabled the building of the Wirral branch of the network was passed in 1793. The canal was opened to passenger traffic in 1795 and to goods in 1796. It ran along the Deva Spillway (also known as the Broxton Valley or Backford Gap) between Chester and the Mersey estuary at Overpool. In 1797 a junction with the Chester Canal which ran from Nantwich was opened. By 1805 canals linked the coasts of England and served most of the industrial centres of the Midlands and the North. It was now possible, by means of a rather tortuous route, carrying loads of coal and limestone, to travel from Shropshire and Wales to the Mersey. In 1835 access to the Black Country was provided when the Birmingham and Liverpool Junction Canal was opened. In consequence of part of the network being called the Ellesmere Canal, the name Ellesmere Port began to be applied to the settlement which grew up at the point where the canal entered the Mersey. In reality, by the second half of the 19th century, the majority of the traffic which passed along the Wirral line was servicing the Staffordshire iron and pottery industries and carrying grain, coal and passengers to Liverpool.

Ellesmere Port grew up as a trans-shipment point for both goods and passengers. As we have seen, by the time Ormerod visited the neighbourhood, it was still sparsely inhabited and quite picturesque: there were bathing houses on either side of the canal terminal and archery butts between the basin and the estuary. There was an inn, a lock-keeper's house, a few small cottages and some warehouses. It was not long, however, before it grew: in 1843 the Shropshire Union Railway and Canal Company wrote a letter to its shareholders and said this about the district:

> Whereas before the new works had been started the place contained only four cottages ... it contains now nearly 100 houses, an extensive range of first class warehouses, a noble dock with wharfs, ship building yards ... and other buildings and houses are constantly erecting. There are frequently congregated at this spot as many as 60 vessels of all denominations forming, with the resident population from 1,000 to 1,500 souls.[10]

It was becoming a distinct settlement. The population altered: by 1851 there were fewer farmworkers and more shop-keepers, tradesmen, canal workers and boat people. Eighteen per cent of the population had been born outside Cheshire—mainly in Scotland, Ireland and Wales. Many people came from other places on the canal network. During the next fifty years, additional warehouses were opened and the port dealt in iron ore from Ireland,

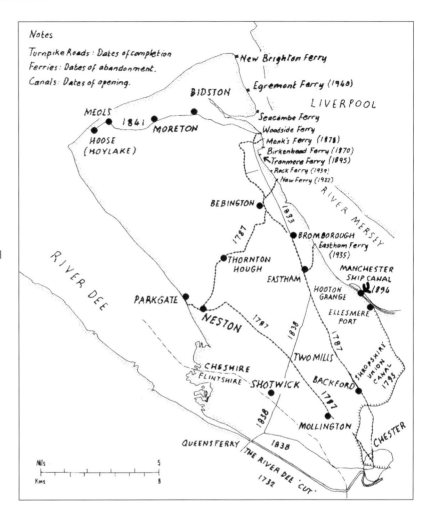

Notes

Turnpike Roads : Dates of completion
Ferries : Dates of abandonment.
Canals : Dates of opening.

69 The road, ferry and canal network.

Spain, Whitehaven and Ulverston and pig iron from America. Local metal working factories were opened between 1879 and 1906.

In January 1894 the economy of the district was boosted even further when the Manchester Ship Canal was opened. It began at Eastham, hugged the south shore of the Mersey estuary and ran parallel to the river all the way to the city which gave it its name. It boosted Ellesmere Port's trade. Preferential charging ensured that large vessels were allowed to sail up the canal and use the town's new pontoon dock which was capable of servicing ships of up to 5,500 tons. In 1894, it saw 686,158 tons of shipping and in 1906 nearly four and a half million. Ellesmere Port flourished as a consequence of its unique position on the Mersey estuary and in relation to the industrial hinterland of the North and Midlands. It was not a by-product of the growth of Birkenhead.

Table 13 summarises the main events in the development of Ellesmere Port and compares it with that of Birkenhead and Wallasey.

Birkenhead's story is best introduced by quoting the words, witten in 1847, of one of its most famous residents, Mr William Williams Mortimer:

70 Manchester Ship Canal above Eastham, *c.*1896. Mount Manisty is visible in the background; it is a spoil heap from the canal excavations and is named after the contractor's agent.

Never were works of immense public utility, grand in conception, and admirable in design, commenced with greater spirit and energy than in Birkenhead: within the last few years the whole neighbourhood has assumed a different aspect,—a town now stands where then only a few scattered houses could be seen. Upon green fields which scarcely served for pasture, stately mansions, and magnificent streets, squares and terraces, have arisen; and where tidal waters, even last year, flowed uninterrupted in their course, hundreds and thousands of labourers are now employed, transforming the sanded shores and weed-clad banks of the Mersey into immense docks, for the accommodation of vessels from every nation and of every clime.

He went on to say that the population of the town had 'so rapidly increased within the last few years, that a reference to the official returns is nearly useless' and noted that of the population of 8,223 people, only 2,752 were natives of Cheshire. He calculated that there was an average of six and a half people living in each house. By 1901 Birkenhead's population had increased at a much faster rate than had the population of Britain.

Every Wirralian knows the story of Birkenhead—of how, all in the space of 90 years, a tiny settlement next to a ruined priory on the banks of a great river turned firstly into a suburb for wealthy Liverpool businessmen and then into a gigantic port, industrial centre and home to over a hundred thousand people. We know that the town has witnessed innovation, success and prosperity as well as disappointment, stagnation and decay, but have we ever stopped and tried to imagine what it must have been like during the first fifty years of its expansion? Mortimer helps us by quoting an extract from *Chambers Edinburgh Journal* of 17 May 1845:

When we had passed a mere frontier of short streets overlooking the river, we were at once launched into a mile's breadth of street building, where unfinished houses, unmade roadways, brickfields, scaffolding, heaps of mortar, loaded wains, and troops of busy workmen meet the eye in every direction. It was like the scene which Virgil describes when he introduces

Table 13: Urban Development along the Mersey

	Wallasey (with Liscard and Poulton Cum Seacombe)	Birkenhead (with Claughton Cum Grange, Oxton and Tranmere)	Ellesmere Port (Comprehending Whitby, Overpool and Netherpool)
Communications	1823–steam ferry to Liverpool; 1875–horse-drawn trams; 1888-95–railway connections to Birkenhead and Wirral lines; 1903–electric trams	1817–steam ferry to Liverpool; 1840–railway to Chester; 1847–first docks; 1860– street railway; 1886–Railway to Liverpool, electrified in 1903, 1901–electric tramway	From late 18th-century coach service between Chester & Woodside. Ferry provided passing trade; 1795–canal between Mersey & Chester & finally linked to the Midlands network; 1816–passenger steamer to Liverpool; 1863–Hooton to Helsby railway; 1894–Manchester Ship Canal
Industries	Early 19th century: flour milling; limekilns. Mid-19th century: Seacombe pottery sugar refining; smalt works; Guano; fertiliser; copper; cement; vitriol; brewing; brickworks	From 1824: iron works; ship-building brickworks; chemicals; abattoirs & animal processing–leather, glue & sausage works; timber; grain; oil-refining; brewing; paintworks; candle factories; 1894-1906 Della Robbia pottery	Boat repair; goods storage & trans-shipment, especially of iron, pottery grain & coal; oil-refining; iron smelting; galvanised corrugated iron; brickworks
Local Government	1845–Commissioners; 1853–Local Board; 1894–Urban District Council; 1910–Municipal Borough; 1913–County Borough	1833–Commissioners; 1843–Claughton cum Grange & parts of Oxton brought into Birkenhead; 1861–Parliamentary Borough; 1877–Charter of Incorporation, became a Borough & included Tranmere & parts of Oxton & Higher Bebington; 1888–County Borough	1902–Ellesmere Port & Whitby Urban District Council; 1908–new council offices
Amenities/ Services	1845—first Court House & Police Station;1860–gas supply begun; 1883–cemetery on Rake Lane 1895–refuse destructor on Gorsey Lane; 1897–electricity; 1914–new electricity station, Town Hall begun	1821–new church; 1841– gasworks; 1845—most of town had sewers; Flaybrick cemetery, new Market Hall; 1847–Park; 1856–first Library; 1863–Tranmere Workhouse; 1868–Argyle Music Hall; 1887–new Town Hall, Hamilton Square; 1895–Fire Station; electricity	1842–New Church for 270 People; 1863–Gasworks; 1869–another new Church and 1871–new parish of Ellesmere Port
Health	1853–Board of Health; 1903–first health visitor; 1885–Cottage Hospital; 1886–Infectious Diseases Hospital; 1899–Victoria Central Hospital; 1914–Leasowe Children's Hospital	1862–Borough Hospital; 1863–Children's Hospital started; opened in 1883	Wirral Union Medical Officer then 1876–Shropshire Union Canal Company Medical Officer; 1909–ambulance; no Hospital until after the First World War
Pop. 1801	663	667	272
Pop. 1851	8,339	33,525	1,004
Pop. 1901	53,579	157,123	4,194
Pop. 1911	78,504	192,758	10,253

Aeneas and his companion into Carthage, but like nothing which had ever met our eyes in real life. Where houses were occupied or shops opened, they all had a peculiarly fresh sparkling look, like furniture in an upholsterer's wareroom as compared with that in private dwellings. The very children playing or walking in the streets looked old beside them. In some streets, traceable as such by buildings posted here and there along a line, the substratum of the roadway was only in the course of being formed; in others the process had advanced as far as the superficies [*sic*] of macadamized trap; but hardly anywhere was a beaten and smoothed road to be seen. You entered a piece of street with a particular name, and half an hour after, walking in quite a different part of the country—for country it still is in some measure—you fall into another piece of street bearing the same name.

We are standing on Bidston Hill in 1870: picture the long straight streets reaching towards its foot. Green fields are being turned first into brown morasses, dotted with groundworks, piles of bricks, scaffolding and labourers and then into lines of dark grey houses and roads, whose intrusive angles will not be mellowed by foliage for another ten years. Further away, the Mersey is visible—full of ships, some with sails, others pushing out plumes of smoke and steam. Some are heading for Liverpool, but others are turning into the Wallasey Pool, a once wild and beautiful creek, but now an increasingly murky host to docks and factories. When we descend the hill and wander the streets, we witness some of the town's human story—yes there are many who prospered from trade and are living in comely and capacious villas, but many more, labourers and artisans, share rooms in tiny terraced houses and others—the unemployed and the starving Irish—who would be glad of the smallest area of dry floorspace upon which to lay their heads and now wander the streets in search of charity, but are probably destined for the workhouse. We are amazed by the people's speech—at how the accents of Lancashire, Scotland, Wales and Ireland are merging with the native Cheshire to form a strange hybrid which will soon

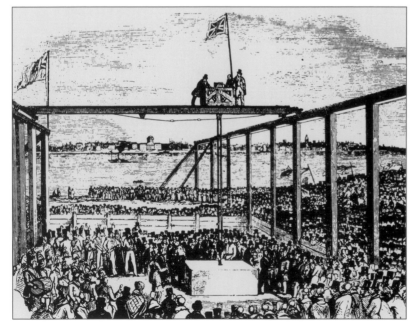

71 An engraving showing the foundation laying ceremony at Birkenhead Docks on 23 October 1844.

72 'Laying the Foundation Stone of Birkenhead Docks on 23 October 1844' was painted by Duncan. The obvious grandeur of the occasion tells us that the investors in the new docks had a clear vision of the significance of their actions for the economic development of Birkenhead.

become so characteristic of the area. Despite the town's problems we are optimistic—God and the Queen are on their thrones; the empire is growing; trade is increasing; science and self-help will always pull us through.

It all began in 1824 when a Liverpool Scotsman, William Laird, purchased a large amount of land from Francis Richard Price and got Mr Gillespie Graham of Edinburgh to produce plans for a new town. Upon land next to Wallasey Pool, Laird built his first boilermaking and shipbuilding yard. In 1829 he launched his first iron ship—a 60-ton lighter for use on the Irish lakes. By 1882, Thomas Helsby was able to write:

> As showing the great trading capabilities of this part of the country, it will be enough to remark that the production of a single yard in vessels of wood and of iron—for trade, exploration, pleasure and war—for the past fifty years, would, together with an account of the numerous engines of all kinds constructed in the same period, quite fill a catalogue as extensive as that of some not inconsiderable libraries.

Laird exploited the business opportunities which were created by Britain's imperial expansion: in 1839 an armed flotilla was built for the East India Company and an iron steam frigate called *Nemesis* was supplied for the Chinese War. Three vessels were supplied for the Niger Expedition and warships were built for use in the Crimea. Numerous vessels were built for customers in America, the most famous of which was, of course, the '290' or *Alabama*, which, between 1862 and 1864, sank 56 Union vessels during the American Civil War. The shipyard was moved to its waterfront site near the Priory in 1856 and by 1882 was employing over 3,000 workers.

Birkenhead's other great asset was its docks. William Laird had spotted the potential of the Wallasey Pool in 1826 when he arranged for a team of engineers to survey the site. Mr Telford of London looked down on the scene from Bidston Hill and was heard to say 'Liverpool [or perhaps 'the docks'] was built on the wrong side of the Mersey'—the Pool was a natural harbour, affording wonderful prospects for development. Plans were then discussed to build a canal between the Pool and the Dee estuary at a possible cost of nearly £1½ million. Liverpool Corporation became alarmed at the prospect of the emergence of a rival port and promptly bought up the land. They put it up for sale in 1843 and it was purchased by John Laird. The Act of Parliament allowing the construction of the docks was

[149]

passed in July 1844 and, amidst great celebrations, the first stone was laid by Sir Philip de Malpas Grey-Egerton on 23 October of that year. The Egerton and Morpeth Docks were opened in April 1847; the Great Float and the Alfred Dock were finished in 1851; and the Wallasey Dock was opened in 1877. In 1857 all docks on both sides of the Mersey were put under the control of the Mersey Docks and Harbour Board. Numerous ware-houses, wharfs, quays and workshops were subsequently built and thousands of people employed.

Birkenhead Park was opened at the same time as the first docks. It was designed by Joseph Paxton who later worked on Crystal Palace and is said to have inspired the designers of New York's Central Park. Again Mortimer provides us with the best summary:

> Nothing could afford stronger proof of the public spirit and sagacity of the Commissioners of Birkenhead than this noble project ... Birkenhead Park is not, like many, a vast tract in the hands of some lordly owner, who too generally pursues a system of exclusion by which the public are debarred the opportunity of beholding its beauties; on the contrary, it contains extensive drives, beautiful walks, and elegant gardens, is adorned with groves, fountains, ornamental waters, and numerous sources of pleasure, all of which ... are freely and gratuitously appropriated in perpetuity to the community ...

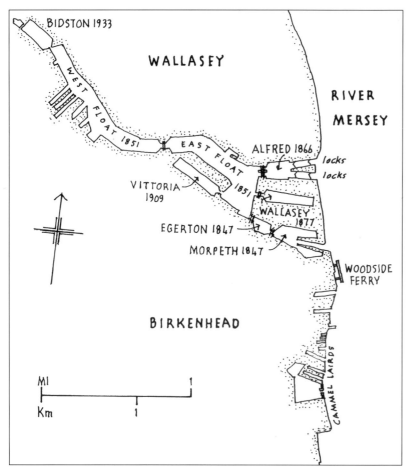

73   Birkenhead and Wallasey Docks.

Table 13 on page 147 lists Birkenhead's other urban developments and also states the salient points in the story of Wallasey's growth. One of Wallasey's industries is worthy of special mention—Seacombe Pottery. Its story illustrates the nature of Merseyside's 'industrial revolution'—it did not occur because of local raw materials and was dependent upon trade. It was founded in 1852 by John Goodwin from Staffordshire, who saw that the proximity of the Great Float would allow both the cheap import of the necessary clay, stone and flint and the speedy export of the finished product. Indeed, the factory specialised in making tough, cheap wares for sale in the colonies. By 1861 it had 115 employees, 79 of whom came from Staffordshire. It closed down in about 1864. Some workers returned to Staffordshire, but others remained in the area and found alternative jobs.

Neston's coalmines were a small part of Wirral's industrial landscape. They first appeared at the middle of the 18th century and worked intermittently until 1927. The 1841 census recorded a total of 94 colliers living in Ness and Great and Little Neston. Ten years later James Gregory was the colliery proprietor and his son Peter was clerk and book-keeper. There were 120 other employees, including seven boys under the age of fourteen, of whom two were only nine years of age. The census also recorded the presence of the coal sloop *Mary* which was moored at Denhall Quay. By 1881 there were 147 colliers in the Neston area. Eighty per cent of them were born outside Neston, mainly in North Wales and Lancashire. In Norman Ellison's words, '... they brought their local dialects, and even today [1955] you will hear words used by men in the *Harp Inn*, on the edge of the marsh, such as cannot be heard elsewhere in Cheshire.' They were tough men who worked on five- and six-foot seams in flooded tunnels, stretching up to two miles under the Dee estuary. Between 1900 and 1910 the mines employed about 200 workers. After the closure of the mines, most of the equipment was scrapped, leaving only the disused quay, some slag and the *Harp Inn* as evidence of their former existence.

In order to complete the picture of the effects of the Industrial Revolution on the face of Wirral, we must mention the role of benevolent industrialists. In 1852 Price's Patent Candle Company of London bought 80 acres of cheap land next to Bromborough Pool and built not just a factory, but a garden village in which to house its employees. In addition to decent housing, it contained allotment gardens, reading rooms, schools and recreation grounds and in this respect presaged the creation of its larger and more famous neighbour, Port Sunlight.

William Hesketh Lever was the son of a Bolton wholesale grocer. In 1885 he bought a soap factory in Warrington and began to produce a new brand called 'Sunlight'. It was made with vegetable oil instead of tallow and given a refreshing scent by the addition of citronella oil. He was soon selling 450 tons of soap per week and was in need of a site for a new factory. He found an unpromising tract of waterlogged ground on the banks of the Mersey in Lower Bebington. On 3 March 1888 his wife cut the first sod and Lever announced his aims:

It is my hope, and my brother's hope, some day to build houses in which our workpeople will be able to live and be comfortable—semi-detached houses, with gardens back and front, in which they will be able to know more about the science of life than they can in a back slum, and in which they will learn that there is more in life than the mere going to and returning from work, and looking forward to Saturday night to draw their wages.[11]

Lever's son said of him, 'Altering the face of nature was with him a passion'.[12] He was stimulated by the challenge of transforming his scrappy bit of wasteland into a model town. Price's village did not impress him—with its regimented rows of terraces and lack of open space, it was simply a more wholesome version of the typical working-class settlement of the day. Lever had higher ambitions—for him a home required a 'greensward' just as much as a 'cup requires a saucer'. By 1900 there were over 400 houses in the new town of Port Sunlight; by 1951 there were 1,372. They were built in small groups and no two groups were the same. The gardens were all open-plan and maintained by a permanent staff. Lever himself settled at Thornton Manor and completely rebuilt the village of Thornton Hough.

Of course, none of the above developments would have been possible without attendant improvements in transport—following the opening of the Liverpool to Manchester Railway in 1830, numerous new lines were built throughout the country. It was not long before Wirral

74 Workers' cottages at Price's Patent Candle Factory village, Bromborough Pool. Wirral's earliest example of a model village for factory workers, later outclassed by Levers' village at Port Sunlight.

75 Levers' General Offices, Port Sunlight, *c*.1931.

76 Workers' cottages at Port Sunlight village, c.1931.

77 The Dell, Port Sunlight village, c.1928. An example of the way in which Lever created a rural environment for his staff.

had its own network, full details of which are depicted in the map on page 155. Not only were docks and factories well served, but people were able to move quickly and cheaply, causing the construction of more Liverpool commuter suburbs in Wirral. By 1882 the annual traffic on the Mersey ferries was about ten million passengers. Four years later the underground link between Liverpool James Street and Birkenhead Green Lane was opened and the route was electrified in 1903.

Reference to the railways introduces the negative side of Wirral's urban development. In 1947 Sir C. Reilly and N.J. Aslan produced their Outline Plan for Birkenhead in which they took stock of the town's successes and failures. They observed that Birkenhead's original planners had entertained great hopes for its prosperity and expansion and had, accordingly, laid out a grandiose network of long, wide streets. But the tidy pattern was severed by the Birkenhead to Chester Railway: 'awkward triangular patches' were created which became 'difficult to utilise' and were ultimately filled with 'builders' yards and

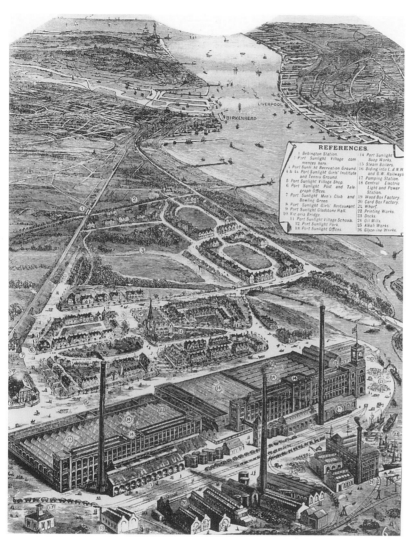

REFERENCES.

1 Bebington Station.
2 Port Sunlight Village commences here.
3 Port Sunlt At Recreation Ground.
4 & 4a Port Sunlight Girls' Institute and Tennis Ground.
5 Port Sunlight Village Shop.
6 Port Sunlight Post and Telegraph Offices.
7 Port Sunlight Men's Club and Bowling Green.
8 Port Sunlight Girls' Restaurant.
9 Port Sunlight Gladstone Hall.
10 Victoria Bridge.
11 Port Sunlight Village Schools.
12 Port Sunlight Park.
13 Port Sunlight Offices.
14 Port Sunlight Soap Works.
15 Steam Boilers.
16 Siding into L. & N.W. and G.W. Railways.
17 Pumping Station.
18 Central Electric Light and Power Station.
19 Wood Box Factory.
20 Card Box Factory.
21 Wharf.
22 Printing Works.
23 Docks.
24 Oil Mills.
25 Alkali Works.
26 Glycerine Works.

78 Port Sunlight in 1898 from the *Illustrated London News*. Not only an excellent summary of Levers' enterprise at Port Sunlight, but an illuminating aerial view of Wirral's Mersey shore all the way to New Brighton Tower.

dumps'. They concluded by saying: 'The ruthless cutting of a diagonal railway across the formal plan of rectangular streets by destroying the meaning of the latter helped to degrade the area and to reproduce the slums with which it is now largely covered'. In addition, they noted how the re-siting of Laird's shipyard deprived the people of Birkenhead of an attractive river frontage. They also felt that the early planners had been over ambitious:

> If all this showed immense optimism as regards the future of the town and can be admired from that point of view, it was, except for Hamilton Square and a few adjacent buildings, little short of a disaster. Never has Birkenhead been able to live up to such paper grandeur, nor indeed could any other provincial city have done so saddled with such a plan. Instead of buildings on the scale of a Parisian boulevard lining these long wide streets, small two-storey cottages appear almost at once, and the area they cover, except in the immediate neighbourhood of the Square is the chief slum of the neighbourhood.

Hilda Gamlin had her own feelings about the town's difficulties. In her 1892 work, *Memories or Chronicles of Birkenhead*, she made this observation:

In the early days of Birkenhead, its people were in a fair way to make a historical name for themselves by patient, quiet plodding; the town gradually rose and enlarged, and small fortunes were realised within its boundaries. But a wicked prophet arose, and blasted our even course by forcasting us as the 'City of the Future'. Pride comes before a fall! From that day forth commenced our sliding scale of decline. Relying on the seer's prediction that we were vaunting our prospective grandeur, and stayed the hand that should have steered us to prosperity, while the prophet laughed merrily in his corner at our misinterpretation of his prevision for 'the future' never arrives!

She also said, 'Fabulous wealth is attributed to many residents of the district. Yet the community at large seems to benefit little by its circulation.' We do not have to search very hard to find the evidence which corroborates the assertion—even random readings of contemporary newspapers reveal a society with problems. Take the *Birkenhead News* of

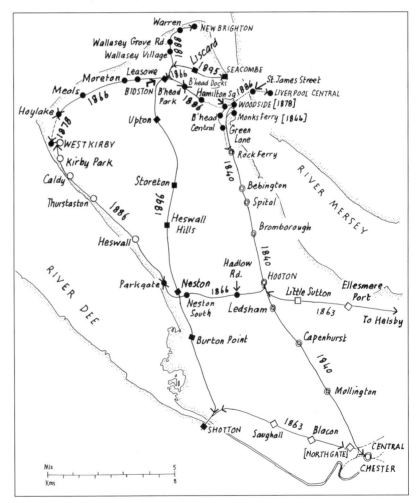

79 The extent of the railways in the Wirral.

9 March 1895: it reported that the Borough Workhouse had 140 inmates, as against 131 during the previous year; and that there had been 37 vagrants during the previous fortnight, compared with seven during the two weeks before that. The rest of Wirral had its share of needy people: the Wirral Guardians met at Clatterbridge Workhouse to discuss problems and noted an increase in vagrancy and the way in which tramps were frightening the people of rural Wirral by knocking on their doors and begging in an intimidating manner. If we are not careful, we can allow ourselves to be insulated from any understanding of the sufferings of the lower classes in Victorian Wirral by the decorous tone of the accepted texts of local history and their concentration upon the superficialities of Wirral's economic 'progress'. They usually failed to consider the huge numbers of people whose lives were certainly not improved and, in many cases, made worse by the growth of the industrial economy and by urbanisation. People like seasonal workers, Irish migrants, the unemployed, the disabled, the elderly and the orphaned often struggled to survive.

Others had regular work and permanant homes, but were paid very little and forced to live in the squalid rows of tiny back-to-back terraced houses, where sunshine was rarely seen and vermin, disease and crime flourished. The *Birkenhead News* of 17 April 1895 reported all the cases which had appeared, during the previous week, at the Borough Police Court: 43 people had committed crimes ranging from playing football and stone-throwing to assault and threatening to murder a baby. The latter case involved one Winifred Woods of St John's Place, who drunkenly argued with the baby's mother and said she would 'twist the child's head off'. She was given seven days in prison and told to pay five shillings' costs. Winifred was one of hundreds of Birkenhead women convicted for drink-related crimes during the spring of 1895. During the above-mentioned week, one man was convicted of such offences, but there were three more women. One was Maria Bowen of Davies Street, who knocked the head of a local salt-dealer against a wall, claiming that he had sold her short. About six weeks prior to this, six women had been arrested for drunkenness at all times of day and throughout the week. Margaret Day of Egerton Street was caught using 'filthy language and would not go away at the request of the officer'. She got 14 days' imprisonment with hard labour. Annie Brown of 8 Oliver Place, Chapel Street was found 'misconducting herself on Grange Road. She had her hat and shawl off, and refused to go away until PC 18 [Gibbons] threatened to take her to the bridewell'. Apparently, the officer then said, 'If your husband does not give you a good punching, I will'. She had to pay a five-shilling fine and 6s. 6d. costs.

There were many cases of domestic violence. George Hamlet of 32 Back St Anne Street assaulted his wife with a pepper box and threatened 'to use his clogs on her'. Thomas Mahon of 35 Lord Street hit his wife on the head when he found her asleep on the couch, then threatened her with a knife and chased her onto the street, where he kicked her on the thigh. He was fined ten shillings.

Street violence was similarly rife. In late April 1895 two policemen grappled with a brawler called Blythe on Grange Road. He knocked PC Taylor down and butted PC Griffith in the mouth. A mob 'of between 500 and 700 people' then gathered and began to taunt the officers and to throw stones, sticks and mud at them. Remarkably, without the aid of cars, radios, shields or guns, the two bobbies persevered and not only got Blythe and Griffith into the bridewell, but returned, unsupported, to Grange Road and dispersed the mob.

Rioting was a well known Birkenhead pastime. Back in 1861, the town had witnessed a virtual civil war. It was the time of Garibaldi's campaign for the unification of Italy.

Birkenhead's substantial population of Irish Catholics objected to Garibaldi's anti-papalism. On 8 October, the Rev. Dr Joseph Baylee, a staunch Irish Protestant and vicar of Holy Trinity church, allowed a public debate, with the provocative title 'Garibaldi and Italy', to be held in one of his parish buildings. By 7 p.m. a crowd of about 4,000 Irish demonstrators had gathered outside the church. They stoned the building and smashed most of its windows before moving off down the side streets, where they stoned the Welsh Chapel and another nonconformist church. The debate was abandoned but re-arranged for 15 October. Hundreds of police, special constables and soldiers were put on alert. The Irish had planned their attack: they drew the Borough constables down the side streets and then the householders 'fired their chimneys' and enveloped the district in smoke. By 8.30 only 29 Borough Policemen out of a force of 55 were left uninjured. Captain Smith of the County Force prosecuted his attack on the main Irish stronghold in Oak Street. At number 21 his officers fought Thomas Larkin who was armed with an iron bar, his wife Catherine who had an axe and Michael Hogan who brandished a poker. At number 6, PC Martin arrested Patrick Fahey who was standing next to enormous pile of stones and a gun. Meanwhile the Protestant meeting had reached a peaceful conclusion and a large party of Orangemen had returned to Liverpool singing *Rule Britannia*. Numerous shops and pubs had been wrecked and, on the next day, 12 Irish people appeared in court and were given sentences of between six months and nine years.[13]

Victorian society was riven with conflict. Even its attempts to enjoy itself were thwarted by the divisiveness of social class. New Brighton was originally conceived as 'The sea-bathing rendezvous par excellence of the Lancashire people of note'. It was laid out by John Atherton and William Rowson on 170 acres of sandhills in 1841. By 1867 it had a promenade and pier and became 'a kind of marine suburb of Liverpool'. However, at its north-eastern edge, a shanty town grew up. Squatters built driftwood shacks and provided donkey rides, beach entertainment and cheap refreshments. Things were not going according to plan—the working class was colonising a district which had been intended for the exclusive use of members of the bourgeoisie and industrial aristocracy. During the next decade, a Manchester syndicate built the 'Ham and Eggs Parade'. Soon the district became notorious for its 'rowdiness, insobriety and prostitution', which was clearly remembered by

80   Aerial view of Holy Trinity church and neighbourhood, Birkenhead, 1969. It was the location of the 1861 Garibaldi Riots. Since the photograph was taken, Holy Trinity church and all the terraced houses have been demolished.

81 Engraving of New Brighton Pier in the 1890s.

82 The impressive New Brighton Tower in 1905.

Norman Ellison in 1955, who betrayed his own class origins when he described it like this: '... a disgraceful collection of low eating houses and oyster stalls where horseplay and vulgarity gained New Brighton an unenviable reputation all over the country'.

A wonderful new tower was planned and provoked the *Liverpool Shipping Telegraph* to ask, 'What is obtained in return except possibly the added risk of attracting hordes of savages from the backwoods of Lancashire who would invade and depreciate its value?' The town began to lose its way. What was it to become, a select resort for the wealthy or a paradise for the the working man eager to spend his hard-earned wages on one of his few annual holidays? Those who favoured the former course supported the New Brighton Improvement Association which aimed to build new gardens, to demolish the Ham and Eggs Parade and to ban undesirable behaviour An ironic letter appeared in the *Wallasey News* in 1912: 'Our aim is to make New Brighton a place of restful gardens and sweet music, a sort of threshold to Paradise, where candidates for celestial glory could come and exercise their embryonic wings'.

In fact, the Tower flourished until the First World War, after which it had badly rusted, was thought to be irreparable and was demolished. We can now see that it was an attraction which could have maintained New Brighton's popularity and enabled it to continue to thrive as a day-trippers' resort well into the 20th century, but class distinctions had made its residents unclear about whether they wanted a Bournemouth or a Blackpool, and ultimately caused it to become 'a distressed gentlewoman of a Liverpool suburb'.[14]

Despite the ambiguities inherent in the development of Wirral's resorts, many people were still able to enjoy themselves. Local Victorian newspapers contain regular reports on the activities of cycling and walking clubs, church youth groups and sporting teams. By the 1880s Association Football and Rugby Union Football seemed to be equally popular in the Birkenhead area. Birkenhead Rugby Club was founded in 1871 and was based in the Park. In 1887 its ground hosted the international fixture between Wales and Ireland. The *Liverpool Echo* of 12 March, with tongue in cheek, gave the reason—'Welshmen and Irishmen flourish wonderfully hereabouts and ought to occupy all the space set apart for spectators

83 & 84 Views of a different kind of Wirral resort—West Kirby at the beginning of the 20th century; approximately the same section of promenade viewed from opposite directions. Marine Lake is on the other side of the railings. West Kirby was a quiet and pleasant seaside town whose rail link with Liverpool enabled it to flourish both as a day-trippers' destination and as a dormitory town.

85 West Kirby shore, *c*.1945. This post-card is a charming reminder of Wirral's importance as a place of recreation. Its sender showed where she was building a sandcastle and where 'Auntie F' was sitting by marking the picture with crosses.

and not leaving any room for a beggarly Saxon at all'. The *Birkenhead News* listed all the day's fixtures—in addition to the international, 11 matches were to be played in Birkenhead and Wallasey. Wales won the match with one goal, one try and three minors to three tries. About 6,000 people had watched the game. In January 1894 Birkenhead Park hosted the England versus Wales match, when the home side won with 24 points to three.

By 1914, Wirral was a divided land. Virtually its entire Mersey coast was encased in bricks, mortar and concrete, while its Dee coast and centre was still rural. It was geographically well-placed to benefit from Britain's growing industrial economy and trade with the Empire. New industries and its proximity to Liverpool attracted many immigrants. Numerous entrepreneurs became rich and many monuments testifying to their ambitions were constructed. Amidst the grey expanse of the growing conurbation there were small indications of the presence of forethought and philanthropy, but many more of exploitation and neglect. Capitalism had been allowed to run without restraint; its energy had created opportunity; but its inability either to meet every human need or to reform the human soul had engendered squalor, poverty and conflict. Much of Wirral was still attractive: the new gentry and the farmers were good stewards of the countryside, but how long were they going to be able to defend it against the advance of the metropolis?

Seven

The Twentieth Century

Part One: War and Society

Without consideration of the role of war, nobody could possibly hope to understand the recent history of the British people. What is true of the nation, is also true of its regions; Wirral is no exception. The author cannot claim that this section of the book will do justice to the exceptionally dramatic, emotive and complex question of how the two World Wars changed the people and landscape of Wirral, but it is hoped that the introduction of certain themes will provoke the reader both to ask questions and to consider carrying out further research. At the time of writing, the First World War has all but disappeared from living memory and even those who were children during the Second World War are now nearly all of pensionable age. On the negative side this means that oral testimony is rapidly becoming more difficult to obtain; on the positive side it means that the growing temporal gap between the historian and those great events is enabling a greater degree of objectivity. We are beginning to be able to interpret the events with detachment and to challenge some of the great myths of the 20th century.

Britain declared war on Germany on 4 August 1914. In order to prevent German conquest of Europe, an army of some 125,000 men was sent to Belgium and France. It dug in and by the time of the Armistice of 11 November 1918, nearly six million men had served in the British Army. About 743,000 of them died. For the first time, killing was carried out on an industrial scale: an average of 5,600 people from all the combatant nations died each day of the War. By 1922, 62,000 British veterans were still being treated for shellshock and 240,000 had received full or partial limb amputations. Every British family was affected. It is not surprising that we are still trying to comprehend 'The Great War for Civilization' and that arguments can become heated when some of its myths are challenged.[1]

The declaration of war was received with enthusiasm. Millicent Jones of Birkenhead remembered how when the troops 'left for service they marched down to Woodside Station with the band playing. People lined the streets, cheered them on and the children waved their Union Jacks'. But, by early 1915, it was clear that the War would be longer and bloodier than expected and '... there was no jubilation. They left in the middle of the night by tram cars'. She recalled civilian sufferings:

> I remember one time my grandmother queued for hours to buy potatoes. When it was her
> turn she was allowed only four, when she cut them open they were half rotten. It wasn't

always this bad though, sometimes we got an egg. Meat was rationed so everyone got a little. There was no butter—only horrible margarine, not a bit like today's kind. I disliked it so much that even today I cannot face margarine.[2]

People went to war for the King and for the Empire, but their immediate feelings were for family, neighbourhood and town. In order to sustain the war effort, the local newspapers combined both types of loyalty. Every edition from the period 1914-18 contains numerous columns listing local men who were serving in the trenches. Extracts from their letters gave first-hand detail of the fighting and helped to stir up local pride and enthusiasm for enlistment. Special emphasis was placed on large families with numerous brothers all 'in the colours'. The *Deeside Advertiser* for 12 November 1915 contained a large article about the four sons of Mr and Mrs Joseph Rainford of Ridley Grove, West Kirby—Sam, Dick, George and Tom. The paper published Tom's most recent letter:

Just a line to tell you that I am still in the land of the living, and in the best of health too. How does the old spot look these days? What a pleasure it would be to get a glimpse of you all ... With patience worthy of Job himself we are waiting for our friend the enemy to come out of his hole and fight us. We are especially anxious for the event, seeing that when he does come he will be accorded a 'warm' reception. But the question is will he come? It is about six weeks since I had my boots off and it is practically the only complaint I have to make.

It is typical of the thousands which were printed in Wirral newspapers. Sergeant Tom Rainford was a common man, but notice the sophistication of his grammar and expression. We are reminded that, not only was the British Army of the First World War the largest that the country had ever produced, but also the most literate—forty years of educational reform had ensured that most people were competent writers. He was also a civilian in uniform. When we put these two facts together, we begin to understand why the horrors of war impinged so powerfully upon the popular imagination, engendering the conviction that the First World War was worse than all its predecessors. It was certainly bigger than any other up to that time, but no 'worse' than the Crimean War, when men also froze and rotted in trenches and were blown to pieces by shells, but—because the Victorian soldiers were professionals who were expected to endure such hardships and were largely uneducated and thus unable to communicate their sufferings – that war did not wound the popular psyche to the same extent.

The 1/4th Battalion of the Cheshire Regiment was Wirral's local unit. The *Deeside Advertiser* of 27 August 1915 carried a long article about it:

... the news that although they only arrived at the Dardanelles less than three weeks ago they have been in action and quitted themselves like true men we have all along known them to be, created quite a sensation throughout Birkenhead and the Wirral ... Undoubtedly the people of Wirral are living through a period of sorrow and anxiety without parallel ... From time to time recruiting appeals have been made on its behalf, and the pride which Wirral takes in its local battalion was reflected in the response to the call for more and more men in order to bring the Establishment at Grange Road West, Birkenhead, to full strength. In all parts of Wirral ... companies of the territorials had been drilling assiduously for years and consequently the stress of war found 'the Fourth' a well-trained high spirited, and sound corps fully able to take its place side by side with the regulars ...

The words of the late Private Dobbing of Birkenhead were quoted: 'I hear the people of Birkenhead started to call us the "Scruffy 4th" and the "Never Budgers" ... Let us have no more unmerited criticism of the gallant lads ... Every fit man ought to come forward.'

He was alluding to the growing recruitment problem: many men were declining to sign up and the newspaper contained repeated appeals for more volunteers. It reported with extreme distaste how one Birkenhead household contained four young men who all refused to join up and said, 'Incidents like that must make even the most ardent voluntarist turn to conscription'. Compulsory military service was introduced in 1916.

During 1917 Birkenhead witnessed a powerful demonstration of popular discontent with the war. The town was home to a large number of Welsh people and played host to the annual Eisteddfod (for the second time—it had done so once before in 1878). It was attended by Prime Minister David Lloyd George, who addressed the crowds in both English and Welsh. Samuel Evans of Rhos near Wrexham was announced. He had conducted a choir of army comrades during the 1915 Eisteddfod. It was now made clear that every one of those lads had been killed on the Somme. The traditional conclusion to the great cultural event—the awarding of the chair to the writer of the year's finest poem—was then announced. The Archdruids summoned the bard to come forward, but nobody came. Eventually, it was announced that the winner was Hedd Wynn, or Private Ellis Humphrey Evans, 6117, C Company, 15th Battalion, Royal Welch Fusiliers (First London Welsh), who had been killed on Pilkem Ridge near Ypres and the chair was draped in black. A lament was sung and other poets read epitaphs. It soon became apparent that the entire performance had been designed to act as a protest to the prime minister against the evils of the war which he was prosecuting with such vigour.[3]

Wirral is also associated with an immensely important shaper of the popular perception of the First World War—the poet Wilfred Owen. He was born in Oswestry but came to Birkenhead in 1897 when his father was appointed supervisor at Woodside Station. He attended Birkenhead Institute and had several friends in the town whom he continued to visit after he moved to Shrewsbury in 1907. He served in the Artists' Rifles and the

86 Commemorative stone for the 1917 Eisteddfod, Birkenhead Park, evidence of the importance of Birkenhead's Welsh population and reminder of a subtle anti-war demonstration made during Lloyd George's visit.

Above from the left: **87** The Wilfred Owen commemorative window, Birkenhead Central Library, reflects the importance of the poet in shaping our concept of the First World War and the high regard in which he is held in Birkenhead. **88** Port Sunlight war memorial is a unique and dramatic representation of the sufferings of the whole of society. It was designed by Sir W. Boscombe John and unveiled in 1921. **89** Birkenhead cenotaph was unveiled on 5 July 1925 and stands on the site formerly occupied by the statue of John Laird. It bears the names of Birkenhead's 1,293 First World War dead. **90** *Left*. Grange Hill war memorial, West Kirby was designed by Charles S. Jagger and unveiled in the 1920s. **91** *Right*. Shotwick Parish war memorial lists five First World War fatalities: William Evans, John Mansley, Ralph Thomas, John Weston and Herbert Wilcoxson; from the Second World War, Frederick Walter Hopwood, who was killed in Arnhem on 18 September 1944.

Manchester Regiment and was killed not long before the Armistice in 1918. His most famous words are 'My subject is war and the pity of War' and eloquently further expressed the sentiment in several shocking and haunting poems, including 'Anthem for Doomed Youth', 'Inspection', 'The Sentry' and 'Dulce Et Decorum Est'. If he had survived the war, Owen might well have become Britain's greatest 20th-century poet. Birkenhead is proud to have been his temporary home: the Central Library has a commemorative window and a Wilfred Owen Drive stands on the site of his former school.[4]

Every district did its bit to support the soldiers: numerous buildings were turned into hospitals. Wounded soldiers, dressed in blue jackets and red ties, became a common sight. Churches, clubs and charities put on shows for them. People raised funds and knitted warm clothing. During March 1918 the Germans looked as though they were going to win. Schoolchildren were asked to pray for the Allies and then, in November, Germany began to collapse. Millicent Jones was now at Birkenhead Girls' School and remembers writing notes in her history book:

> Nov. 11 10:00am—no news yet 10.30am—still waiting 10.45am—still no armistice 10.50am—(we were almost beside ourselves with excitement) 10:55am—nothing 10:59am—? 11:00am—Every church bell rang out, the one o'clock gun went off and Laird's whistle blew. We jumped up and cheered and then went into the garden and danced and hugged one another. Miss Laird, one of the governors came to tell us that the rest of the day was a holiday. November 14th was my twelfth birthday and I thought, 'What a lovely birthday present!'.

Celebrations were short-lived. There was universal grief. Many of the lads who had marched away never returned. Armistice Day was fixed as a day of commemoration and a multitude of memorials began to appear throughout Wirral. The most spectacular of them all is probably the one in Port Sunlight; it was designed by Sir W. Boscombe John and completed in 1921. It is a huge granite structure surmounted with bronze figures of women, children and soldiers and is, therefore, a true representation of the way in which the First World War involved the whole of society. Birkenhead has a plain and dignified cenotaph in Hamilton Square. The monument at Grange Hill dominates the local landscape. It was designed by Charles S. Jagger (who also designed the Royal Artillery Memorial in London). It bears the words, 'In gratitude to God and to the men and women from these parts who laid down their lives in the great war 1914-1919. They were a wall unto us both by night and day.' Amongst the 334 First World War names can be found those of five Johnstone brothers, the sons of Mr and Mrs Benjamin Johnstone of West Kirby.

Herbert Kemp played the cornet in the Wallasey Village Silver Band. His memories of participation in Wallasey's annual remembrance ceremonies during the inter-war years are typical:

> I saw this parade as a great social leveller. In the ranks were men I knew well, others I only knew about, and some I saw as occupying posts of power: policemen, teachers, school attendance officers, park-keepers, shopkeepers, bank clerks, shipping clerks, fishermen, railway men, tram drivers. Others I knew worked in market gardens down Leasowe Road: grooms, blacksmiths, wheelwrights ..., but the majority were unemployed ... Our bass drummer had served in both the Boer War and the Great War, but his distinction for me was his playing of the drum on that march: he produced a hair-raising, spine-chilling, never-to-be forgotten sound. For the first two bars only the sound of gently shuffling feet and the swaying chink of medals could be heard, when into this awesome silence the band entered with the full

92   Argyle Street, Birkenhead in the 1930s.

sonorous chords of 'Sondon'. It was deeply moving—I could not see the music for my eyes filled with tears ... I attended my last service in 1938 and it held for me the same sense of awe it had held ten years earlier; the next time I attended I wore my own medals.

Once the formalities were over, the participants retired to the pub and the 'chinking of medals was augmented by the chinking of glasses' and 'Wallasey Village had once again remembered them'.[5]

On 3 September 1939, for the second time that century, Britain declared war on Germany. Once again, in order to resist the German conquest of Europe, an army was despatched to France, where it dug in and awaited the attack, which did not come until May 1940. Within a month, the army was defeated and forced to come home via Dunkirk. France was occupied and Britain stood alone. It was another total war, but one in which British land forces had not been engaged with the enemy for as long as they had during the First World War. Along with the rest of Britain's population, the people of Wirral were deeply involved in the war effort. Many also became casualties.

Even before the declaration of hostilities, people were already preparing for total war. As early as 1938 the sixth-form boys of Park High School in Birkenhead were digging trenches around their rugby pitch and placing sandbags around their gymnasium.[6]

Others had been told that 'the bomber would always get through' and invested in protection. In March 1939 the headmaster of Mostyn House School in Parkgate sold off the swimming pool and used the proceeds to pay for an air-raid shelter. Balcony House in the same town was reinforced with beams that can still be seen today.[7] By late 1939, anti-aircraft guns had been lodged in many places and most of the coastline had been fortified with barbed wire, tank traps and minefields. During the summer of that year, in order to train the emergency services and to prepare the people for the worst, the Birkenhead authorities arranged a mock air raid.

On 29 July 1940 Wirral received its first German bombs—on fields around Neston, Irby and Thurstaston. Ironically, the first person to die during an air raid was a German-born maid in Prenton on 8 August 1940. Every rural area of Wirral has its own stories of stray bombs landing in fields. The bombers were heading for the shipping and docks of the Mersey, but were sometimes diverted from their routes by imperfect navigation, anti-aircraft fire or by frayed nerves and were inclined to jettison their bombs in the wrong place. However, between August 1940 and November 1941, Birkenhead, Wallasey and the Mersey shore were attacked with tremendous ferocity. Four hundred and sixty-four Birkenhead people were killed and 661 seriously injured. Wallasey had 355 people killed and 311 seriously injured. Out of a total of 35,727 houses in Birkenhead, 2,079 were destroyed and 26,000 badly damaged. After Bootle, Birkenhead was the second most badly hit town on Merseyside. On 31 August 1940 Wallasey Town Hall received a direct hit and the great organ, worth £3,000, was destroyed. On 8 May 1941 the ferryboat *Royal Daffodil* was sunk at her moorings by a direct hit. By March 1941 Wallasey had 10,000 homeless

93 & 94 Two happier images of life in inter-war Wirral. Crowds enjoying the warm weather at Derby Pool in Wallasey, *c.*1933 and at New Brighton Baths, *c.*1935.

95 Victory celebrations, Birkenhead Town Hall in 1945.

people. One story stuck in people's minds—the rescue of a baby from the ruins of her home. She had lain buried in rubble next to her dead parents for four days before rescuers heard her muffled cries, dug her out and took her to some relations. In 1955 Norman Ellison wrote that by then she was 'a handsome, cheerful girl living with her grandparents'. Eastham and Ellesmere Port were damaged by bombers aiming for the lock gates of the Manchester Ship Canal and the oil storage tanks.

Aeroplanes played a huge role in the Second World War. Wirral was home to an important air base at Hooton Park. By 1930 it was Liverpool's official airport, but, from 1936, it played a military role when it became home to Number 610 (County of Chester) Squadron, Auxiliary Air Force, who, on the eve of war, were equipped with Spitfires and went on to fight in the Battle of Britain. During the Battle of the Atlantic escort planes flew from Hooton.[8]

Local people sometimes witnessed air combat. Eileen Griffiths of Backford saw a German 'Heinkel or Junkers' being shot down: 'Bullets ricocheted from nearby ivy on the wall. I rushed the children indoors—we were all very lucky that night'.[9] Children liked to collect shell fragments and aeroplane debris. The proximity of the large airbase at Burtonwood near Warrington ensured that the skies were rarely free of allied planes.

Some 30 aeroplanes are reported to have crashed in Wirral. Fred Roberts of West Kirby was, like most of his wartime schoolmates, a great admirer of the Spitfire. One day he was enjoying a day out on Little Eye in the Dee estuary. He heard the growing roar of a diving Spitfire and confidently told his companion, Reg. Feeley, that the plane would soon make a spectacular recovery and soar off into the clouds. It did not and crashed with a sickening explosion into the sea just north of Hilbre Island. The two boys were shocked. In Fred's words, 'We never heard anything more about it; that's the way things were in the war. It was probably hushed up and anyway death was pretty much taken for granted during those terrible years.'[10] On 4 October 1944 an American Liberator with 24 airmen on board exploded over Landican. The fields were littered with body parts, personal property, tins of corned beef and plane fragments. Mr Freddy Bowden picked up a head and placed it on a sack. His daughter-in-law told him that he would never sleep that night. The bodies were taken to Clatterbridge Hospital mortuary and, for a long time afterwards, many a local mantelpiece was adorned with brass shell-cases and other souvenirs from the wreck.[11]

Surprisingly, many memories of wartime experiences are positive: N.H.C. Tomlinson used these words:

> It was an amazing period of history which will never again be repeated ... It was also a time when everyone was a comrade. People were helpful and friendly under fire and all classes of society were involved and affected. This is something which vanished after the war and will never happen again. Without doubt it was a most wonderful experience to have lived through the Blitz, although I feel sure my mother, being of an older generation, took a different view.[12]

The sentiments are echoed by many other informants as they recall pulling together with a common purpose, making do with what they had and living life as fully as they possibly could. It must also be remembered that the War gave even those who were unfit or were either under or over military age the chance to get involved. Many people have fond memories of serving in the Home Guard. The Wallasey detachment manned the

96 *Above left.* Wallasey Town Hall was designed by Briggs, Wolstenholme and Thornley of Liverpool. Its foundation stone was laid by King George V on 25 March 1914; it was not opened until 3 November 1920. Between 1916 and 1919 it acted as a hospital and 3,500 wounded soldiers were treated here.

97 *Above right.* Birkenhead Town Hall was designed by C.O. Ellison and Son of Liverpool, its foundation stone was laid in 1883. The completed building was opened in February 1887; the original clock tower was destroyed by fire in 1901 and replaced by the one seen here in the photograph.

anti-aircraft rocket range on Warren Drive. Other platoons were more humbly equipped and given more modest responsibilities. The Backford/Chorlton Platoon was originally armed with 12-bore shotguns and sticks and was required to patrol the railway line as far as Capenhurst. Later the men acquired one American First World War rifle. One night they were told that the Germans had landed in Parkgate: 'the whole platoon was mobilised to help, with their one gun and many sticks'.

The Home Guard was more than a Dad's army—it was a citizens' army. It gave men from the most humble backgrounds status and responsibility. They often acted as a kind of auxiliary police force and were noted for the alacrity with which they manned roadblocks and checked people's papers. Many of them welcomed the opportunity to demonstrate the military skills which they had acquired during the First World War. Harold Jager recorded how the first uniformed parade of the Hoylake Platoon was 'profoundly interesting'. There were 38 men who had served during the First World War. Four of them were wearing the Military Cross; one was wearing a D.S.O. and another a D.C.M. He made the interesting observation that the Platoon's major contribution to the war effort was probably the training of younger men in basic military skills, which later proved useful when they joined the regulars.

Jager's highly enjoyable account of the 'Rise and Ascent' of the platoon contains many descriptions of comradeship, fulfilment and fun. For many of the men it was the happiest time of their lives, especially the older men, who were suddenly lifted out of the sluggish routines of the final days of their working lives and given a reason to get out of the house, get some exercise and fresh air and meet new friends. Here is a typical passage:

> We continued for a time to hold weekly meetings at the Green Lodge Hotel; but soon after our formation, the Royal Liverpool Golf Club most generously gave us the use of their splendid Club House as our Headquarters, setting apart an 'orderly room' for our exclusive use. This was a great and appreciated privilege. Then commenced the weekly Platoon meetings in the Clubroom which became an institution. That spacious lofty luxuriously furnished chamber with its long line of windows overlooking the historic links, the beautiful estuary of the Dee, the Welsh Mountains, Hilbre Island and the Irish Sea, became the Parliament House of Number Two Platoon. There the members disposed themselves at great ease, with their tankards of ale and became firmer and truer friends and more loyal and efficient soldiers as the months and years of war went by.

However, the men also knew the true nature of their calling and received training in 'strangling, scalping, gouging, bone-smashing, face-stamping, kicking, scratching and generally making mincemeat of hostile sentries, paratroops or other enemy personnel'. One night they assembled at Calday Grange Grammar School and listened to 'a most blood curdling address by a foreign gentleman who had been through the Spanish Civil War. His description of the methods used by those warm-blooded southern warriors was gruesome in the extreme.'[13]

Another by-product of the war was social mixing. Evacuation had not always been a success. In Mollington, Bernard Green's mother had accommodated some Londoners, but 'they soon returned, hating the distance from any shops, especially the fish and chip shop'. But refugees from Liverpool, Birkenhead and Wallasey often had no choice but to stay with families in western and southern Wirral, with the result that town-dwellers and country people were forced to learn about each other. Members of different classes served together in the various auxiliary forces and on the many local boards and committees. In addition, for the first time, many people were able to meet foreigners. Polish soldiers were entertained at Backford and Greg Dawson recalls how, on his Thingwall Farm, three Bretons from the Free French Army, encamped in Arrowe Park, were the best workers his 'Dad ever had'. The same camp later accommodated American soldiers. G.I.'s were based at many other sites throughout the peninsula. Carlett Park was appropriated by the Ministry of Defence and became Number 76 Transit Camp. Roger Dowdswell was a newspaper delivery boy from Allport Lane. He remembered delivering papers to the camp and seeing how the black and white soldiers were segregated. He also recalled spotting tanks and Bren gun carriers in the adjoining woods.[14] The Americans were famous for driving around in jeeps and prompting cries of 'Any gum chum?' from local pedestrians.

American troops arrived in Wallasey in 1942. Wilkie's New Palace on the promenade became their maintenance depot and numerous other buildings became storage parks. Some soldiers were lodged in empty or bomb-damaged houses. Their camp was known as Depot 0616 and was commanded by Colonel Earl Zwingle. In 1944 the U.S. Army was given the freedom of the town and commemorative flags were lodged in the Town Hall. The flags have since been renewed. There is also a map depicting the origins of soldiers who stayed in Wallasey.[15]

The War in Europe came to an end in May 1945 and in Asia in August. Britain had dedicated its economy and society to the war effort to a greater extent than any other of the participating nations.

When considering the full effects of the World Wars upon Britain in general and upon its regions in particular we should probably agree with Mao Xedong's judgement on the effects on the world of the French Revolution and say that 'it is too early to tell'. Historiographically and with regard to Wirral the judgement is certainly true. It is not claimed that the foregoing discussion constitutes an adequate analysis of this vitally important topic, but it is hoped that certain issues have been highlighted and that other researchers will be motivated to publish their work.

Part Two: Economic Developments

Following the First World War there was an economic slump. Lloyd George's 'Land Fit for Heroes' did not materialise. By the late 1920s, Britain's economy was recovering, but, in October 1929, the Wall Street Crash pitched the world into an appalling period of economic recession which became known as the Great Depression. Like Liverpool, with its dependence upon trade and manufacturing, Wirral suffered. Leslie Scott Jones was born in Birkenhead in 1927 and lived some 300 yards away from Birkenhead Dock Gates. He remembers life during the Depression:

> In my estimation we were poor, but in the locality there were people worse than us. I remember going to the Dock Gates when the dockers were going home and saying 'Any bread mister?' [Many people have written about those times, but never mentioned that saying.] There was a docker who used to give us a 'Buttie' wrapped in a piece of newspaper. In it was two thick pieces of dry bread with half a sausage in it, we used to eat the sausage and throw the hard bread over the dock wall. If my mother had found out what I was doing, we would have got the cane out.

Like many other women of the time, his mother had to find ways of earning some money for her family:

> ... she used to make 'Ice Cream' and we used to push her iron wheeled cart up to Bidston Hill. She used to stop at the opening by the drink fountain. We used to play about until she sold out, then pushed it home. She also made 'Balm Beer'. I can remember going to the Birkenhead Brewery in Price Street for the Balm. Also she used to go to the 'Toffs' houses and ask to buy any second hand clothes. She used to push a pram around. I think half the time they gave her them. She sold them to locals on tick.

Maggie Gallagher was a character who stuck in Leslie's mind:

> She wore hobnailed boots and a long black skirt with a black shawl. Her complexion—if that is what you could call it—was like the proverbial farmer's backside. She used to sell fish and cockles; she carried them in a wicker basket on her head, an 'Echo' rolled up, then made into a circle was what she used on her head – she wore it like a crown. My mother gave her a cup of tea and a 'buttie'. She used to say 'Poor Maggie'. She was found dead on the foreshore at Hoylake. She must have got caught by the tide.

Others created more spectacular employments for themselves:

> Another character was a chap who dived off a crane into the dock. He only had one arm. How he got up to the gib I'll never know. Other chaps used to break concrete slabs on their chests and bend iron bars around their necks—anything for a few bob.

Birkenhead people were tough in those days. Men made their own entertainment:

> There was another piece of waste ground behind Myrtle Street, Beckwith Street and Brassey Street, where the men used to play pitch and toss and cards; there was only two entrances to it. One from Brassey Street, down about four steps, where there was always a lookout for the 'scuffer' (policeman) [and] another lookout placed at the Myrtle Street entrance. I can remember two men having a fight there—shirts off and about 30 men forming a ring. I think it was an illegal professional fight.[16]

People in the supposedly better-off districts of western Wirral suffered as well. Mrs Jacqueline Roberts (née Hadwin) of West Kirby remembers her father cycling around the entire peninsula in search of a job as a bricklayer. A family photograph of the time shows him attempting to put on a nonchalant pose and happy smile, but his face betrays his inner strain.

Farming families suffered either because demand for produce fell or due to the fact that the customers were not paying on time. Fred Jones of Backford remembered how milk from local farms was taken in churns to Mollington station and then to Rock Ferry for bottling, before going to Liverpool, where the retailers were notorious for not settling their bills. Only when the Milk Marketing Board was created in 1932 did the problem begin to be solved. Some farmers went bankrupt and had to sell off their lands at knockdown prices. This is how so many of Wirral's acres fell into the hands of developers.

Greg Dawson records how the farmers of his native Thingwall supplemented their meagre incomes by hiring themselves out to do odd jobs for local 'toffs'. In 1927 Birkenhead Borough Council paid his father for harvesting corn in Arrowe Park. All the farmers felt that

98 Stanlow Oil Docks, c.1951; the larger dock was opened in May 1933.

they were 'in the same boat' and attempted to help each other out on 'a tit for tat basis'. The products of a night's 'mooching' occasionally supplemented meagre diets—poaching.

With their dependence upon trade and manufacturing industries, Birkenhead and Wallasey suffered the highest rates of unemployment. Ellesmere Port faired better due to its growing variety of industries. A thousand jobs were lost after 1921 when the Shropshire Union Canal Company closed down, but new companies came to the town and provided alternative employment. There was a cement works during the 1920s and oil was imported for the first time in June 1922 at the new Stanlow Oil Dock. Shell Mex got its first foothold in the town. By 1926 the facilities next to the Manchester Ship Canal were capable of storing 34.5 million gallons of oil; by 1934, following the construction of another oil dock, they could hold 90 million gallons. Oil refining began in 1934. Three years later Shell Mex and B.P. bought 51 acres of the old Canal Company's land and 1,500 acres of land east of the river Gowy and extended their works. Ellesmere Port was now home to one of the biggest refining complexes in the world. Between 1929 and 1947 the number of men employed in the oil industry rose from 70 to 5,000. Other industries flourished because of the proximity of the oil trade—engineering, papermaking, and chemical manufacture.

Ellesmere Port became both a destination for people seeking work and a place of work for people who lived further afield—in Wirral, Liverpool and North Wales. In 1934 the first Mersey road tunnel was opened. It had cost £8 million to build and by 1935 was being used by well over three million vehicles per year. Some of these must have been carrying commuters from Lancashire to Ellesmere Port, but by far the largest group of users was commuters from Wirral to Liverpool. The great city was the largest single destination for Wirral's commuting population. Most of them lived around the northern and western coast, which was served by the railway and where the environment was salubrious.

By 1961 over 20 per cent of Wirral's population was travelling daily into Liverpool to work. Birkenhead employed some 22,400 workers from the surrounding areas and Ellesmere Port 9,610. By 1967 the trend had continued—nearly 19 million vehicles were using the Mersey Tunnel each year; a further tunnel was required. It was opened in 1971 and avoided the congestion of the town centres by using land beside Wallasey Pool. Its

99 Bidston Dock in 1969 specialised in transferring iron ore and scrap iron to the rail link with Shotton Steel Works. Workers in the vicinity of the ships were always covered in red iron dust.

link to the M53 mid-Wirral motorway enabled quicker journeys between Liverpool, Ellesmere Port, Cheshire and North Wales.

Despite its continuing importance as a port and shipbuilding centre and the large number of people who found work within its boundaries, Birkenhead was in fact declining. Great investments had been made in the dock system. During the 1890s the Queen's Channel was laid out, some 12 miles out from the shore. Huge dredgers and barges were employed in scooping out millions of tons of sand and silt from the seabed. By the early part of the 20th century, the channel was 1,000 yards wide and 15 feet deeper than the natural spring tide low water mark. Huge ships were more easily able to sail into the Mersey Docks. Vittoria Dock was built in 1909 and Bidston Dock opened in 1933. Great investments were made after the Second World War. A radar station, which enabled all the Mersey's shipping to continue to function even in the foggiest conditions, was built at Gladstone Dock in Liverpool in 1948. Birkenhead specialised in trading with the Far East and with Southern Africa. Ships belonging to such companies as the Bibby Line, the Clan Line and Brocklebanks were impressive sights. Bidston Dock eventually specialised in importing scrap metal and iron ore which was transported by rail to John Summers' Iron and Steel Works at Shotton.

In 1903 Laird's shipbuilding company amalgamated with Charles Cammell and Co. to become Cammell Laird and Co. Ltd. The firm continued to produce an impressive range of ships for customers all over the world. Before the First World War, it had begun to build submarines. There were few orders during the 1930s, but, later, the yard built the *Prince of Wales* and the *Ark Royal* for the Royal Navy and the *Mauretania*, which was the largest mercantile vessel ever built in England up to that date. During the Second World War the yard serviced and repaired numerous merchant vessels and, of course, there was full employment.

Since 1945, the number of people employed by the shipbuilding yards and the docks and their subsidiary industries has declined. All such businesses have invested in new technologies which do not require so much manpower: they have become capital intensive instead of labour intensive. In addition, numerous firms have gone out of business—during the last two decades of the 20th century, despite its many modernisations, Cammell Laird's itself was forced to contract and eventually to close completely. Changes in trading patterns away from the old empire routes and towards the European continent and the increasing use of containers have enabled new ports such as Felixstowe to expand at Birkenhead's expense.

While Birkenhead was declining, the area between the A41 (Birkenhead to Chester Road) and the Mersey was expanding. In 1954 the Queen Elizabeth II Dock was opened at Eastham. It enabled ships which were too large to travel up the Manchester Ship Canal to pump their cargoes of oil along a pipeline to the Stanlow refinery in Ellesmere Port. Tranmere Oil Jetty was opened four years later. The area between Port Sunlight and Ellesmere Port became home to a wide range of industries, which were fed by raw materials imported via Bromborough Pool—soap and detergent manufacture, cooking fats and margarine production, vehicle parts, domestic appliances, chemicals, packaging, cake mixes and paper. A private oil-fired power station at Bromborough provided the necessary energy for the area.

The story of the rise and fall of the Vauxhall Motor Works at Hooton Park illustrates the complex nature of interactions between government, economics and the local environment and people. By the late 1950s it became apparent that Merseyside was perennially suffering from an above average rate of unemployment. At the same time the government was keen to encourage the motor car industry to export its products and

100   Three tankers discharging oil at Queen Elizabeth II Dock at Eastham, 1955.

101   The Wallasey ferry boat *John Joyce* at Egremont Pier, *c.*1914. One of the sturdy vessels which helped to transport Wirral's thousands of daily commuters to Liverpool. New Brighton Tower is in the background.

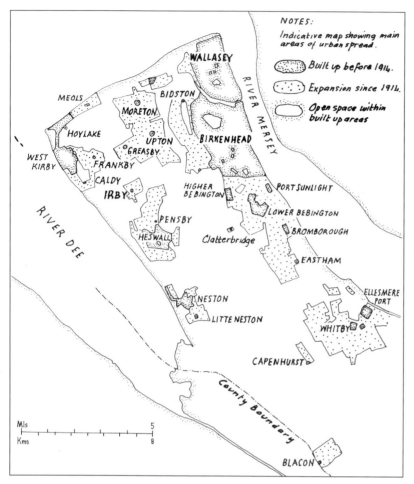

NOTES:
Indicative map showing main areas of urban spread.

Built up before 1914.

Expansion since 1914.

Open space within built up areas

102   Urban development throughout Wirral.

thereby remove the balance of trade deficit. Wirral was seen as a good place in which to place a new factory because of the availability of land, the proximity of potential employees and the accessibility of markets. Three hundred acres of Green Belt land at Hooton Airfield, which straddled the local authority boundary between Bebington and Ellesmere Port, were appropriated. By 1963, the first phase of the factory was open. Three years later, it was employing 9,212 people and, by 1970, 12,000 workers. It specialised in making the Viva. Employees came from Liverpool, Chester, North Wales and from throughout the Wirral peninsula, but disappointingly, in the year 1964-5, only 8.7 per cent of new recruits to the factory had actually been unemployed. Most of the workforce had left other jobs in order to benefit from the higher wages and better conditions offered by the new factory. The laudable aim of attacking the unemployment problem had not, therefore, been achieved. At the time of writing, the factory is about to shut down.[17]

During the factory's heyday, it was fashionable to describe all such industrial and urban developments as 'progress'. It was thought that, in view of the material rewards which were bound to accrue, the countryside and local sites of natural and historical interest were expendable. We now have an opportunity objectively to assess the consequences of such assumptions and to ask ourselves what was gained and what was lost? For some forty years a lot of people had relatively secure jobs; doubtless a small number of senior managers became exceedingly wealthy and a large number of cars was sent into the world, enabling factory workers elsewhere on the globe to travel from the suburbs to work, thereby adding to the amount of carbon dioxide in the atmosphere and increasing the rate of global warming. A once beautiful section of the banks of the Mersey is now a hideous wasteland of semi-derelict concrete car parks and giant buildings and a large number of people yet again face unemployment.

Part Three: Town and Country

Before further discussion of the unhappier aspects of Wirral's social and economic development, we would do well to remember an important event which was made possible by the generosity of Birkenhead Corporation. In 1908 General Baden Powell gave a lecture at the Y.M.C.A. on Grange Road in Birkenhead about his experiences during the South African War and described his plans for a new association for boys. By 1929 the Scouts were a worldwide movement which held international gatherings called Jamborees. In that year Birkenhead offered its newly acquired 450-acre Arrowe Park as a free venue. On 31 July the Duke of Connaught opened the great convention. Over 50,000 scouts from all over the world camped in the park for two weeks and received 320,000 visitors, including the King, the Prince of Wales and the Archbishops of Canterbury and Westminster. Incessant rain turned much of the park into a quagmire, prompting Baden Powell to tell the Duke of Connaught, 'You see, any ass can be a good scout on a fine day, but the thing is to make the best of conditions on a bad day'. His final address was moving:

> Today, I send you from Arrowe to all the world, bearing my symbol of peace and fellowship, each one of you my ambassador bearing my message of love and fellowship on the wings of sacrifice and service, to the ends of the Earth. From now on, the Scout symbol of peace is the Golden Arrow. Carry it fast and far, so that all men may know the brotherhood of man.[18]

103 Upton, a quieter part of mid-20th-century Wirral when the motor car was still rare.

104 Frankby, like Upton, a quiet mid-20th-century village.

How poignant to think that millions of scouts throughout the world have worn the arrow symbol—a play on a word introduced by Scandinavian settlers to describe a tiny corner of their Wirral colony about 1,000 years prior to the Jamboree. It is pleasant also to remember the foresight of the council in buying the park for the public and its generosity in loaning it to the scouts.

One of the most controversial developments in the modern history of Wirral was the change in its local authority boundaries. By 1921 the following local authorities, the relative sizes of which are indicated by their acreages and populations, administered the peninsula:

	Area in acres	Population 1921
Birkenhead County Borough	3,909	145,577
Wallasey County Borough	3,324	90,809
Bebington and Bromborough U.D.	3,446	19,104
Ellesmere Port and Whitby U.D.	3,449	13,063
Hoylake and West Kirby U.D.	1,979	17,068
Neston and Parkgate U.D.	3,331	5,195
Wirral Rural District Council	36,761	24,753
Chester Rural District (Part of)	10,763	2,744
Total	**66,964**	**318,313**

Wallasey and Birkenhead came under what today would be called unitary authorities, which administered every local amenity, including education, police and emergency services. The other councils were district authorities, whose police, education and emergency services were provided by Cheshire County Council.

Later on, Ellesmere Port also became a borough. By the 1970s it was thought that many of the old counties no longer represented the true dispositions of populations. There were two county boroughs at the northern end of the peninsula and the rest of the land came under Cheshire County Council, but the majority of the population had far more to do with Liverpool than they did with Chester. As we have seen, vast numbers of Wirralians travelled to the city daily to work; it was also the main venue for shopping and entertainment. In 1974 the new Metropolitan County of Merseyside was created. Wirral Borough Council, with its headquarters at Wallasey Town Hall, became one of its constituent parts. The new council did not embrace the entire peninsula—its southern portion was placed within the bounds of Neston and Ellesmere Port District Council which remained in Cheshire. It led to the erroneous and hurtful road sign on the side of the A540 at Gayton which welcomed motorists—who by then had already travelled some eight miles into the peninsula—to Wirral. The more southerly villages along the Dee were now apparently somewhere else.

Oddly enough, the boundary between Merseyside and Cheshire looked a little bit like the possible boundary which had existed between Norse and Anglo-Saxon Wirral 1,000 years previously. There is a tenuous connection between the two: the reader will remember how southern Lancashire has a similar proportion of Norse place-names as Wirral and the way in which there seems to have been a continuing exchange of populations between the two districts right up to the early modern period. The population movements of the 19th and 20th centuries could be viewed as the latest stage in that tradition. Certainly, by that time, the speech of north Wirral was almost indistinguishable from that of Liverpool. However, boundaries cannot be redrawn without hurting people's feelings. For as long as Cheshire had been in existence Wirral had been a part of it. It seemed arrogant and heartless suddenly to divide the peninsula. Some people resented the official connection with Liverpool, believing that the city was socially and economically very different from Wirral; others found the name 'Merseyside' itself cumbersome and contrived; and so many continued to write 'Cheshire' at the end of their postal addresses. The government of Margaret Thatcher in 1986 abolished Merseyside itself. Wirral and Ellesmere Port and Neston Borough Councils are now unitary authorities. Presumably no part of the peninsula is now entitled to use Cheshire as an address. At the time of writing the issue still excites emotion—Kenneth Burnley wrote this in the spring of 2002:

> The first essential step is to scrap Wirral Borough Council and Ellesmere Port Borough Council and replace them with a new unit that covers the whole of the peninsula—from top to tail—under the aegis of our rightful county of Cheshire. This will help to ensure that the future demands made upon the place are seen and implemented as a corporate whole, and will help re-create that sense of oneness and belonging that we used to have, but which has disappeared since 1974. Then all residents of the peninsula, acting with pride in the place in which they live, will feel encouraged to strive and work together to ensure that this small, fragile, but very special peninsula settles into becoming the community of prosperity and happiness that it deserves to be.[19]

Wirral's history is a microcosm of England's history. Just like the country as a whole, the peninsula carries the evidence for its transmogrification from a rural to an industrial and thence to a post-industrial land. It contains a representative of most of the environments which can be found within the wider nation: decaying former docks and factories, Victorian middle- and working-class suburbs, once elegant coastal resorts and residences, 20th-century semi-detached private and council housing estates, parks, farmland, heathland and a few exceedingly precious tiny remnants of wilderness. The cyclist can travel in a northerly direction along the A41 during the early part of a November evening and pass through Great and Little Sutton, thinking that there can be no end to the suburbs, but then a left turn is taken and the unremitting line of houses is broken. The sun is sinking and its rays are fractured through the black branches. The Clwydian Hills become stunningly apparent for the first time. A winding route through the heart of the peninsula is followed and its quiet countryside begins to invade the senses—copses, ponds and murky morasses pleasingly disrupt the clipped hawthorn-cordoned pastures. Tyres splatter through the film of earth and dung which the feet of cattle have painted over the road. A farmyard is passed and there is a reassuring hum from the milking sheds and the sweet smell of barns. Further on, tiny hedgerow birds have their final twittering arguments before the night. Blackbirds skitter in alarm; crows caw and head for their gaunt roosts. A fox shouts and a pheasant coughs. Home is achieved and it feels that this land has not changed since the days when the workers smoked clay pipes. Soon life's routine takes hold again and time is spent on the streets, in the offices and at the shops—we remember that the peninsula is also urban and we wonder for how long and by what means its rurality will be preserved.

Wirral's charms are delicate. It began to be colonised on a large scale because people who worked in towns wanted to live in the country. Paradoxically, just by settling here they were helping to destroy the very beauty they had come to enjoy. The author well remembers the formation of an environmental protection group in Greasby in 1975. A meeting was convened in order to protest against a vast new housing development. An elderly man interrupted the proceedings to denounce all the protestors as hypocrites—were they not living in houses which had been built on once beautiful fields? To reinforce his point he described how one of the main residential areas, between Wood Lane and Upton, had been orchards and how the sight and smell of the blossom in spring had made it, for him, the most gorgeous place on earth and there it was now—a large middle-class estate, whose inhabitants were resisting the creation of another one just like it in another part of the village.

The suburbs began seriously to expand during the inter-war years. Some of the original colonisers of places like Moreton and Thingwall lived in caravans which were turned into permanent houses later on. Other new developments were the result of local authority action. The *Liverpool Daily Post* of 13 March 1928 reported a meeting of the Wirral Rural District Housing Inspection Committee. It was announced that 10,000 new houses had been built since 1921. The council had 'advanced over 300,000 pounds to occupiers for purchase of their properties'. The Fender Valley Sewer of 1902 was 'the largest of any ever attempted by any local authority up to that time' and was designed to cope with the increased population. At the time of the article, another £250,000 was being spent on sewerage improvements. A great many of the 20th century's typical dwellings— the semi-detached house with driveway and adjoining garage—were built before the Second World War. Following the War there was another wave of development which has continued to this day. Many thousands of acres of farmland have disappeared. In certain areas, numerous settlements have coalesced into great amorphous sprawls: we think of Thingwall, Irby, Pensby and Heswall or Greasby, Moreton, Upton and Woodchurch. Neston is now indistinguishable from Little Neston, Ness and Parkgate and Great and Little Sutton have merged with Ellesmere Port, which itself used to be several smaller townships.

Former agricultural districts now have no working farms whatsoever. Greg Dawson informs us that Pensby now has no farms and only one piece of ground which has anything like an agricultural use—a paddock upon which ponies graze. It is a remarkable phenomenon. Think about Norman Ellison's 1955 words:

> The large country houses and small estates of the wealthy mid-Victorian merchants have made way for avenues of attractive villas, and development is by no means finished. Such is the story of the immediate surroundings of all our cities: our population is increasing and

people must live somewhere. When the acreage of fertile agricultural land buried under bricks and mortar becomes so great that we are all in grave danger of starvation, then perhaps somebody in authority will realise that we should build vertically and not horizontally.

Wirral now has less agricultural land than ever before, but we have more food and at lower prices than ever before. Economies have developed in a far more complex manner than Ellison could ever have imagined: as a result of scientific and technological advancement, agricultural yields are now huge. Ellison would have been very surprised to hear that, not long after his death, farmers were being subsidised to produce food which nobody ever ate and lay rotting in warehouses.

We can understand that the growth of population has necessitated the construction of more houses and that the loss of some countryside has been inevitable, but many Wirralians have been disgruntled with the assumption that all forms of urban development, regardless of the heritage which they destroy and the ugliness they create, are synonymous with 'progress'. In 1981 in his *Portrait of Wirral* Kenneth Burnley reflected on changes which had occurred in the north of the peninsula:

> Much has been said and written about the disastrous planning (if indeed it can be called planning) which has resulted in the virtual destruction of Bidston's immediate environment; suffice it to say that the damage has been done. It is to be hoped, though, that lessons have been learnt by many; not only by the local authority, but by those ordinary folk of Wirral who should have done something, who should have stood up and shouted long and loud, to save Bidston from the ravishes of insensitive planning. Some did fight; as a result of a 'Save Bidston' campaign in the late 1960s the Council declared the village the first conservation area in 1971. Yet even as I write, plans are afoot to convert one of the old cottages into a restaurant and the Hall into a country club.

Mr Burnley is introducing an important point: people have got to make choices. Do they believe that uninhibited urban development is truly progress? Is it right that ease of travel by motor car and the accessibility of consumer goods, at any time of the day or night, in superstores should take priority over the preservation of the natural world in which we live? Do we want totally to expunge every remnant of the human past from the landscape?

During the last quarter of the 20th century, by their acquiescence to a whole range of hideous and irreversible road and retail development schemes—on Upton Meadow, at Bidston Moss, on the edge of Ellesmere Port—the majority of people seemed to answer those questions in the affirmative. The small minority who answered in the negative—the voices in the wilderness—were labelled as reactionaries and cranks. By enabling us objectively to view the effects of man's decisions over time, the study of history enables us to determine the true nature of progress. This and the previous chapter have told the stories of how people believed that their huge urban and industrial development projects were bound to benefit mankind. We have seen how the rewards of these enterprises were at best ambiguous and at worst non-existent. Furthermore, currently, it is becoming increasingly apparent that the supposed creation of material wealth by the exploitation of natural resources is gradually making the earth uninhabitable. It seems that the conservationist is not a crank after all, but simply someone who would like to ensure that the human race has a home.

Alienation is a modern problem—from nature, from each other and from communal heritage. Material security provides only a degree of satisfaction. People also need to be

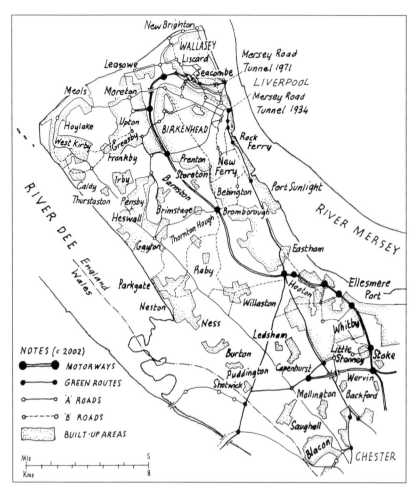

105 The motorways and roads network of 20th-century Wirral.

spiritually nourished by their environment and to have a sense of where they fit in space and time. Rapid urban development has detached them not only from the natural world, but also from their roots. Wirral has seen the exponential growth of an unhealthy by-product of this detachment—nostalgia. There seems to be an unlimited market for sentimentally annotated collections of old photographs and columns of purple prose eulogising the 'good old days'. Nostalgia is a false friend—it cannot return us to the past for which we yearn, partly because that past never existed; it creates nothing but a transient emotion and, by misrepresenting our past, it makes our present less understandable and, thereby, increases our alienation.

Nostalgia needs to give way to history. Objective study of the past can lend meaning to the present and enable wiser decisions about the future. We cannot return to the past, but, by studying its people and their relationship with that part of the earth's surface upon which we live, we will have a better chance of building healthy and peaceful relationships both with each other and with our planet. At no stage has it been assumed that this work is the final word on the story of the people and land of Wirral. It is hoped that some degree of curiosity has been satisfied and more has been aroused and that many more people will be provoked both to study our local history and to value our heritage.

Appendix 1

Roman Wirral

A) Roman Coins Discovered in Wirral. From Shotter, D., *Roman Coins from North-West England*

Where Found	When Found	Description	Century
		(Imperial Roman Coins in descending order of value with equivalent value of next denomination in brackets: *Aureus* (25), *Denarius* (4), *Sestertius* (2), *Dupondius* (2), *As* (2), *Semis* (2), *Quadrantes;* Other Coins: *Radiate* = an inflationary 'double-*sestertius*', introduced in the A.D. 240s; *Antoninianus* = an inflationary 'double-*denarius*', introduced by Caracalla)	(All A.D. unless otherwise stated
Birkenhead	*c*.1900	A hoard about which no details have survived.	?
		Hadrian	2nd
	1952	Constantine I	4th
	1965	A Coin?	?
Backford	*c*.1920	*Aes* of Maximian	3rd
Bebington (Church)	1876	*Antoninianus* of Valerian	3rd
Bebington	1971	*Radiate* of Posthumus	3rd
Blacon	1953	*Denarius* of Nerva	1st
	1934	Greek *Aes*—issue of Geta	3rd
	?	*Sestertius* of Gordian III	3rd
	?	*Radiate* of Victorinus	3rd
Bromborough	1900	Domitian	1st
	1936	Vespasian	1st
	1969	*Sestertius* of Marcus Aurelius	2nd
	?	?	4th
Childer Thornton	1990	*Denarius* of Vespasian	1st
Chorlton-by-Backford	1999	*Denarius* of Domitian	1st
	1818	?	?
Eastham	*c*.1889	Hoard consisting mainly of coins of Constantine.	4th?
	1956	Constantius Gallus	4th
Ellesmere Port	Pre-1976	?	?
Heswall	?	*As* of Antoninus Pius ?	2nd
Hooton	1889	Hoard of coins of Constantine	4th
		Sestertius of Antoninus Pius ?	2nd
Hoylake	?	*As* of Nero	1st
Meols	19th cen.	91 coins	1st to 5th
	1980s	Republic;	1st B.C.
		Claudius I 2;	1st
		Domitian;	1st
		Hadrian 3;	2nd
		Antoninus Pius (?);	2nd

[183]

Where Found	When Found	Description	Century
Meols (contd.)		Marcus Aurelius; *As.*	2nd Probably 2nd
Mockbeggar Wharf	1979 ? ? 1991	*Denarius* of Trajan; *Denarius* of Caracalla; *Radiates* of Gallienus and Tetricus I; *Aes*-issue of Philip I from Antioch, Syria	2nd 3rd 3rd
Mollington	1940	*As* of Domitian	1st
Moreton Beach	1998	*Denarius* of Septimus Severus	3rd
Ness	?	*Aes* of Hadrian	2nd
Neston	? ? *c.*1930 1866	*Sestertius* of Marcus Aurelius A Coin ? *Tetradrachm* Diocletian Hoard, including 2 of Constantine I	2nd ? 3rd 4th
Oxton, Arno Hill	1834	Antoninus Pius, Honorius, Marius Victorinus?	2nd to 4th?
Parkgate	1867	*As* of Claudius	1st
Saughall	Pre-1966	*As* of Titus as Caesar	1st
Shotwick	1999	*Sestertius* of Antoninus Pius ?	2nd
Thingwall	?	*Sestertius* of Antoninus Pius	2nd
Thurstaston	?	Constantine I	4th
Wallasey	1979 *c.*1955 1939	*Denarius* of Trajan *Antoninianus* of Gordian III Valentinian	2nd 3rd 4th
West Kirby	c.1937	Constantius II	4th
Willaston	1997/8	*Aes* coins of Constantine	4th
Wirral ?	?	*Denarius* of Marcus Antoninus	1st

B) Roman Tombstone Discovered in 1887 in the East Part of the Northern Wall of the City of Chester

A lower block of cream Keuper Sandstone of a monumental tomb; the mouldings below the inscription have been broken away and a deep cist has been cut into the upper surface.

> *...] Pub(lilia tribu) c(enturio) leg(ionum) V Macid(onicae) et*
> *VIII Aug(ustae) et II Aug(ustae) et XX V(aleriae) V(ictricis)*
> *Vixit annis LXI Aristio*
> *Lib(ertus) h(eres) f(aciendum) c(uravit)*

'... Of the Pubilian voting-tribe, centurion of the Legions Fifth Macedonica, Eighth Augusta, Second Augusta and Twentieth Valeria Victrix, lived 61 years. His freedman and heir Aristio had this set up.'

This centurion served with the first two legions probably in Germany, with the Second Augusta at Caerleon, Monmouthshire and with the Twentieth at Chester. Mention of a voting tribe tells us that he was a Roman citizen. He did not have a cognomen, or extra name indicating to which branch of the family he belonged, with the name of the voting-tribe, so it might be an early inscription.

The stone upon which the inscription has been carved came from Wirral. This does not mean that the soldier had anything personally to do with Wirral, but it does imply that the Roman garrison exploited the resources of the peninsula and perhaps designated it as a *prata legionis*. See Chapter 2 for full details.

From: The Grosvenor Museum, Chester, 'The Roman Inscriptions in the Grosvenor Museum, Chester' (1978); Reprinted from Collingwood, R.G. and Wright, R.P., *The Roman Inscriptions of Britain* (Oxford University Press, Oxford, 1965).

Appendix II

The Battle of Brunanburh

from Garmonsway, G.N. (Trans.), *The Anglo-Saxon Chronicle* (Dent, London, 1953)

937: In this year king Athelstan, lord of Warriors,
Ring-river of men, with his brother prince Edmund,
Won undying glory with the edges of swords,
With their hammered, blades, the sons of Edward
Clove the shield-wall and hacked the linden bucklers,
As was instinctive in them, from their ancestry,
To defend their land, their treasures and their homes,
In frequent battle against each enemy.
The foemen were laid low: the Scots
And the host from the ships fell doomed. The field
Grew dark with the blood of men after the sun,
That glorious luminary, God's bright candle,
Rose high in the morning above the horizon,
Until the noble being of the Lord Eternal
Sank to its rest. There lay many a warrior
Of the men of the North, torn by spears,
Shot o'er his shield; likewise many a Scot
Sated with battle, lay lifeless.
All through the day the West Saxons in troops
Pressed on in pursuit of the hostile peoples,
Fiercely, with swords sharpened on grindstone,
They cut down the fugitives as they fled.
Nor did the Mercians refuse hard fighting
To any of Anlaf's warriors, who invaded
Our land across the tossing waters,
In the ship's bosom, to meet their doom
In the fight. Five young kings,
Stretched lifeless by the swords,
Lay on the field, likewise seven
Of Anlaf's jarls, and a countless host
Of seamen and Scots. There the prince
Of Norsemen, compelled by necessity,
Was forced to flee to the prow of his ship
With a handful of men. In haste the ship
Was launched, and the king fled hence,
Over the waters grey, to save his life.
There, likewise, the aged Constantine,
The grey-haired warrior, set off in flight,

North to his native land. No cause
Had he to exult in that clash of swords,
Bereaved of his kinsmen, robbed of his friends
On the field of battle, by violence deprived
Of them in the struggle. On the place of slaughter
He left his young son, mangled by wounds,
Received in the fight. No need to exult
In that clash of blades had the grey-haired warrior,
That practised scoundrel, and no more had Anlaf
Need to gloat, amid the remnants of their host,
That they excelled in martial deeds
Where standards clashed, and spear met spear
And man fought man, upon a field
Where swords were crossed, when they in battle
Fought Edward's sons, upon the fateful field.
The sorry Norsemen who escaped the spears
Set out upon the sea of Ding, making for Dublin
O'er deep waters, in ships with nailed sides,
Ashamed and shameless back to Ireland.
Likewise the English king and the prince,
Brothers triumphant in war, together
Returned to their home, the land of Wessex.
To enjoy the carnage, they left behind
The horn-beaked raven with dusky plumage,
And the hungry hawk of battle, the dun-coated
Eagle, who with white-tipped tail shared
The feast with the wolf, grey beast of the forest.
Never before in this island, as the books
Of ancient historians tell us, was an army
Put to greater slaughter by the sword
Since the time when Angles and Saxons landed,
Invading Britain across the wide seas
From the east, when warriors eager for fame,
Proud forgers of war, the Welsh overcame,
And won for themselves a kingdom.

The above verses appear next to the date 937 in the *Anglo-Saxon Chronicle*. They do not describe the exact location of the battle, but scholars seem broadly to agree that *Brunanburh* was Bromborough. Historically and linguistically, it fits: by 937, the Wirral Norse colony would have been strong enough to act as a safe bridgehead for a combined Norse and Scots attack upon the Anglo-Saxons. At this time, Mercia was a particular target for attempted Norse invasions. The 'Sea of Ding' or *Dingesmere* could have been the Irish Sea. Local topographical details are further evidence for the battle having been fought in Wirral. The ridge of high ground on the border between Higher Bebington and Storeton is thought to be the possible heart of the battlefield. Local folklore certainly speaks of a great battle having been fought there and contains references to places called Red Hill (so-called because of the blood of dying warriors which ran down its slopes), 'Soldiers' Hill', 'Battlefields' and 'King's Road'. See Harding's *Ingimind's Saga* (pp.121-37) and Cavill et al., *Wirral and its Viking Heritage* (pp.4 and 123).

Appendix III

Domesday Book: Wirral Manors

('In *Wilaveston* Hundred'). Transcribed from *Domesday Book*: *Cheshire* edited by Philip Morgan (1978). See Chapter Four for analysis.

The Bishop of Chester holds:

(GUILDEN) SUTTON (*Sudtone*) himself. 1 hide paying tax. Land for 3 ploughs. In Lordship 1; 5 villagers and 2 smallholders with 1 plough. Meadow, 6 acres. Value before 1066, 40s; now 20s.

St Werburgh's Church has 13 houses in the City of Chester, exempt from all customary dues; one is the churchwarden's; the others are the Canon's. The Church itself holds and held before 1066:

WERVIN (Wiverene). 1 hide and two parts of 1 hide. Land for 3 ploughs. 4 villagers and 2 smallholders have 1½ ploughs. Meadow, ½ acre. Value before 1066, 30s; now 20s.

CROUGHTON (Crostone). 1 hide paying tax. Land for 1 plough. 1 rider, 2 villagers and 1 smallholder have 1 plough. Meadow 1 acre. The value was and is 10s.

LEA (Wisdelea) itself. 1 hide paying tax. Land for 3 ploughs. In lordship 1; 2 slaves; 2 villagers and 2 smallholders with 1 plough. Meadow, 1 acre. Value before 1066,10s; now as much.

(GREAT) SUTTON (Sudtone) itself and held it before 1066. 1 hide paying tax. Land for 5 ploughs. In lordship ½ plough; 5 villagers and 9 smallholders with 2 ploughs. Value before 1066, 40s; now 30s.

SAUGHALL (Salhare). 1 hide paying tax. Land for 1 plough. It is there, in lordship; 2 slaves; 1 villager and 1 smallholder. Value before 1066, 16s; now as much.

SHOTWICK (Sotoviche). 1 hide paying tax. Land for 3 ploughs. 4 villagers and 2 smallholders with 1 plough. Meadow, 1 acre. Value before 1066, 16s; now 13s 3d.

(GREAT) NESTON (Nestone). William holds from the (Church). A third part of 2 hides paying tax. Land for 1 plough. It pays and paid 17s 4d in revenue.

RABY (Rabie) William holds from the (Church). ½ hide paying tax. Land for 1 plough. It pays and paid 6s 8d revenue.

Earl Hugh holds:

EASTHAM (Estham) Earl Edwin held it. 22 hides paying tax. Land for as many ploughs. In lordship 2 ploughs; 4 slaves; 14 villagers and 10 smallholders with 6 ploughs. A mill, 2 riders and a priest. Mundret holds 2 hides of this manor's land, Hugh 2 hides, William 1 hide, Walter ½ hide, Hamo 7 hides, Robert 1 hide and Robert ½ hide. In lordship 4 ploughs; 8 ploughmen; 22 villagers, 11 smallholders, 5 riders and 2 Frenchmen with 9 ploughs. Total value of the manor before 1066 £24; later £4; now the value of the Earl's lordship £4, of his men's 112s.

(MICKLE) TRAFFORD (Traford) Ording held it; he was a free man. 2 hides paying tax. Land for 6 ploughs. In lordship 2; 2 slaves; 4 villagers and 2 smallholders with 1 plough. Value before 1066, 100s; now 40s; found waste.

HADLOW (Edelaue) Earl Edwin held it. 1 hide paying tax. Land for 1 plough. It was waste; now a man
  ploughs it and pays 2s.

UPTON (BY CHESTER) (Optone) Earl Edwin held it. 4½ hides paying tax. Land for 12 ploughs. In
  lordship 1; 2 ploughmen; 12 villagers and 2 riders with 5 ploughs. Of this land, Hamo holds 2 parts of
  1 hide of this manor; Herbert ½ hide; Mundret 1 hide. In lordship 4 ploughs; 8 ploughmen. 2 villagers
  and 2 smallholders with 1 plough. Meadow 1 acre. Value of the whole manor before 1066, 60s; now the
  Earl's lordship 45s, his men's 40s.

(GREAT and LITTLE) STANNEY (Stanei). Restald holds from him. Ragenald held it like a free man.
  1 hide paying tax. Land for 2 ploughs. In lordship 1; 2 ploughmen; 2 villagers and 2 smallholders. A
  fishery. Value before 1066, 12s; now 14s. The fifth acre of this land was and ought to be St Werburgh's
  church's, as the county witnesses; the Canons claim it, because they lost it wrongfully.

Robert Son of Hugh holds:

(LITTLE) SUTTON (Sudtone). Toki held it; he was a free man. 1 hide paying tax. Land for 3 ploughs.
  In lordship 1; 3 smallholders with 1 (plough?). Meadow, 6 acres. Value before 1066, 40s; later 6s; now it
  pays 64d in revenue.

Robert of Rhuddlan holds:

(LITTLE) MOLLINGTON (BANASTRE) (Molintone). From Earl Hugh. Godwin held it; he was a
  free man. 1½ hides paying tax. Land for 3 ploughs. In lordship 1; 3 slaves; 3 villagers and 3 smallholders.
  Meadow, 2 acres; woodland, 2 acres. Before 1066 it was waste; value when acquired 20s; now 15s.

(GREAT) MOLLINGTON (TARRANT) (Molintone). Lambert holds from him. Gunner and Ulf held
  it as 2 manors; they were free men. 1 hide paying tax. Land for 2 ploughs. In lordship 1, with 2 slaves.
  Meadow, 2 acres. Value 14s; it was waste; found waste.

LEIGHTON (Lestone). William holds from him. Leofnoth held it; he was a free man. 1 hide paying tax.
  Land for 2 ploughs. In lordship 1 plough, with 1 slave. 1 Frenchman and 2 smallholders. 2 fisheries. The
  value was and is 15s.

THORNTON (MAYEU later HOUGH) (Torintone). William holds from him. Ulfketel held it; he was
  a free man. ½ hide paying tax. Land for 2 ploughs. 1 rider, 1 villager and 1 smallholder have ½ plough.
  The value was 10s; later and now 5s.

GAYTON (Gaytone). William holds from him. Leofnoth, a free man, held it. 1 hide paying tax. Land for
  2 ploughs. 2 villagers and 3 smallholders have 1 plough. 2 fisheries. The value was 15s; later 2s; now
  3s.

HESWALL (Eswelle). Herbert holds from him. Ulfkel held it; he was a free man. 2 hides paying tax. Land
  for 4 ploughs. In lordship 1; 2 ploughmen; 3 villagers and 1 smallholder with 1 plough. Value before
  1066, 16s; later 20s; now 22s.

THURSTASTON (Turstanetone). William holds from him. Leofnoth held it; he was a free man. 2 hides
  paying tax. Land for 4 ploughs. In lordship 1; 2 ploughmen; 4 villagers and 4 smallholders with 1½
  ploughs. Value before 1066, 30s; later 8s; now 16s.

(GREAT) CALDY (Calders). Leofnoth held it; he was a free man. 3 hides paying tax. Land for 10
  ploughs; 5 villagers and 5 smallholders have 2 ploughs; 1 Frenchman with 1 servant has 2 ploughs. In
  lordship 2 oxen. Meadow, 2 acres. Value before 1066, 50s; later 10s; now 24s.

(LITTLE) MEOLS (Melas). Leofnoth held it. 1 hide paying tax. Land for 1½ ploughs. 1 rider, 2 villagers
  and 2 smallholders have 1 plough. Value before 1066, 15s; now 10s; found waste.

(GREAT) MEOLS (Melas). Leofnoth held it. 1 hide paying tax. Land for 3 ploughs. 1 rider, 3 villagers
  and 3 smallholders have 1 plough. Value before 1066, 10s; later 8s; now 12s.

WALLASEY (Walea). Uhtred held it; he was a free man. 1½ hides paying tax. Land for 4 ploughs. 1
  villager and 1 smallholder with ½ plough; 1 Frenchman has a plough with 2 ploughmen; 1 rider and 1
  smallholder. (Value ...)

Robert Cook holds:

NESTON (*Nestone*) from the Earl. Osgot held it; he was a free man. 1 hide paying tax. Land for 3 ploughs. In lordship 2; 1 slave; 2 villagers and 4 smallholders with 1 plough; 1 Frenchman. Value before 1066, 13s 4d; now 16s; found waste.

HARGRAVE (*Haregrave*). Osgot held it. 1 hide paying tax. Land for 2 ploughs. 3 villagers and 2 smallholders have 1 plough. Value before 1066, 6s 8d; now 10s; value when acquired 4s.

Richard of Vernon holds:

PICTON (*Pichetone*). Toki held it. He was a free man. 1 hide paying tax. Land for 3 ploughs. In lordship 1; 2 ploughmen; 1 rider and 3 smallholders with 1 plough. Meadow, ½ acre. Value before 1066, 40s; later 5s; now 20s.

HOOTON (*Hotone*). Toki held it. 1 hide and two parts of 1 hide paying tax. Land for 3 ploughs. 4 riders, 1 villager and 4 smallholders with 2 ploughs. Value before 1066, 30s; later 5s; now 16s.

Walter of Vernon holds:

NESS (*Nesse*). Erngeat held it. 1½ hides paying tax. Land for 2 ploughs. In lordship 1; 2 ploughmen; 5 villagers and 3 smallholders with 2 ploughs. Meadow, ½ acre. Value before 1066, 20s; now 16s.

LEDSHAM (*Levetesham*) Erngeat held it. 1 hide paying tax. Land for 2 ploughs. In lordship ½ plough; 1 slave; 1 rider and 1 smallholder with ½ plough between them. Value before 1066, 5s; later 8s; now 10s.

PRENTON (*Prestune*) Wulfgeat, Edric and Luvede held it as 3 manors; they were free. 1½ hides paying tax. Land for 3 ploughs. In lordship 1; 2 ploughmen; 2 smallholders. A mill which serves the court; woodland 1 league long and 1 wide. The value was 7s; now 5s.

William Malbank holds:

WERVIN (*Wivrevin*). Colbert held it; he was a free man. A third part of a 1 hide paying tax. Land for 1 plough. 2 villagers with ½ a plough. The value was 8s; now 4s.

(OVER- and NETHER-) POOL (*Pol*). Ernwin held it as a manor. Land for 4 bovates paying tax. 1 villager and 1 smallholder have ½ plough. The value was and is 4s.

SAUGHALL (*Salhale*). Leofing held it; he was a free man. 6 hides paying tax. Land for 6 ploughs. In lordship 1½; 1 slave; 7 villagers, 1 rider and 4 smallholders with 3½ ploughs. A fishery. Value before 1066, 20s; later 22s; now 45s.

LANDICAN (*Landechene*). Aescwulf held it; he was a free man. 7 hides paying tax. Land for 8 ploughs. In lordship 1; a priest, 9 villagers, 7 smallholders and 4 Frenchmen with 5 ploughs between them. Value before 1066, 50s; now 40s; found waste.

UPTON (OVERCHURCH)(*Optone*). Colbert, who also held it as a free man, holds from him. 3 hides paying tax. Land for 5 ploughs. In lordship 1; 4 slaves; 2 villagers, 1 rider and 4 smallholders with 1 plough. Meadow, 2 acres. Value before 1066, 25s; now 20s.

THINGWALL (*Tvigvele*). Durand holds from him. Winterlet held it; he was a free man. 1 hide paying tax. Land for 2 ploughs. In lordship 1; 2 slaves. 1 villager and 1 smallholder have another (plough). Value before 1066, 8s; now 5s.

NOCTORUM (*Chenoterie*). Richard holds from him. Colbert held it; he was a free man. ½ hide paying tax. Land for 1 plough, which is there, in lordship, with 2 ploughmen; 2 villagers. The value was 15s; now 10s; it was waste.

William son of Nigel holds:

NESTON (*Nestone*). Arni held it; he was a free man. 2 parts of 2 hides paying tax. Land for 4 ploughs. In lordship 2 ploughs; 1 slave. A priest, 4 villagers and 2 smallholders have 3 ploughs. Value before 1066, 20s; later as much; now 25s.

RABY (*Rabie*). Hardwin holds from him. Arni held it. ½ hide paying tax. Land for 1 plough. It is there, in lordship; 1 slave; 2 villagers and 2 smallholders with 1 plough. Value before 1066, 10s; later 14s; now 20s.

CAPENHURST (*Capeles*). David holds from him. ½ hide paying tax. Arni held it. Land for 1 plough. It is there , with 1 villager and 2 smallholders. Value before 1066 and later 5s; now 8s.

BARNSTON (*Bernestone*). Ralph holds from him. Ravenswart and Leofgeat held it as 2 manors; they were free men. 1 hide paying tax. Land for 2 ploughs. In lordship 1; 2 ploughmen; 3 smallholders. Value, 10s; found waste.

Hugh of Delamere holds:

(LITTLE) CALDY (*Calders*) Erngeat held it; he was a free man. 1 hide paying tax. Land for 3 ploughs. In lordship 1, with 1 smallholder. The value was 5s; now 10s.

Ranulf (Mainwaring) holds:

BLACON (*Blachehole*) from Earl Hugh. Thored held it; he was a free man. 2 hides paying tax. Land for 4 ploughs. In lordship 2; 4 ploughmen. 4 villagers and 4 smallholders have 1 plough. A fishery. Value before 1066, 14s; now 40s.

Osbern son of Tezzo holds:

POULTON (LANCELYN) (*Pontone*). Roger holds from him. Gamel held it; he was a free man. 2 hides paying tax. Land for 4 ploughs. In lordship 1; 2 slaves; 1 rider, 1 villager, a priest and 4 smallholders with 1 plough between them. Value before 1066, 25s; later it was waste; value now 25s.

Nigel (of Burcy) holds:

GREASBY (*Gravesberie*). Dunning held it. 2 hides paying tax. Land for 3 ploughs. In lordship 1; 2 slaves. 3 villagers, 2 Frenchmen and 1 smallholder with 1 plough between them. Value before 1066, 25s; later 10s; now 20s.

STORETON (*Stortone*). Dunning held it. 2 hides paying tax. Land for 3 ploughs. In lordship ½ plough; 1 slave; 5 villagers and 3 smallholders with 1½ ploughs. Value before 1066, 15s; now 20s; it was waste.

Erroneously Placed in Eddisbury (*Risedon*) Hundred:

The Bishop holds **BURTON** (*Burtone*) himself, and held it before 1066. 3 hides paying tax. Land for 7 ploughs. In lordship 2 ploughs; 7 villagers, 4 smallholders, a priest and 1 rider with 3 ploughs. Meadow, 1 acre. Value before 1066, 40s; now as much; when acquired 15s.

Erroneously Placed in Nantwich (*Warmundestrou*) Hundred:

Hamo of Mascy holds **PUDDINGTON** (*Potitone*) from Earl Hugh. Wulfric held it; he was a free man. 2½ hides paying tax. Land for 3 ploughs. In Lordship 1: 1 slave; 4 villagers, 4 smallholders and 1 rider with 1 plough. Value 20s; it was waste.

Notes

(Full references given only to works not appearing in the main bibliography)

One: From Creation to the First Settlements

1. Young, in *A Perambulation of the Hundred of Wirral*, gives the popularly accepted account in which he implies that there was only one such find. There were four quarries on Storeton Hill. The largest and commercially by far the most important was the North Quarry, worked from 1838 until the 1880s. The footprints, however, came from two of the smaller quarries. The earliest finds, in 1838, came from the South Quarry, the oldest of the four, which lay in the parish of Higher Bebington. The second spate of finds, from 1906 to 1912, came from the Higher Bebington White Freestone Quarry, situated immediately to the north of the by-then-disused South Quarry. Between them, these two quarries must have yielded several hundred footprints, although only a fraction of these still survive. An exhaustive account of the quarries and footprint finds can be found in Tresise and Sarjeant, *Tracks of Triassic Vertebrates* (Stationery Office, N.M.G.M.,1997). The author is indebted to Alan Bowden and Dr Geoff Tresise from the Liverpool Museum for supplying this information.
2. Jermy and Rickards, *Quarries and Brickfields*.
3. Greswell and Lawton, *Merseyside*, p.6.
4. Greswell, *Physical Geography* (Longman, London, 1974)
5. Gresswell and Lawton, *op. cit.*, p.8.
6. Hewitt, *The Wirral Peninsula*.
7. Ellison, *The Wirral Peninsula*, p.87.
8. Hewitt, *op. cit.*
9. Greswell and Lawton, *op.cit.*, p.10.
10. Plater, A.J. et al., 'The Land of the Mersey Basin: Sea Level Changes' in Greenwood, *A History of the Mersey Basin*.
11. Kenna, R., *Early Settlement on the North Wirral Coastal Area*; *An Old Woodland Floor Beneath the Sea—The Peat Beds of the North Wirral Coast*; Innes, J., *Woodlands Beneath the Sea*.
12. Ashton, *Evolution of a Coast Line*, p.124.
13. Kenna, *op. cit.*, 1978, p.32.
14. Rideout, *Wirral Watersheds and River Systems*, p.107.

Two: From the First Settlers to the Romans

1. Rasmus Nyerup (1759-1829), Danish antiquarian, quoted in McIntosh, J., *The Practical Archaeologist* (Thames and Hudson, London, 1999) p.9. Details about Thomsen and the ages of man are also contained in this work.
2. Sulley, *The Hundred of Wirral*, p.2.
3. For fuller details about the formation of the ancient environment and about the methods employed in investigating it see: Kenna, *Early Settlement on the North Wirral Coastal Area*; *An Old Woodland Floor Beneath the Sea—The Peat Beds of the North Wirral Coast*; Innes, J., *Woodlands Beneath the Sea—An Ancient Forest Reveals its Secrets*; Greenwood, *Ecology and Landscape Development: A History of the Mersey Basin*.
4. The author is indebted to Ron Cowell and Rob Philpott who have freely provided him with copies of their interim reports and been willing to show and discuss the artifacts. They are still analysing their findings from the sites; complete reports will be published in due course. Please see bibliography

for full details of their relevant interim reports and articles, all of which have been used in the composition of this chapter.

5. Mithen, S., 'Hunter Gatherers of the Mesolithic' in *The Archaeology of Britain: An Introduction from the Upper Palaeolithic to the Industrial Revolution* (Routledge, London, 1999).
6. Cowell, *The Wetlands of Merseyside*.
7. Varley, *Cheshire Before the Romans*, p.21.
8. See Gazetteer in *V.C.H.*, p.39.
9. Roeder, *On a Newly Discovered Neolithic Settlement at the Red Noses*.
10. Higham, *The Origins of Cheshire*, p.17.
11. Dodgson, *The Place-Names of Cheshire*, p.255.
12. *V.C.H., ibid.*
13. Chitty, *Wirral Rural Fringes etc.*, p.4.
14. Booth, *Burton in Wirral* and *V.C.H., ibid.*
15. Shotter, *Roman North West England: The Process of Annexation*.
16. Shotter, D., *Roman Britain* (Lancaster Pamphlets, Routledge, London, 1998).
17. Shotter, *Roman Coins From North-West England*.
18. Philpott, *A Romano-British Brooch Type*.
19. Jermy, *The Roman Road in Wirral*.

Three: Celtic, Saxon and Viking Wirral, A.D. 400-1066

1. Suggested reading on Dark-Age England: Stenton, F., *Anglo-Saxon England* (Oxford University Press, Oxford, 1971); Morris, J., *The Age of Arthur* (Phillimore & Co. Ltd, Chichester, 1977).
2. Philpott, *Three Byzantine Coins etc.*
3. *A Pilgrim Flask of St Menas*, J.C.A.S.
4. Bu'Lock, *Pre-Conquest Cheshire*; Dodgson, *The English Arrival in Cheshire*; Higham, *The Origins of Cheshire*.
5. Chitty, *Wirral Rural Fringes etc.* and V.C.H.
6. Bu'Lock, *Pre-Conquest Cheshire*, p.8.
7. It is also argued that it is an Irish name. See Cavill et al., *Wirral and Its Viking Heritage*, p.138; Coates, *Liscard and Irish Names in Wirral*.
8. Bu'Lock, *op.cit.*, p.24; Dodgson, *The Place Names of Cheshire*, p.266; Cavill et al., *op.cit.*, p.137.
9. Bu'Lock, *ibid.*; V.C.H.
10. Dodgson, *The English Arrival in Cheshire*. Higham (*op. cit.*) criticises Dodgson's thesis as relying too heavily upon a 'migrationary' interpretation of events. In other words, it assumes that the numbers of English settlers simply increased and that this both forced them to move into British-occupied areas and enabled them to conquer the indigenous population. In actual fact, Dodgson did not propound such a crude thesis: he stated clearly in his article that the English take-over was political. The English were able to dominate the area because British control and organisation were weak. He contrasted this with the reverse situation of the 10th century, when English political institutions were strong enough to absorb the Scandinavian immigration, thus allowing the survival of the existing language and culture which, as a result, had gained a Scandinavian flavour.
11. Sherley-Price, L. (trans.), *Bede—A History of the English Church and People* (Penguin, Harmondsworth, 1978), pp.103-4.
12. Professor Williams used this as a title for a section of Chapter 2 of *When Was Wales? A History of the Welsh* (Penguin, Harmondsworth, 1985).
13. Pantos, 'Meeting Places in *Wilaveston* Hundred'.
14. Cox, E.W., *Overchurch and Its Runic Stone*.
15. Philpott, R.A., Unpublished Reports on the Excavations at Moreton 1987-8.
16. All quoted by Norman Ellison in *The Wirral Peninsula*, p.78.
17. Stephen Harding can be thanked for returning the important topic of Viking Wirral to the public's attention and for co-ordinating the genetic research. He is joint editor with Paul Cavill and Judith

Jesch of *Wirral and its Viking Heritage*, which contains classic articles by the great scholars of a previous generation—F.T. Wainwright, J. Mc.N. Dodgson, J.D. Bu'lock and W.G. Collingwood as well as others by Simon C. Bean and Andrew Wawn.

18. Dodgson, J. McN., *The Background of Brunanburh* in Cavill et al., *op. cit.*
19. Griffiths, D., *Coastal Trading Ports of the Irish Sea*.
20. Collingwood, W.G., *Early Monuments of West Kirby* in Cavill et al., *op. cit.*
21. *Ibid.*
22. Bu'Lock, J.D., *Pre-Norman Crosses of West Cheshire and the Norse Settlements Around the Irish Sea* in Cavill et al., *op. cit.*
23. Web site address: http—www.nottingham.ac.uk-~sczsteve

Four: Medieval Wirral 1066-1500

1. Garmonsway, G.N. (trans.), *The Anglo-Saxon Chronicle* (Dent, London, 1953).
2. *Ibid.*
3. Booth, *Burton in Wirral*. All Burton references are from this work.
4. Barraclough, *The Earldom and County Palatinate of Chester*.
5. Stewart-Brown, *The Royal Manor and Park of Shotwick*.
6. Booth, *Chester Chamberlain's Account*.
7. Morgan, *War and Society in Medieval Cheshire*.
8. Hewitt, *Cheshire Under the Three Edwards*, pp.110-1.
9. Morgan, *op.cit.*, p.210.
10. Stewart-Brown, *The Wapentake of Wirral*.
11. Irvine, *Notes on the Old Halls of Wirral*.
12. Booth, *Calendar of Cheshire Trailbaston Proceedings*.
13. Booth, *Taxation and the Public Order*; Bennett, *A County Community etc.*
14. Tait, *The Chartulary or Register of the Abbey of St Werburgh*.
15. Brownbill, *West Kirby and Hilbre*. All references to West Kirby are from this work.
16. Ormerod, p.457.
17. *Ibid.*
18. Mortimer, p.259.
19. Hewitt, *Medieval Cheshire*.
20. Ormerod, *ibid.*
21. Booth, *The Financial Administration etc.*
22. Harding, *Ingimund's Saga*; Cavill et al., *Wirral and its Viking Heritage*; notes provided by private researcher Mr S. Hornby to Stephen Harding.
23. Dobson, R.B., *The Peasants' Revolt* (Macmillan, London, 1983).
24. Stewart-Brown, *Calendar of County Court etc. Rolls*.
25. Place, G., *The Fields and the Forest* in Booth, *Burton*.
26. Chitty, *Wirral Rural Fringes Survey Report*.
27. Woods and Brown, *The Rise and Progress of Wallasey*.
28. *Wirral A to Z Street Atlas* (A-Z Maps, Sevenoaks, 2000).
29. Stewart-Brown, *op. cit.*
30. Spoken at an Archaeological Conference held at Lancaster University 9/3/2002.
31. Cox, *Traces of Submerged Lands etc.*

Five: Early Modern Wirral 1500-1800

1. Mortimer.
2. Cheshire Quarter Sessions, p.36.
3. Unless otherwise stated, all documentary references in this chapter were obtained from *Wirral Notes and Queries*, which has comprehensive indexes.

4. Mortimer.
5. Brownbill, *West Kirby and Hilbre.*
6. Rideout, *The Growth of Wirral.*
7. Booth, *Burton in Wirral.* All Burton references were obtained from this work.
8. Woods and Brown, *The Rise and progress of Wallasey,* p.134.
9. *Ibid.,* p.135.
10. Hume, *Rural Life and Manners etc.*
11. Marker, *The Dee Estuary etc.*
12. Place, *The Rise and Fall of Parkgate.*

Six: 1800-1914
1. Hess, *George Ormerod.*
2. All details about Hawthorne were obtained from Forster, *An American in Cheshire.*
3. Dawson, *Arwe.*
4. *Ismay, Dawpool and the Titanic Connection* in *W.J.*
5. Place, *Neston 1840-1940.* All references to places within Neston parish are from this work.
6. Woods and Brown, *The Rise and progress of Wallasey.*
7. Fussell, *Four Centuries of Cheshire Farming Systems.*
8. Porter, *The Marketing of Agricultural Produce.*
9. Jermy and Rickards, *Brickfields.*
10. Aspinall et al., *Ellesmere Port,* pp.13-14.
11. Ellison, p.152.
12. Hubbard and Shippobottom, *A Guide to Port Sunlight Village.*
13. Neal, *The Birkenhead Garibaldi Riots.*
14. Perkin, *The 'Social Tone' of Victorian Seaside Resorts.*

Seven: The Twentieth Century
1. Birkenhead is home to a distinguished historian of the Great War, Graham Maddocks, who has written about its most important myth in his book *Bloody Red Tabs* (with Frank Davies, Leo Cooper, London, 1995); casualty figures were obtained from Gilbert, M, *The First World War* (Weidenfeld and Nicolson, London, 1994).
2. Le Pan (Jones), *The 1914-18 War Seen through a Child's Eyes.*
3. Mon Hughes, *The Eisteddfod of the Black Chair.*
4. Harris, *A Poet of the First World War.*
5. Kemp, *We Will Remember Them.*
6. Tomlinson, *Walking the Blitz.*
7. Place, *Neston 1840-1940.*
8. Parsons, *Hooton Airfield.*
9. Hess, *Parish Reminiscences*; all subsequent references to Backford are taken from this work.
10. Unpublished quotations result from private conversations with the author.
11. Dawson, *Tingvelle.* All references to Dawson and to Thingwall are from this work.
12. Tomlinson, *Walking the Blitz.*
13. Jager, *The Rise and Ascent of Number Two Platoon.*
14. Hutchings, *Carlett Park.*
15. Smith, *Almost an Island.*
16. Unpublished autobiography kindly lent to the author.
17. Aspinall et al., *Ellesmere Port.*
18. Rickards, *Arrowe's Jamboree.*
19. *WCJ,* 11:1 (2002).

Bibliography

Abbreviations

BC	=	Birkenhead Central Library
JCAS	=	*Journal of the Chester Archaeological Society*
CBA	=	Council for British Archaeology
CRO	=	Cheshire County Records Office
CS	=	*Chetham Society* (Manchester); (OS = Old Series; NS = Ne Series; TS = Third Series;)
HS	=	*Historic Society of Lancashire and Cheshire* (Liverpool)
LRO	=	Liverpool Records Office
NMGM	=	National Museums and Galleries on Merseyside (Liverpool)
PRO	=	Public Records Office
RS	=	*Records Society of Lancashire and Cheshire* (Manchester)
THSLC	=	*Transactions of the Historic Society of Lancashire and Cheshire*
TLCAS	=	*Transactions of the Lancashire and Cheshire Antiquarian Society*
WCJ	=	*Wirral Champion Journal*
WJ	=	*Wirral Journal*

1) Primary Sources

a) Printed (listed by editors' names)

Barraclough, G., 'Facsimiles of Early Cheshire Charters', *R*S, (1957)

Barraclough, G., 'The Charters of the Norman Earls of Chester, *c*.1071-1237', *RS* 126, Alan Sutton, Gloucester (1988)

Bennett, J.H.E. and Dewhurst J.C., 'Quarter Sessions Records with Other Records of the Justices of the Peace for the County Palatinate of Chester 1559-1760', *RS* 94 (1940)

Booth, P.H.W., 'Calendar of Cheshire Trailbaston Proceedings, 1353', *Cheshire History*, 9 (1983)

Booth, P.H.W. and Carr, A.D., 'Account of Master John de Burnham the Younger, Chamberlain of Chester and Flint, 1361-2', *RS* 125 (1991)

Brownbill, J., 'List of Clergymen etc. in the Diocese of Chester, 1691, Recorded at the First Visitation of Nicholas Stratford, Bishop of Chester', *CS*, NS 73

Craig, R. and Jarvis, R., 'Liverpool Registry of Merchant Ships 1786-89', *CS*, TS 15 (1967)

Harley, J.B. and Laxton, P., 'A Survey of the County Palatine of Chester by P.P. Burdett', *HS*, Occasional Series (1777)

Hopkins, A., 'Selected Rolls of the Chester City Courts, Late Thirteenth and Early Fourteenth Centuries', *CS*, TS 2 (1950)

Jarvis, R.C., 'Customs Letter Books of the Port of Liverpool', *CS*, TS 6 (1954)

Raines, F.R., ' "Notitia Cestriensis", or Historical Notices of the Diocese of Chester, by the Right Reverend Francis Gastrell, D.D., Lord Bishop of Chester, 1: Cheshire', *CS*, OS 8 (1845)

Sanders, F. and Irvine, W.F., 'Wirral Notes and Queries Being Local Gleanings Historical and Antiquarian Relating to the Hundre of Wirral from many Sources' (Reprinted from *The Birkenhead News*, Willmer Bros., Birkenhead, 1892 and 1893)

Stewart-Brown, R., 'Accounts of the Chamberlains and Other Officers of the County of Chester, 1301-60', *RS* 59 (1910)

Stewart-Brown, R., 'Calendar of County Court, City Court, and Eyre Rolls of Chester, 1259-1279, With an Inquest of Military Service, 1288', *CS*, NS 84 (1925)

Tait, J., 'The Domesday Survey of Cheshire', *CS*, NS 75 (1916)

Tait, J., 'The Chartulary or Register of the Abbey of St Werburgh' Part 1—*CS*, NS 79 (1920) and Part 2—*CS*, NS 82 (1923)

Various Editiors: 'Cheshire Sheaf: Being Local Gleanings Historical and Antiquarian From Many Scattered Fields' (Originally appearing in the *Chester Courant*, Chester, from 1878 onwards)

b) Manuscript

Census Returns from Wirral Townships 1841-1901 PRO, CRO, BC—on microfilm

Newspapers: Files of local and national newspapers, 18th to 20th centuries, National Newspaper Library, Colindale, LRO and BC—usually on microfilm

Registers of Baptisms, Marriages and Burials from Wirral Parishes, CRO—usually on microfilm

Tithe Maps and Apportionments for Wirral Townships in the 1840s, CRO-EDT

Wills Proved at the Consistory Court of Chester 1545-1837 from Wirral, listed by *RS* in 19 volumes, CRO. W.S. Index also available online at CRO

2) Secondary Sources

Anon, 'Notice of Coins Found at Leasowe Castle in 1834', *THSLC* 1 (1848-9)

Anon, 'A Palstave from Great Sutton', *JCAS* 39 (1952)

Anon, 'A Pilgrim Flask from Meols', *JCAS* 43 (1956)

Anon, 'A Stone Axe from Oxton', *JCAS* 44 (1957)

Anon, 'A Flint Arrowhead from Thurstaston', *JCAS* 49 (1962)

Anon, 'Ismay, *Titanic* and the Wirral Connection', *WJ* 4:8 (1989), 5:1-2 (1990)

Anon, 'Wirral's Patchwork Quilt', *WJ* 5:3 (1990)

Aldridge, C., 'The Priory of the Blessed Virgin and Saint James, Birkenhead', *THSLC* 42 (1890)

Allen, J.R., 'The Early Christian Monuments of Lancashire and Cheshire', *THSLC* 45 (1893)

Allison, J.E., 'Sidelights on Tranmere' (Birkenhead Historical Society, Birkenhead, 1976)

Ashby- Pritt, W.C., 'An Account of Wallasey, Based on that of Mr Henry Robinson School-master there 1720; With Notes on the Parish from the Registers', *THSLC* 43 and 44 (1891-2)

Ashton, W., 'The Battle of Land and Sea' (Manchester, 1909)

Ashton, W., 'Evolution of a Coastline' (Stanfords, London, 1920)

Aspinall, P.J., Hudson, D.M. and Lawton, R., 'Ellesmere Port the Making of an Industrial Borough' (Ellesmere Port Borough Council, Ellesmere Port, 1982)

Atherton, J., 'Church and Society in the North West 1760–1997', *TLCAS* 93 (1997)

Baines, T., 'Historical Notes on the Valley of the Mersey Previous to the Norman Conquest', *THSLC* 5 (1852-3)

Barber, E., 'Parkgate: an Old Cheshire Port', *JCAS* 18 (1911)

Barraclough, G., 'The Earldom and County Palatine of Chester', *THSLC* 103 (1952)

Beazley, F.C., 'Notes on the Parish of Burton in Wirral', *THSLC* 59 (1907)

Beazley, F.C., 'Irby Windmill', *THSLC* 61 (1909)

Beazley, F.C., 'Arms and Epitaph—Woodchurch', *THSLC* 63 (1911)

Beazley, F.C., 'The Overchurch Chalice', *THSLC* 64 (1912)

Beazley, F.C., 'Notes on Shotwick in the County of Cheshire', *THSLC* 66 (1914)

Beazley, F.C., 'Thurstaston in Cheshire, An Account of the Parish, Manor and Church', *THSLC* 75 (1924)

Beazley, F.C., 'Wirral Records of the 17th Century', *THSLC* 77 (1925)

Beazley, F.C., 'Wirral Records Supplement', *THSLC* 78 (1926)

Beck, J., *Tudor Cheshire* (Cheshire Community Council, Chester, 1969)

Behrend, J., *John Ball of Hoylake* (Grant Books, Worcestershire, 1989)

Behrend, J., *Golf at Hoylake* (Grant Books, Worcestershire, 1990)

Bennett, M.J., 'The Lancashire and Cheshire Clergy 1379', *THSLC* 124 (1972)

Bennett, M.J., 'A County Community: Social Cohesion Amongst the Cheshire Gentry 1400-1425', *Northern History*, 8 (1973)

Bidlake, W., 'Neston Church in the 18th Century', *THSLC* 87 (1935)

Birkenhead, Second Earl of, *F.E.: The Life of F.E. Smith, 1st Earl of Birkenhead* (Eyre and Spottiswoode, London, 1960)

Blair, A., *Wirral Fieldpaths and Byways* (Phillip Son and Nephew, Liverpool, 1949)

Booth, J.E., 'A Wirral Account Book and Notary's Register 1761-90', *THSLC* 118 (1966)

Booth, P.H.W., 'Taxation and Public Order: Cheshire in 1353', *Northern History* 12 (1976)

Booth, P.H.W., 'The End of Wirral Forest: an Anniversary, July 1376', *Cheshire History Newsletter* 12 (1977)

Booth, P.H.W., *Burton Manor: The Biography of a House* (Burton Manor, 1978)

Booth, P.H.W., 'Farming for Profit in the Fourteenth Century: The Cheshire Estates of the Earldom of Chester', *JCAS* 62 (1979)

Booth, P.H.W., 'The Financial Administration of the Lordship and County of Chester, 1272-1377', *CS*, TS 28 (1981)

Booth, P.H.W. (ed.), *Burton in Wirral: a History* (The Burton and South Wirral Local History Society, Burton, 1984)

Bott, O. and Williams, R., *Man's Imprint on Cheshire* (Cheshire County Council, Chester, 1975)

Bower, F., *Rolling Stonemason* (Jonathan Cape, London, 1936)

Brack, A., *The Wirral* (Batsford, London, 1980)

Bridge, J.C., *Cheshire Proverbs and Other Sayings and Rhymes Connected with the City and County Palatine of Chester* (Phillipson and Goulder, Chester, 1917)

Brockbank, L. (ed.), *Dee Wildfowler The Last Professional: A Lifetime's Recollections by Harold Gill of Parkgate 1883-1961* (West Kirby, 1982)

Brotherton-Ratcliffe, E.H., 'Excavations at Grange Cow Worth, Ellesmere Port 1966 and 67', *JCAS* 58 (1975)

Brownbill, J., 'Cheshire in the Domesday Book', *THSLC* 51 (1899)

Brownbill, J., *West Kirby and Hilbre—A Parochial History* (Henry Young and Sons, Liverpool, 1928)

Brownbill, J., 'A History of the Old Parish of Bidston Cheshire', *THSLC* 88 (1936)

Bu'lock, J.D., 'Pre-Norman Crosses of West Cheshire', *TLCAS* 58 (1958)

Bu'lock, J.D., 'The Celtic, Saxon and Scandinavian Settlement of Meols in Wirral', *THSLC* 112 (1960)

Bu'lock, J.D., *Pre-Conquest Cheshire 383-1066* (Cheshire Community Council, Chester, 1972)

Budden, C.W., *The Beauty and Interest of Wirral* (Philip Son and Nephew, Liverpool, 1921)

Budden, C.W., *Rambles Round the Old Churches of Wirral* (Edward Howell, Liverpool, 1922)

Burnley, K., *Portrait of Wirral* (Robert Hale, London, 1981)

Bushell, W.F., 'The Ancient Graveyard of Birkenhead Priory', *THSLC* 108 (1956)

Caine, N., *The History of the Royal Rock Beagle Hunt* (By Private Subscription, 1895)

Campbell, A. (ed.), *The Battle of Brunanburh* (London, 1938)

Carrington, P., 'The Roman Advance into the North Western Midlands Before A.D. 71', *JCAS* 68 (1986)

Carson, P.A. and Garner, C.R., *The Silver Screens of Wirral: 1 Wallasey, Hoylake, West Kirby and South Wirral; 2 Birkenhead and Bebington* (Countyvise, Birkenhead, 1990)

Caton, A.G., *The Romance of Wirral* (Philip Son and Nephew, Liverpool, 1946)

Cavill, P. et al. (eds.), *Wirral and Its Viking Heritage* (English Place-Name Society, Nottingham, 2000)

Chapman, V., 'Open Fields in West Cheshire', *THSLC* 104 (1952)

Chitty, G. and Warhurst M., 'Ancient Meols', *JMAS* 1 (1977)

Chitty, G., 'Irby Mill', *JMAS* 3 (1979)

Chitty, G., 'Bromborough Court House a Further Note', *JMAS* 2 (1978)

Chitty, G., *Wirral Rural Fringes Survey Report* (Merseyside Archaeological Society, Liverpool, 1980)

Clarke, J.W., 'Mollington Hall', *JCAS* 41 (1954)

Clayton, D.J., 'The Administration of the County Palatine of Chester, 1442-85' (*CS*, TS 35, 1990)

Coates, R., 'Liscard and Irish Names in Northern Wirral', *Journal of the English Place-Name Society* 30 (1997-8)

Coward, B., 'The Stanleys, Lords Stanley and Earls of Derby, 1385-1672: The Origins, Wealth and Power of a Landowning Family' (*CS*, TS 30, 1983)

Coward, T.A., *Picturesque Cheshire* (Sherratt and Hughes, London and Manchester, 1903)

Cowell, R., 'Greasby, North Wirral, Merseyside 1987-90: Interim Report on the Excavation of an Early Mesolithic Site', *Archaeology North West, Bulletin of the CBA North West* 4 (1992)

Cowell, R. and Innes, J.B., *North West Wetlands Survey 1* (Lancaster Imprints, Lancaster, 1994)

Cowell, R.W., 'The Prehistory of Merseyside', *JMAS* 7 (1991)

Cox, E.W., 'Notes on the History of Wallasey Church', *JCAS* 1 (1887)

Cox, E.W., 'Overchurch and its Runic Stone', *THSLC* 43 and 44 (1892-3)

Cox, E.W., 'Birkenhead Priory', *THSLC* 46 (1894)

Cox, E.W., 'Traces of Submerged Lands on the Coasts of Lancashire, Cheshire and North Wales', *THSLC* 46 (1894)

Cox, E.W., 'Birkenhead Priory' (*ibid.*)

Cox, E.W., 'The Architectural History of Bebington Church', *THSLC* 49 (1897)

Cox, E.W., 'The Antiquities of Storeton in Wirral' (*ibid.*)

Craggs, J.D., *Hilbre the Cheshire Island* (Liverpool, 1982)

Craig, R., 'Some Aspects of the Trade and Shipping of the River Dee in the 18th Century', *THSLC* 114 (1962)

Craig, R., 'Shipping and Shipbuilding in the Port of Chester in the 18th and Early 19th Centuries', *THSLC* 116 (1964)

Crosby, Alan, *A History of Cheshire* (Phillimore, 1996)

Cross, E.W., 'Fragments of a Saxon Cross Found at West Kirby and Flints Found in Wirral', *JCAS* 5 (1893-5, Part i)

Curry, A.E., 'Cheshire and the Royal Demesne 1399–1422', *THSLC* 128 (1978)

Cust, E., 'Description of Horse Racing in the 17th Century at Leasowe Castle', *THSLC* 1 (1848-9)

Dallow, W., 'Notes on the Overchurch Runic Stone', *JCAS* 3 (1888-90 and 'Proceedings of the Session 1889-90' in same volume)

Darby, H.C. and Maxwell, I.S., *Domesday Geography of Northern England* (Cambridge University Press, Cambridge, 1962)

Davies, C. S., 'The Agricultural History of Cheshire 1750-1850', *CSTS* 10 (1960)

Davies, J., 'The Celtic Elements in the Dialects of the Counties Adjoining Lancashire', *Archaeologia Cambrensis*, 5th Series, 1 (1884)

Dawson, G., *Tingvelle: A History of Thingwall and Other North Wirral Farming Villages* (Dawson Publishing, Irby, 1993)

Dawson, G., *Arwe: The Story of Arrowe, Pensby and the Liverpool Slave Trade* (Dawson Publishing, Irby, 1994)

Dawson, G., *Wirral Gleanings* (Dawson Publishing, Irby, 1998)

Dawson, G., *Wyrale* (Dawson Publishing, Irby, 1999)

Dodgson, J.McN., 'The Background of Brunanburh', *Sagabook* XIV (1957)

Dodgson, J. McN., 'The English Arrival in Cheshire', *THSLC* 119 (1967)

Dodgson, J.McN., *The Place Names of Cheshire, Part 4 The Place-Names of Broxton Hundred and Wirral Hundred* (English Place Name Society, 47, Cambridge, 1972)

Dodgson, J.McN., *The Place Names of Cheshire, Part 5 Section 2: Introduction, Linguistic Notes and Indexes with Appendices, Completed by Alexander R. Rumble* (English Place-Name Society, 74, Nottingham, 1997)

Dolley, R.H.M., 'The Anglo Saxon Coins from Meols Sands', *THSLC* 113 (1961)

Driver, J.T., *Cheshire in the Later Middle Ages* (Cheshire Community Council, Chester, 1971)

Earwaker, J.P., 'The "Progress" of The Duke of Monmouth in Cheshire, In September 1682', *THSLC* 46 (1894)

Eastwood, J., *Wirral Born and Bred: The Old Life of the Countryside in Wirral* (Winterbourne Press, Bridport, 1993)

Ellis, J.W., 'Medieval Fonts of the Hundreds of West Derby and Wirral', *THSLC* 53 (1901)

Ellison, N., *The Wirral Peninsula* (Robert Hale, London, 1955-1976)

Fellows-Jensen, G., 'J.McN. Dodgson and the Place-Names of Cheshire', *Northern History*, 38 (2001)

Foster, C., 'Cheshire Cheese: Farming in the North West in the 17th and 18th Centuries', *THSLC* 143 (1993)

Forster, W., 'An American in Cheshire', *Cheshire Round* 1:6 (1966)

France, P., 'Roman Roads in Wirral', *WJ* 3:1, 2 (1986)

Freke, D., 'Bromborough Court House Moated Site Excavations 1979', *JMAS* 2 (1978)

Fussell, G.E., 'Four Centuries of Cheshire Farming Systems 1500–1900', *THSLC* 106 (1954)

Gahan, J.W., *Steel Wheels to Deeside: The Wirral Railways Past and Present* (Countyvise, Birkenhead, 1983)

Gamlin, H., *Memories or Chronicles of Birkenhead: The Scenes and People of Its Early Days* (Edward Howell, Liverpool, 1892)

Gamlin, H., *Twixt Mersey and Dee* (D. Marples, Liverpool, 1897)

Gelling, M., 'Paganism and Christianity in Wirral', *Journal of the English Place-Name Society*, 25 (1992-3)

Gillespie, J.L., 'Richard II's Cheshire Archers', *THSLC* 125 (1974)

Glazebrook-Rylands, T., 'Ptolemy's Geography of the Coast from Carnarvon to Cumberland', *THSLC* 30 (1878)

Goodacre, E.B., 'Three Notes on Bidston and the Stanleys', *THSLC* 91 (1939)

Gould, W.T.S. and Hodgkiss, A.G., *The Resources of Merseyside* (Liverpool University Press, Liverpool, 1982)

Green, P.G., 'Charity, Morality and Social Control: Clerical Attitudes in the Diocese of Chester 1715–1795', *THSLC* 141 (1999)

Greenwood, E.F. (ed.), *Ecology and Landscape Development—A History of the Mersey Basin: Proceedings of a Conference Held at Merseyside Maritime Museum, Liverpool, 5th-6th July 1996* (Liverpool University Press and NMGM, Liverpool, 1999)

Gresswell, R.K., 'The Origin of the Dee and Mersey Estuaries', *Geological Journal* 4 (1964)

Gresswell, R.K. and Lawton, R., *Merseyside* (The Geographical Association, Sheffield, 1964)

Greville, M.D., 'Chronological List of the Railways of Cheshire 1837-1957', *THSLC* 56 (1954)

Griffiths, D., 'The Coastal Trading Ports of the Irish Sea' in Graham-Campbell, J.(ed.), *Viking Treasure from the North West: The Cuerdale Hoard in its Context— Selected Papers from 'The Vikings of the Irish Sea' Conference, Liverpool 18th-20th May 1990* (NMGM, Liverpool, 1992)

Grosvenor Museum, Chester, 'The Roman Inscriptions in the Grosvenor Museum, Chester' (1978); Reprinted from Collingwood, R.G. and Wright, R.P., *The Roman Inscriptions of Britain* (Oxford University Press, Oxford, 1965)

Hance, E.M., 'Notes on the Ancient Cheshire Families of Bennett of Saughall Massie and Bennett of Barnston with their Collateral Branches', *THSLC* 38 (1886)

Harding, S., *Ingimund's Saga: Norwegian Wirral* (Countyvise Publications, Birkenhead, 2000)

Harley, J.B., 'Maps of Early Georgian Cheshire', *Cheshire Round* 1:8 (1967)

Harley, J.B., 'Cheshire Maps', *Cheshire Round* 1:9 (1968)

Harris, B.E. and Clayton, D.J., 'Criminal Procedure in Cheshire in the mid 15th Century', *THSLC* 128 (1978)

Harris, B.E. and Thacker, A.T. (eds.), *The Victoria County History of the County of Chester* (University of London Institute of Historical Research, Oxford University Press, Oxford, Volume 1–1987; Volume 2–1979; Volume 3–1980)

Harris, C., 'A Poet of the First World War', *WJ* 7:8 (1996)

Harrison, W., 'The Development of the Turnpike System in Lancashire and Cheshire', *TLCAS* 4 (1886)

Harrison, W., 'Pre-Turnpike Highways in Lancashire and Cheshire', *TLCAS* 9 (1891)

Haworth, D.W. and Comber, W.M., *Cheshire Village Memories* (Cheshire Federation of Women's Institutes, Tilston Court near Malpas, 1952)

Hess, J.P., *George Ormerod—Historian of Cheshire* (Herald Printers, Whitchurch, 1989)

Hess, J.P., *Backford C.E. Aided Primary School 1844-1996* (Published by the School, 1996)

Hess, J.P., *Parish Church of St. Oswald's Backford, Cheshire—Survey of Memorial Inscriptions 1997* (Parochial Church Council, Backford, 1997)

Hess, J.P., *Parish Reminiscences From the Cheshire Townships of Backford, Mollington, Chorlton-by-Backford, Lea-by-Backford and Caughall* (Festival 2000, Backford, 2000)

Hess, J.P., *Chorlton Hall* (4th edn., John Hess, Backford, 2000)

Hess, J.P., St. *Oswald's Church in the Parish of Backford* (The Parochial Church Council, Backford, undated)

Hewitt, H.J., *Medieval Cheshire* (*CS*, NS, 88, 1929)

Hewitt, H.J., *Cheshire Under the Three Edwards* (Cheshire Community Council, Chester, 1967)

Hewitt, W., *The Wirral Peninsula* (The University Press of Liverpool, Hodder and Stoughton, London, 1922)

Hewitt, W., 'Marl and Marling in Cheshire', *Proceedings of the Liverpool Geological Society* 13 (1923)

Higgins, G.P., 'The Government of Early Stuart Cheshire 1590-1640', *Northern History* 12 (1976)

Higham, N.J., *The Origins of Cheshire* (Manchester University Press, Manchester, 1993)

Highet, C., *The Wirral Railway* (The Oakwood Press, Lingfield, 1961)

Hislop, M.J.B., 'A Medieval Building Contract from Storeton', *JCAS* 74 (1996-7)

Hodson, J.H., *Cheshire 1660-1780—Restoration to Industrial Revolution* (Cheshire Community Council, Chester, 1978)

Hoey, D.J., 'Three Cruck Buildings in Lancashire and Cheshire', *THSLC* 117 (1965)

Hole, C., *Traditions and Customs of Cheshire* (Williams and Norgate, London 1937 and S.R. Publishers, Wakefield, 1970)

Holland, H., *General View of the Agriculture of Cheshire* (Richard Phillips, London, 1808)

Hubbard, E., 'Commuter Country: 1837', *Cheshire Round* 1:6 (1966)

Hubbard, E. and Shippobottom, M., *A Guide to Port Sunlight Village Including Two Tours of the Village* (Liverpool University Press, Liverpool, 2000)

Hume, A., 'Notice of Certain Mineral Springs at Leasowe', *THSLC* 1 (1848-9)

Hume, A., 'Lancashire and Cheshire Men in the 16th Century', *THSLC* 6 (1853-4)

Hume, A., 'Outline of the Sea Coast of Cheshire', *THSLC* 11 (1858-9)

Hume, A., 'The Hilbre Cross', *THSLC* 15 (1862-3)

Hume, A., 'Rural Life and Manners in the Neighbourhood of Bidstone and Upton a Hundred Years Ago', *THSLC* 27 (1874-5)

Hume, A. and Jones, F.S.A., 'Notes of the Hundred Court of Wirral' (*ibid.*)

Hume, A., *Ancient Meols or Some Account of the Antiquities Found Near Dove Point, on the Sea Coast of Cheshire; Including A Comparison of them With Relics of the Same Kinds Respectively Procured Elsewhere* (John Russell Smith, London, 1863)

Hunt, R., 'Shipping was his world: The Story of William Inman and his famous Shipping Line', *WJ* 4:3 (1988)

Husain, B.M.C., *Cheshire Under the Norman Earls* (Cheshire Community Council, Chester, 1973)

Hutchings, H., *Carlett Park: A College With a History* (Countyvise, Birkenhead, 1994)

Innes, J.B., 'Woodlands Beneath the Sea—an Ancient Forest Reveals its Secrets', *WJ* 1:6 (1983)

Innes, J.B. and Tomlinson, P.R., 'Environmental Archaeology in Merseyside', *JMAS* 7 (1991)

Irvine, W.F., 'The Place Names of the Hundred of Wirral', *THSLC* 43 and 44 (1891-2)

Irvine, W.F., 'Notes on the Ancient Parish of Bidston', *THSLC* 45 (1893)

Irvine, W.F., 'Notes on the Domesday Survey so far as it Relates to the Hundred of Wirral', *JCAS* 5 (1893-5, Part i)

Irvine, W.F., 'Notes on Parish Churches', *THSLC* 47 (1895)

Irvine, W.F., *Village Life in West Kirby 300 Years Ago* (1895)

Irvine, W.F., 'Notes on the Old Halls of Wirral', *THSLC* 53 (1901)

Irvine, W.F. and Beazley, F.C., *Notes on the Parish of Woodchurch* (*ibid.*)

Irvine, W.F., *Notes on the Old Halls of Wirral* (Henry Young and Sons, Liverpool, 1903)

Irvine, W.F., 'Church Discipline After the Restoration', *THSLC* 64 (1912)

Irvine, W.F., 'Trespassers in the Forest of Wirral 1351', *THSLC* 101 (1949)

Irvine, W.F., 'The Early Stanleys', *THSLC* 105 (1954)

Jarvis, R.C., 'The Customs Cruisers of the North West in the 18th Century', *THSLC* 99 (1947)

Jarvis, R.C., 'The Head Port of Chester and Liverpool, Its Creek and Member', *THSLC* 105 (1953)

Jermy, K.E., 'The Roman Road in Wirral', *JCAS* 48 (1961)

Jermy, R. and Rickards J., 'Wirral Quarries and Brickfields', *WJ* 1:4 (1982)

Jermy, R., *A Portrait of Wirral's Railways* (Countyvise, Birkenhead, 1987)

Jones, G.D.B., 'The Romans in the North West', *Northern History* 3 (1968)

Jones, K., 'Bromborough Manor Houses', *JMAS* 2 (1978)

Jones, R.N. and Booth, P.H.W., 'Burton-in-Wirral: From Domesday to Dormitory', *Cheshire History Newsletter* 11 (1976)

Jones, W.G.H., 'Overchurch Parish Church and the Township of Upton', *THSLC* 111 (1959)

Kemp, H., 'We Will Remember Them: Recollections of Wallasey's Armistice Day', *WJ* 6:3 (1992)

Kenna, R., 'Early Settlement on the North Wirral Coastal Area', *JMAS* 2 (1978)

Kenna, R., 'Coastal Change and Early Settlement on the North Wirral', *JMAS* 3 (1979)

Kenna, R., 'An Old Woodland Floor Beneath the Sea—the Peat Beds of the North Wirral Coast', *WJ* 2:8 (1985)

Kenna, R., 'The Flandrian Sequence of North Wirral', *Geological Journal* 21 (1986)

Kerr, J. Lennox, *Wilfred Grenfell: His Life and Work* (George G. Harrap, London, 1959)

Laing, J. and L., 'A Mediterranean Trade with Wirral in the Iron Age', *Cheshire Archaeological Bulletin* 9 (1983)

Lawton, R. and Cunningham, C., *Merseyside Social and Economic Studies* (Longman and the University of Liverpool, London, 1970)

Le Pan (Jones), M., 'The 1914-18 War As Seen Through a Child's Eyes', *WJ* 9:4 (1999)

Leigh, E., *Legends and Ballads of Cheshire* (Longman, London, 1867)

Leigh, E., *A Glossary of Words Used in the Cheshire Dialect* (Hamilton Adams, London and Minshull Hughes, Chester, 1877)

Lomas, J., 'On Some Flint Implements Found in Glacial Deposits of Cheshire and North Wales', *THSLC* 50 (1898)

London, M.E., 'Landing Places Used by the Eastham Ferry Boats', *Cheshire History Newsletter* 12 and 13 (1977)

McIniss, J., *Birkenhead Park* (Countyvise, Birkenhead, 1984)

McIntyre, W.R.S., *Birkenhead Yesterday and Today* (Philip Son and Nephew, Liverpool, 1948)

McNiven, P., 'The Men of Cheshire and the Rebellion of 1403', *THSLC* 129 (1979)

Mabrey, A., 'Two Taxations in Wirral', *Cheshire History* 6 (1980)

Marker, M.E., 'The Dee Estuary: Its Progressive Silting and Salt Marsh Development', *Transactions of the Institute of British Geographers* 41 (1967)

Mason, B., *A Little Oasis: The Early History of Ashton Park West Kirby* (Countyvise, Birkenhead, 1996)

Mason, D.J.P., 'The *Prata Legionis* at Chester', *JCAS* 69 (1986)

Mason, D.J.P., '*Prata Legionis* in Britain', *Britannia* 19 (1988)

Mawer, A. (ed.), *The Chief Elements used in English Place-Names Being the Second Part of the Introduction to the Survey of English Place-Names, Volume 1 Part 2* (English Place-Name Society, Cambridge, 1930)

Mayer, J., 'On British Urns Found at West Kirby', *THSLC* 1 (1848-9)

Mayer, J., 'On the Old Halls of Cheshire No. 1 Tranmere Hall', *THSLC* 3 (1850-1)

Mayer, J., 'On Shotwick Church and its Saxon Foundation', *THSLC* 6 (1853-4)

Mayer, J., 'On the Arming of Levies in the Hundred of Wirral', *THSLC* 11 (1858-9)

Merseyside Railway History Group, *The Hooton to West Kirby Branch Line and the Wirral Railway* (Metropolitan Borough of Wirral, 1982)

Merseyside Railway History Group, *Railway Stations of Wirral* (I. and M. Boumphrey, undated)

Mitford Abraham, E., 'The Old Flour Mills of Wirral', *THSLC* 55 (1903)

Mon Hughes, G., 'The Eisteddfod of the Black Chair', *WJ* 6:3 (1992)

Morgan, P.J., 'Cheshire and the Defence of the Principality of Aquitaine', *THSLC* 128 (1978)

Morgan, P., *War and Society in Medieval Cheshire, 1277-1403*, CS, TS 34, 1987

Morrill, J.S., *Cheshire 1630-1660: County Government and English Society During the English Revolution* (Oxford University Press, Oxford, 1974)

Morris, D., 'Willaston—New Light on an Old Village', *Cheshire History* 5 (1980)

Mortimer, W.W., 'Memoir of the Family of Holme, especially of the various Randle Holmes, the Cheshire Antiquaries of the 17th century', *THSLC* 1 (1848-9)

Mortimer, W.W., *The History of the Hundred of Wirral* (Whittaker and Co., London, 1847; and E.J. Morten, Didsbury, 1972 and 1983)

Morton T.N., 'Extracts from the Parish Registers of the Parish Church of St. Hilary, Wallasey with Notes Thereupon', *THSLC* 35 (1882-3)

Mountfield, A.S., 'Admiral Denham and the Approaches to the Port of Liverpool', *THSLC* 105 (1953)

Neal, F., 'The Birkenhead Garibaldi Riots of 1862', *THSLC* 131 (1982)

Neilson, H.B., *Auld Lang Syne* (Willmer Bros., Birkenhead, 1935)

Newstead, R., 'Excavations at Hilbre 1926', *THSLC* 78 (1926)

O'Donald-Mays, J., *Mr Hawthorne Goes to England* (New Forest Leaves, Burley, Ringwood, 1983)

O'Neil, J.T., *Operation Pump Lane* (Jim O'Neil, Hoylake, 1982)

O'Neil, J.T. (ed.), *Victorian Hoylake: Changes in the History of Hoylake. Articles Appearing in the Hoylake Free Press 1914-15 by Charles Roberts a Native of the Place* (Jim O'Neil, Hoylake, 1986)

Ormerod, G., *The History of the County Palatine and City of Chester* (Three volumes ed. by Helsby, T., London, 1882; Available on C.D. ROM. from the Family History Society of Cheshire)

Pantos, A., 'Meeting Places in *Wilaveston* Hundred', *Journal of the English Place-Name Society*, 31 (1998-9)

Parsons, S., 'Hooton Airfield', *WCJ* 5 (2001)

Patmore, J.A. and Hodgkiss, A.G. (eds.), *Merseyside in Maps* (Longman for the University of Liverpool, London, 1970)

Pearson, J., *Neston and Parkgate* (Countyvise, Birkenhead, 1985)

Pearson, J., *Wirral—An Illustrated Review* (Bluecoat Press, Liverpool, 2000)

Perkin, H.J., 'The 'Social Tone' of Victorian Seaside Resorts in the North West', *Northern History* 11 (1976)

Pevsner, N. and Hubbard E., *The Buildings of England—Cheshire* (Penguin, Harmondsworth, 1971 and 1978)

Phillips, C.B. and Smith, J.H., *Lancashire and Cheshire From A.D. 1540* (Longman, London, 1994)

Philpott, F., 'A Thousand Years Ago: What Evidence for a Viking Invasion?', *WJ* 5:2 (1990)

Philpott, R.A., 'Unpublished reports made on the Excavations at Moreton of 1987-8' (N.M.G.M., Liverpool, 21/03/88 and 02/08/88)

Philpott, R.A., 'Discovering the Past: Recent Archaeological Work on a Romano-British Farmstead in Irby', *WJ* 6:6 (1993)

Philpott, R.A., 'New Light on Roman Settlement: Recent Aerial Photography in Cheshire', *Cheshire Past* 3 (1994)

Philpott, R.A., 'A New Roman Fortlet Near Stanlow, Cheshire', *Cheshire Past* 4 (1995)

Philpott, R.A., 'Three Byzantine Coins Found Near the North Wirral Coast in Merseyside', *THSLC* 148 (1998)

Philpott, R.A., 'A Romano British Brooch Type from North Western and Northern England', *Britannia* 30 (1999)

Philpott, R.A. and Adams, M.H., 'A Romano-British Farmstead in Irby, Wirral and its Place in the Landscape, An Interim Statement' in Nevell, M. (ed.), 'Living on the Edge of Empire—Models, Methodology and Marginality', *Archaeology North West, Bulletin of the CBA North West* 3, Issue 13 (1998), (Manchester and Chester, 1999)

Place, G., 'Parkgate and the Royal Yachts: Passenger Traffic Between The North West and Dublin in the 18th Century', *THSLC* 138 (1988)

Place, G., *This is Parkgate* (Parkgate and District Society, Parkgate, 1999)

Place, G., *The Rise and Fall of Parkgate, Passenger Port for Ireland, 1686-1815*, CS, TS 39, 1994

Place, G. (ed.), *Neston 1840-1940* (Burton and South Wirral Local History Society, 1996)

Potter, C., 'Observations of Geology and Archaeology of the Cheshire Shore', *THSLC* 4 (1875-6)

Potter, C., 'Antiquities of the Meols Shore', *THSLC* 40 (1888)

Potter, C., 'Leather, Bronze and Pewter Ornaments from the Cheshire Shore', *THSLC* 41 (1889)

Potter, C., 'Agricultural and Mechanical Implements found on the Meols Shore', *THSLC* 43 and 44 (1892-3)

Poole, M.E., 'The Poole Family of Poole Hall, Wirral', *THSLC* 52 (1900)

Porter, R.E., 'The Marketing of Agricultural Produce in Cheshire during the 19th century', *THSLC* 126 (1976)

Radcliffe, R.D., 'An Old Racing Stable at Wallasey in Wirral', *THSLC* 45 (1893)

Randall, D., *The Search for Old Wirral* (Countyvise, Birkenhead, 1984)

Randall, D. (ed.), *The Wirral Society 60 Years On* (The Wirral Society, Wallasey, 1988)

Reilly, Sir C. and Aslan, N.J., *Outline Plan for the County Borough of Birkenhead* (Birkenhead, 1947)

Rickards, J., 'Arrowe's Jamboree—Mudboree', *WJ* 1:8 (1983)

Rideout, E., 'The Account Book of The New Haven Chester 1567-8', *THSLC* 80 (1928)

Rideout, E.H., *The Growth of Wirral* (E.A. Bryant, Liverpool, 1927)

Rideout, E.H., 'Wirral Watersheds and River Systems and their influence on Local History', *THSLC* 74 (1922)

Rideout, E.H., 'Wirral Field Names', *THSLC* 76 (1924)

Rideout, E.H., 'The Sites of Ancient Villages in Wirral', *THSLC* 77 (1925)

Rimmer, A., 'The Ancient Domestic Architecture of Lancashire and Cheshire', *THSLC* 3 (1851-2)

Roberts, S.J., *Hoylake and Meols Past* (Phillimore & Co. Ltd, Chichester, 1992)

Roberts, T.W., *Ellesmere Port 1795–1960* (Gisborne, New Zealand, 1960)

Robinson, A.M., 'Cheshire in the Great Civil War', *THSLC* 47 (1895)

Robinson, A.M., 'The Birkenhead Priory Reparation', *THSLC* 55 and 56 (1903-4)

Roeder, C., 'On a Newly Discovered Neolithic Settlement at the Red Noses in New Brighton Near Liverpool', *THSLC* 50 (1898)

Rylands, J.P. and Brown, C.D., 'The Ancient Parish of West Kirby', *THSLC* 37 (1885)

Rylands, J.P. and Beazley, F.C., 'The Monumental and Other Inscriptions in the Churches of Stoak, Backford and Thornton-le-Moors in the County of Chester', *THSLC* 57 (1905)

Rylands, J.P., 'Armorial Panels in Eastham Church', *THSLC* 61 (1909)

Scard, G., *Squire and Tenant: Rural Life in Cheshire 1760–1900* (Cheshire Community Council, Chester, 1981)

Senar, K.B., *The 'Farmers' at Frankby: A History of the 'Farmers' Arms' Inn at Frankby, Wirral* (Ken Senar, Gayton, 1993)

Shaw, G.T., 'Nathaniel Hawthorne's House in Rock Park', *THSLC* 58 (1906)

Shaw, G.T., 'Shotwick Church Bells', *THSLC* 76 (1924)

Shaw, G.T., 'Thornton Grange in Wirral' (*ibid.*)

Shone, W., *Prehistoric Man in Cheshire* (Minshull and Meeson, Chester, 1911)

Shotter, D., 'Roman North-West England: The Process of Annexation', *THSLC* 148 (1998)

Shotter, D., *Roman Coins from North-West England—Second Supplement* (Lancaster University Centre for North-West Regional Studies, Lancaster, 2000)

Shrubshole G.W., 'List of Prehistoric Remains found in Cheshire', *JCAS* 4 (1890-1)

Singleton, W.A., 'Traditional House Types in Rural Lancashire and Cheshire', *THSLC* 104 (1952)

Smith, H.E., 'Notice of an Early Conventual Cemetery in Wirral', *THSLC* 17 (1864-5)

Smith, H. E., 'Produce of the Cheshire Shore', *THSLC* 18 (1865-6)

Smith, H.E., 'Archaeology of the Mersey District 1866', *THSLC* 22 (1869-70)

Smith, H.E., 'Reliques of the Anglo-Saxon Churches of St Bridget and St Hildeburga West Kirby, Cheshire', *THSLC* 22 (1869-70)

Smith, H.E., 'Archaeology of the Mersey District and Liverpool Notabilia 1874', *THSLC* 27 (1874-5)

Smith, N.E., *Almost an Island—The Story of Wallasey* (published by the author, Wallasey, 1998)

Smith, W. (ed.), *A Scientific Survey of Merseyside* (Liverpool University Press, Liverpool, 1953)

Stallworthy, J., *Wilfred Owen* (Oxford Lives, Oxford University Press, Oxford, 1983)

Stephens, W.B., 'The Overseas Trade of Chester in the Early 17th Century', *THSLC* 120 (1968)

Stewart-Brown, R., 'The Disafforestation of Wirral', *THSLC* 59 (1907)

Stewart-Brown, R., *The Wapentake of Wirral: A History of the Royal Franchise of the Hundred of Wirral in Cheshire* (Henry Young and Sons, Liverpool, 1907)

Stewart-Brown, R., 'The Royal Manor and Park of Shotwick in Cheshire', *THSLC* 64 (1912)

Stewart-Brown, R., *The Royal Manor and Park of Shotwick* (HS, 1912)

Stewart-Brown, R., *Birkenhead Priory and the Mersey Ferry* (The State Assurance Company, Liverpool, 1925)

Stewart-Brown, R., 'The Charter and Horn of the Master Forester of Wirral', *THSLC* 87 (1935)

Stewart-Brown R., 'Further Notes on the Deafforestation [*sic*] of Wirral', *THSLC* 89 (1937)

Sulley, P., *The Hundred of Wirral* (B. Haram and Co., Birkenhead, 1889)

Sulley, P., *A History of Ancient and Modern Birkenhead* (Liverpool, 1907)

Sylvester, D., 'Rural Settlement in Cheshire: Some Problems of Origin and Classification', *THSLC* 101 (1949)

Sylvester, D., 'The Open Fields of Cheshire', *THSLC* 108 (1957)

Sylvester, D., 'The Manor and the Cheshire Landscape', *TLCAS* 70 (1960)

Sylvester, D., 'Cheshire in the Dark Ages', *THSLC* 114 (1962)

Sylvester, D., 'Parish and Township in Cheshire and North East Wales', *JCAS* 54 (1967)

Sylvester, D. and Nulty, G. (eds.), *The Historical Atlas of Cheshire* (Cheshire Community Council, Chester, 1958)

Sylvester, D., *A History of Cheshire* (Darwen Finlayson, Henley-On-Thames, 1971)

Taylor, H., 'On Some Early Deeds Relating to the Families of Hoton of Hooton and Stanley of Storeton', *JCAS* 6 (1899, Parts ii-iii)

Terret, I.B., 'The Domesday Woodland of Cheshire', *THSLC* 100 (1948)

Thompson, F.H., *Roman Cheshire* (Cheshire Community Council, Chester, 1965)

Thornton, C.E., 'Roman Discoveries in Wirral', *WJ* 1:4 (1982)

Tigwell, R.E., *Cheshire in the 20th Century* (Cheshire Community Council, Chester, 1985)

Timbrell, W.F.J., 'The Medieval Stall-End in Hawarden Church and Contemporary Panels in Eastham Church', *JCAS* 23 (1920)

Tomlinson, N.H.C., *Walking the Blitz* (I. and M. Boumphrey, Prenton, 1996)

Travis, C.B., 'The Peat and Forest Beds of Leasowe, Cheshire', *Proceedings of the Liverpool Geological Society* 15 (1929)

Varley, W.J. and Jackson, J.W., *Prehistoric Cheshire* (Cheshire Rural Community Council, Chester, 1940)

Varley, W.J., *Cheshire Before the Romans* (Cheshire Community Council, Chester, 1964)

Vipond, P., 'Harrow Fields in Heswall-cum-Oldfield', *Journal of the English Place-Name Society* 25 (1992-3)

Wainwright, F.T., 'North West Mercia A.D. 871-924', *THSLC* 94(1942)

Wallasey History Society, *Wallasey at War 1939-45 Including Moreton & Leasowe* (Ian and Marilyn Boumphrey, Prenton, undated)

Wardle, A.C., 'The Customs Collection of the Port of Liverpool', *THSLC* 99 (1947)

Wark, K.R., *Elizabethan Recusancy in Cheshire, CS*, TS 19 (1971)

Watkin, W.T., *Roman Cheshire: A Description of Roman Remains in the County of Chester* (Liverpool, 1886 and Wakefield, 1974)

Webb, W. et al., *King's Vale Royal of England or the County Palatine of Chester etc.* (Daniel King, London, 1616, included in Ormerod [1819 and 1882])

Whitaker, H., *A Descriptive List of the Printed Maps of Cheshire, 1577-1900, CS*, NS 106 (1942)

White, R.H., 'Viking Period Sculptures at Neston, Cheshire', *JCAS* 69 (1986)

Wilkinson, T.T., 'On the Battle of Brunanburgh, and the probable locality of the Conflict', *THSLC* 9 (1856-7)

Williams, H., 'The Seacombe Pottery 1852-64', *Journal of Ceramic History*, Stoke-on-Trent City Museums 10 (1978)

Williams, J., *The Story of Greasby* (John Williams, Greasby, 1978)

Wilson, C., *The History of Unilever: A Study in Economic Growth* (Three volumes, Cassell, London, 1970)

Wirral Society, *Wirral—Yesterday, Today and Tomorrow* (Wirral, 1979)

Woods, E.C., 'The Journal of John Hough of the Manor of Liscard', *THSLC* 72 (1920)

Woods, E.C., 'Leasowe Castle Its Owners and History', *THSLC* 73 (1921)

Woods, E.C., 'Further Notes on the Penkett Family', *THSLC* 78 (1926)

Woods, E.C., 'Smuggling in Wirral', *THSLC* 79 (1927)

Woods, E.C., 'Some History of the Coastwise Lights of Lancashire and Cheshire', *THSLC* 96 and 97 (1944-5)

Woods, E.C. and Brown, P.C., *The Rise and Progress of Wallasey, a History of the Borough* (Wallasey Borough Council, Wallasey, 2nd edn. 1960)

Woodward, D.M., 'The Overseas Trade of Chester 1600-1650', *THSLC* 122 (1970)

Young, H.E., *A Perambulation of the Hundred of Wirral in the County of Chester* (Henry Young and Sons, Liverpool, 1909)

Index

Page numbers in **bold** refer to illustrations or their captions